Unbecoming Human

D1610026

Plateaus – New Directions in Deleuze Studies

'It's not a matter of bringing all sorts of things together under a single concept but rather of relating each concept to variables that explain its mutations.'
Gilles Deleuze, *Negotiations*

Titles available in the series
Christian Kerslake, *Immanence and the Vertigo of Philosophy: From Kant to Deleuze*
Jean-Clet Martin, *Variations: The Philosophy of Gilles Deleuze*, translated by Constantin V. Boundas and Susan Dyrkton
Simone Bignall, *Postcolonial Agency: Critique and Constructivism*
Miguel de Beistegui, *Immanence – Deleuze and Philosophy*
Jean-Jacques Lecercle, *Badiou and Deleuze Read Literature*
Ronald Bogue, *Deleuzian Fabulation and the Scars of History*
Sean Bowden, *The Priority of Events: Deleuze's Logic of Sense*
Craig Lundy, *History and Becoming: Deleuze's Philosophy of Creativity*
Aidan Tynan, *Deleuze's Literary Clinic: Criticism and the Politics of Symptoms*
Thomas Nail, *Returning to Revolution: Deleuze, Guattari and Zapatismo*
François Zourabichvili, *Deleuze: A Philosophy of the Event* with *The Vocabulary of Deleuze* edited by Gregg Lambert and Daniel W. Smith, translated by Kieran Aarons
Frida Beckman, *Between Desire and Pleasure: A Deleuzian Theory of Sexuality*
Nadine Boljkovac, *Untimely Affects: Gilles Deleuze and an Ethics of Cinema*
Daniela Voss, *Conditions of Thought: Deleuze and Transcendental Ideas*
Daniel Barber, *Deleuze and the Naming of God: Post-Secularism and the Future of Immanence*
F. LeRon Shults, *Iconoclastic Theology: Gilles Deleuze and the Secretion of Atheism*
Janae Sholtz, *The Invention of a People: Heidegger and Deleuze on Art and the Political*
Marco Altamirano, *Time, Technology and Environment: An Essay on the Philosophy of Nature*
Sean McQueen, *Deleuze and Baudrillard: From Cyberpunk to Biopunk*
Ridvan Askin, *Narrative and Becoming*
Marc Rölli, *Gilles Deleuze's Transcendental Empiricism: From Tradition to Difference*, translated by Peter Hertz-Ohmes
Guillaume Collett, *The Psychoanalysis of Sense: Deleuze and the Lacanian School*
Ryan J. Johnson, *The Deleuze-Lucretius Encounter*
Allan James Thomas, *Deleuze, Cinema and the Thought of the World*
Cheri Lynne Carr, *Deleuze's Kantian Ethos: Critique as a Way of Life*
Alex Tissandier, *Affirming Divergence: Deleuze's Reading of Leibniz*
Barbara Glowczewski, *Indigenising Anthropology with Guattari and Deleuze*
Koichiro Kokubun, *The Principles of Deleuzian Philosophy*, translated by Wren Nishina
Felice Cimatti, *Unbecoming Human: Philosophy of Animality After Deleuze*, translated by Fabio Gironi
Ryan J. Johnson, *Deleuze, A Stoic*

Forthcoming volumes
Justin Litaker, *Deleuze and Guattari's Political Economy*
Nir Kedem, *A Deleuzian Critique of Queer Thought: Overcoming Sexuality*
Jane Newland, *Deleuze in Children's Literature*
Sean Bowden, *Expression, Action and Agency in Deleuze: Willing Events*
Andrew Jampol-Petzinger, *Deleuze, Kierkegaard and the Ethics of Selfhood*

Visit the Plateaus website at edinburghuniversitypress.com/series/plat

UNBECOMING HUMAN
Philosophy of Animality After Deleuze

Felice Cimatti

Translated by Fabio Gironi

EDINBURGH
University Press

Edinburgh University Press is one of the leading university presses in the UK. We publish academic books and journals in our selected subject areas across the humanities and social sciences, combining cutting-edge scholarship with high editorial and production values to produce academic works of lasting importance. For more information visit our website: edinburghuniversitypress.com

Edinburgh University Press Ltd
The Tun – Holyrood Road, 12(2f) Jackson's Entry, Edinburgh EH8 8PJ

First published in hardback by Edinburgh University Press 2020

Typeset in 11/13 Sabon LT Std by
Servis Filmsetting Ltd, Stockport, Cheshire
and printed and bound by CPI Group (UK) Ltd,
Croydon, CR0 4YY

A CIP record for this book is available from the British Library

ISBN 978 1 4744 4339 5 (hardback)
ISBN 978 1 4744 4340 1 (paperback)
ISBN 978 1 4744 4341 8 (webready PDF)
ISBN 978 1 4744 4342 5 (epub)

Published with a contribution from the Department of Humanistic Studies of the University of Calabria.

Contents

Introduction: Animals Do Not Exist

Bien sûr, l'homme fut animal; et pourtant il ne l'est plus
[Of course, man was an animal; and yet he is no longer]

(Bimbenet 2011: 22)

Animals are not others. Let us be clear about this: *Unbecoming Human* is neither exclusively nor mainly about nonhuman animals – like cats and jellyfish. The book you are holding deals with *our* animality, with *human* animality. *Unbecoming Human* attempts to delineate the still-unknown features of human animality. That is to say, all those *inhuman* characters that must be cut off by the apparatus (the 'anthropologic machine', as Agamben defines it) through which we become human, for otherwise we could neither become, nor *define* ourselves as, human. The double process of de-animalisation on the one hand and linguisticisation on the other, which we all must go through (for otherwise we could not be defined as properly human), produces a peculiar entity: the human psychological *subject*. The subject – which, as we will see, is nothing but a body referring to itself as an 'I' – speaks, and only in virtue of this is it indeed a subject. For this reason, animality concerns language: on the one hand language engenders the 'subject', on the other animality is animal (i.e., nonhuman) precisely because it is not traversed by language.

The purpose of this book, then, is that of describing the difficult – if not impossible – relationship established between *Homo sapiens* and other animals (and animality in general) from different points of view: those of philosophy, science, art, literature, cinema, and psychoanalysis. This relationship is impossible more than it is difficult because, ultimately, *Homo sapiens* simply means 'the living being that is *not* an animal' or 'the living being that continuously expels its own animality'. However, since every individual of the species *Homo sapiens* is, clearly, an animal – a vertebrate and a mammal, to be precise – to be human also means to be something intrinsically contradictory. It follows, therefore, that *Unbecoming Human* will *also* deal with nonhuman animals, but only insofar as this will help

1

in drawing the contours of human animality. When we speak of animality, therefore, we should certainly think about animals, but also – and perhaps mainly – about all those circumstances wherein something eludes the grasp of thoughts and words. Animality avoids our grasp, it cannot be captured; it is indeed the very elusiveness of life. It is for this reason that we will find animality in the most unsuspected places, where we would never think of encountering it, since animality abides even where no animals dwell.

In order to track human animality, however, it is necessary to start from that of nonhuman animals. This book will, then, also deal with cats and jellyfish. As Derrida (2008) warned us, this is a risky operation. Because the animal of which we speak is never the animal as it is in and of itself: the animal is always an *'animot'*, the spoken-of animal, metaphorised and idealised. That is, it is always the animal as thought and feared by human beings. In this sense, as we will see, the animal does not exist. In fact, the *'animot'* is literally made up by language, since our talking about animals (humans always talk about animals, and indeed it could be said that they invented language in order to speak *about* animals, and distance themselves from them) requires the hypothesis that, in the world, a referent for the word 'animal' can be found. The concept of *'animot'* allows us to subvert the common supposition according to which language simply nominates objects, independently existing in the world. As Derrida, like Hegel before him, observes, there are no cats, or viruses, in the world. Rather there is *this* living being in front of my eyes, or *this* particular virus that I can examine through the lenses of an electronic microscope. Clearly, *the animal* does not exist. Indeed, the category ANIMAL is a linguistic invention. We will return time and again to the relationship between language and animality, but for now it should be clear that the question of animality cannot be separated from that of language.

Let us come back to how to talk about animality. We have just seen that this is an unknown animality – still and perhaps forever unknown. This does not mean questioning the many scientific discoveries that have put our belonging to the animal kingdom beyond any doubt. But this is not the point. Darwin notwithstanding, the definition of the humanity of the human always implies, more or less explicitly, a radical differentiation from the world of animals. Even in prehistoric human cultures, for example, 'animals act primarily as metaphors' (Russell 2012: 11). An animal is a *metaphor* when it functions as a mere 'vehicle' for a meaning that transcends it. Thus, the flesh-and-blood living creature vanishes, and becomes an abstract and symbolic entity, an *animot*. In particular, the animal-metaphor is used by the human in order to think and to think itself: so, every thought about the animal necessarily oscillates between anthropocentrism and anthropomorphism (Russell 2012: 4). That is to say between, on the one hand, a thought about the animal that always refers back to the human standard, a thought that completely ignores all that, in the animal, cannot be referred to the human; and, on the other hand, a thought that attributes to the animal its own characteristics, and that therefore can only discern that which is attributed to it. But this means that there has never been a time when, for human beings, the animal was just an *animal*, and the human *another animal* among animals. If, since the beginning, the animal was a metaphor, then the animal was never an animal. As always, there was never a beginning, since every 'beginning' keeps beginning again and again, and was never a pure origin:

> This is the original mythologem and, at the same time, the aporia the speaking subject clashes with: language presupposes something nonlinguistic, and this something unrelated is presupposed, however, by giving it a name. The tree presupposed in the name 'tree' cannot be expressed in language; we can only speak *of* it starting from its having a name. (Agamben 2018b: 3)

The animal is the prototype of this unreachable non-linguistic origin; on the one hand there is no doubt that the human is an animal, and indeed both *Homo sapiens* and its language derive from this non-linguistic presupposition. But on the other hand this non-linguistic foundation enters the representational field simply as an 'animal', i.e., as a word, as language and representation. The unrepresentable is only present *qua* linguistic representation. Thus, the animal is both wild and domesticated, unsayable and metaphorised, constantly elided but always recalled, since 'we can think a being entirely without relation to language only through a language without any relation to being' (Agamben 2018b: 3). *Homo sapiens* is this aporia. It is impossible, or at least counterproductive, to think the animal and ignore the fact that this is always an *animot*. From this point of view the contemporary *animal* and *nonhuman* turns (Ritvo 2007; Weil 2010; Grusin 2015; Ingold 2016; Bjørkdahl and Parrish 2018) must come to terms with this paradox, intrinsic to any discourse on the animal.

It is now necessary to consider a few examples, in order to highlight the traps that await every reflection on animality. In §55 of his

Metaphysics of Morals, Kant writes that 'anyone has an incontestable property in anything the substance of which he has himself made'. Immediately after, Kant goes on to clarify that 'there are various natural products in a country that must still be considered artifacts (*artefacta*)'. He then proposes a curious comparison between potatoes and nonhuman animals: 'vegetables (e.g., potatoes) and domestic animals are, as regards their abundance, a product of man, which he can use, wear out or destroy (kill)' (Kant 1991: 345–6). Animals, like potatoes, are human 'products', i.e., things we can freely dispose of. The only way to consider animals is radically anthropocentric. This pattern of thought is still widespread even today. According to contemporary Italian legislation, for example, an 'animal companion' is 'any animal kept, or meant to be kept, by man for companionship or affection with no reproductive or feeding purposes, including those performing activities useful to man, like guide dogs, dogs for disabled people, animals meant for pet-therapy and rehabilitation, or employed for TV commercials. Wild animals are not to be considered companion animals' (article 1, comma 2, D.P.C.M. 28 February 2003). According to this definition the animal literally exists only to fulfil human needs, whether emotional or therapeutic. It should be noted how this same legislation excludes so-called 'wild' animals from any advantage given by this juridical standing. From the biological point of view, whether a cat lives in a human house or in the woods, whether it has been given a name and registered with a vet or not, makes no difference whatsoever. A cat is a cat, whether it is a house cat or not, whether it has been neutered or not. However, the law establishes – between these two cats – an enormous juridical difference, solely grounded in human interests. This is most disheartening when we consider that this legislation has been promoted by people and institutions who 'love' animals. Anthropocentrism seems difficult to avoid. At the same time, this example shows how the problem of animality has more in common with law than it does with biology. The question is never that of the animal per se, but rather concerns the human way of legislating about animal life. This is especially true when it comes to human animality – and indeed human life itself.

Anthropomorphism too is always lurking. Let us consider a famous example, the so-called 'mirror test' for nonhuman animals (Brandi 2016). The first experiment was originally designed by a psychologist looking for an 'objective' test to study the elusive phenomenon of consciousness (Gallup 1970). After having sedated a chimp with a narcotic, two odourless red stains were applied to its face, above one eyebrow and one ear. On waking up, the animal looked at itself in the mirror in the cage, which it had already been trained to use, and tried to scratch the colour stains away with its fingers. Gallup, and many after him, interpreted this behaviour as proof that chimps are capable of self-recognition. According to Gallup, 'insofar as self-recognition of one's mirror image implies a concept of self, these data would seem to qualify as the first experimental demonstration of a self-concept in a subhuman form' (1970: 87). The first point in need of clarification is: why should it be so important for an animal to pass the self-recognition test? Does self-recognition add something to an animal's value? Secondly, when a cat scratches itself with a paw, surely it somehow 'knows' that the paw is 'its' paw, but this does not mean that the cat knows itself to be *someone* with a paw. The concept of self-recognition has nothing to do with what one sees, but rather with what is thought about what is seen (or is believed to be seen). After all, the very concept of 'personal identity' is a historical-religious one (Martin and Barresi 2008), not a perceptual one. Self-consciousness, the awareness of oneself as a 'subject', has nothing to do with biology or psychology; it has to do rather with ethics and religion. What is most interesting is not so much whether or not some animals (why the chimp and not the gorilla?) are able to use a mirror to inspect 'their' body, but rather why we humans assign so much importance to self-recognition in the first place. What kind of life is a life unaware of itself? Our shared terror of Alzheimer's syndrome (Behuniak 2011) is, at base, the fear of an *animal life without consciousness*: the life of an ant, or a leaf, an inhuman impersonal life, but no less vital. It is for this reason that we constantly try to project our characteristics upon nonhuman animals, or at least those we believe to be our 'better' characteristics. Once again, we are not so much interested in animals as in exorcising the possibility of a different life – a radically different one compared to our human life. Anthropomorphism is the polite face of a more cruel and obtuse anthropocentrism. The challenge of this book is the attempt to think human animality while being mindful of these two pitfalls.

Returning to Derrida and his cat, it is now clear why we cannot talk about ourselves without imagining a radically different 'other'. We cannot talk about human beings, about their animality, without referring to nonhuman animals. Even if Derrida's cat is, precisely, 'Derrida's', that animal exists, it moves and observes. The fact that we can describe it, and that it cannot tell us what it thinks about itself, does not hinder the confrontation between the naked philosopher and 'his' cat. The crucial point is that that cat *exists*. In an extraordinary scene in the movie *Dogman* (2018), by the Italian director Matteo Garrone, we see some dogs in cages. In a dramatic moment when a murder takes place, these caged dogs – at once indifferent and preoccupied – witness the struggle between two men, victim and murderer. These dogs, like Derrida's cat, exist. This is the point: these animals exist. It is not a matter of interpreting their gazes, looking for some kind of hidden meaning or value in their eyes. They are eyes, and there is life in them – a life that captures the audience's attention precisely insofar as it is a nonhuman life. Animality is inhuman, and therein lies its charm. Every attempt to humanise those gazes is not just useless – since animality is indifferent to humanity – but harmful, since it would elide the radical alterity of the animal. *Dogman* does not show the saccharine humanity of the animal, but instead reminds us of its unthinkable and intolerable inhumanity, beginning with the most unknown of animals, the animal body of *Homo sapiens*.

If *Unbecoming Human* has a conceptual location, the only possible one would perhaps be in the undefined space that opens between us as observers and *Dogman*'s caged animals, not properly looking at us even while, as the audience, we feel observed. An impossible confrontation between humanity and animality is always underway. The philosophy of animality is, ultimately, an exploration of this impossibility. Human animality, whatever that is, is found *between* the philosopher and the cat, *between* an inevitable anthropocentrism and a just-as-inevitable anthropomorphism, *between* ethics and ethology. This point requires a further disclaimer.

It seems difficult to speak of animals and animality without immediately becoming preoccupied with the animal condition, animal rights and the ethical dilemma of the human treatment of animals. It is doubtless an urgent problem, but not one that properly pertains to the question of animality. In a ruling dated 14 June 1794, in Clermont, France, a pig who had bitten an infant in his cradle to death was sentenced to death by hanging. The text of the ruling explained that: 'we, in detestation and horror of said case, and in order to exemplify and preserve justice, have said, judged, sentenced, pronounced and appointed, that said pig be held prisoner and locked up in the abbey, and will be hanged and strangled in a wooden fork by the executioner' (cited in D'Addosio 1992: 186). The case of the pig sentenced to death is morbidly interesting, since it exemplifies the paradox that implicitly lies within every attempt – no matter how fully justified by the conditions under which nonhuman animals live – to give animality a juridical standing. In this case the judge was able to sentence the pig to death because he could consider it somehow 'responsible' for its actions. The fact that a modern reader considers this trial to be a nonsensical farce does not make it any less exemplary: to give legal rights to animals can lead to extreme consequences. Even at the time of this trial, animal advocates stressed how animals could not be considered responsible for their actions. In his *Tractatus de exorcismis*, the famous fourteenth–fifteenth century exorcist, Felix Hemmerlein, also known as Malleolus, recounts an invasion of so-called Spanish flies (*Lytta vescicatoria*) in the lands belonging to the Electorate of Mainz, and how the farmers whose plantations were threatened sued the flies. Unlike in the pig trial, however, in this case the judge, 'in consideration of their small size and the fact that they had not yet reached their majority', assigned the flies a small patch of uncultivated land for them to live on freely (Payson Evans 1896: 111). In this case, the leniency towards the flies is no less arbitrary, or absurd, than the merciless punishment inflicted upon the pig. In both cases, the animal is in the same predicament as *Dogman*'s dogs, mutely witnessing the absurdity of human actions, all the more meaningless as they pretend to respect the principles of *human* law. From this point of view, even the praiseworthy collection *The Great Ape Project* (Cavalieri and Singer 1994) does not – and cannot – subtract itself from the paradox described by Agamben: the paradox incurred by those who want to safeguard the non-linguistic, and in this case the nonhuman, at the price of fully reinscribing it within human (in this case, legal and ethical) discourse.

A helpful gesture, no doubt, but one that also implies forfeiting what one is independently of such a gesture. Let us consider the famous opening of Cavalieri and Singer's volume, which marked a turning point in the ethical-political debate on animal rights:

> we are human, and we are also great apes. Our membership of the human species gives us a precious moral status: inclusion within the sphere of moral equality. Those within this sphere we regard as entitled to special moral protection. There are things that we may not do to them. They have basic rights that are denied to those outside this sphere. (Cavalieri and Singer 1994: 1)

The aim of enlarging the 'sphere of moral equality' to include other species is clearly a noble and agreeable one; however, to define a gorilla as a human being implies that a gorilla *is not* a gorilla. After all, the project's placement between anthropocentrism and anthropo-morphism is explicitly declared by the authors: 'we seek an extension of equality that will embrace not only our own species, but also the species that are our closest relatives and that most resemble us in their capacities and their ways of living' (1994: 1). The contentious point lies in this resemblance between 'us' and the great apes: 'if you are like me, I will save you. You are not like me? Then there is no hope for you.' The scientific reasoning motivating this request for an extension of (at least some) human rights to animals is even more 'merciless'. As they put it: 'we now have sufficient informa-tion about the capacities of chimpanzees, gorillas and orang-utans to make it clear that the moral boundary we draw between us and them is indefensible. Hence the time is ripe for extending full moral equality to members of other species, and the case for so doing is overwhelming' (Cavalieri and Singer 1994: 1). If, in Malleolus's days, one appealed to divine authority, today it is science that has the last word. But science, due to its very nature, often changes its mind, so that what was an incontrovertible fact yesterday can become an outdated – if not downright false – notion tomorrow. Let us imagine that one day it is discovered that nonhuman animals have no interior life and that, as Descartes argued, they are nothing but complex bio-mechanical automata. Bracketing the contemporary debate around the possibility of granting 'rights' to robots and to artificial intelligence (Anderson and Leigh Anderson 2011), the fact remains that subordinating legal rights to science implies the ground-lessness of the ethical principle, which would depend on an 'opinion' (since scientific consensus is an opinion too, as well-supported as it might be), and like all opinions, it would be prone to revision. Behind this opinion lies the anthropocentric and anthropomorphic principle prompting us to see 'some nonhuman animals as persons' (Cavalieri and Singer 1994: 2). It should be evident that this is not a mere observation, but rather a sentence: a life sentence for some animals, and a death sentence for many others. Some animals will be saved, sure, but we should not forget the arbitrary violence implicit in such a sentence (for it is arbitrary to hold that having a conscious-ness is more ethically relevant than having a 'simple' central nervous system). We once again encounter a theme that will recur throughout the rest of this book: the intrinsically contradictory nature of any discourse on animality (Cimatti 2015; Cavalieri 2015).[1]

But what is a 'person'? Roberto Esposito has shown, in his *Persons and Things* (2015), that this is actually a juridical-religious concept rather than a psychological or scientific one. Ultimately, deciding what counts as a person and what doesn't, and therefore who has rights and intrinsic value and who doesn't, is a political decision. The concept of the 'person' is an apparatus that engenders dualisms: 'not a union but a separation. It separated not only some from others on the basis of particular social roles, but also the individual from its own biological entity' (Esposito 2015: 30). As we will see in greater detail later on (Chapter 2), the person is a kind of biopolitical machinery that produces the split, on the one hand, between the subject-person – a subject that sets itself apart from every other person – and its 'own' body on the other. Indeed, the mind-body dualism – where the mind controls the body like the tamer controls the lion – is the main product of the personal machinery: thus 'the concept of the person [works by] splitting the living organism into two' (Esposito 2015: 35). One becomes a person by learning to control the body, i.e., by adapting 'its' needs to the 'will' of the subject-person. But the tamed body is nothing but the animal body, human animality. This dualism is identical to the one established between human and nonhuman, or *Homo sapiens* and the ANIMAL. Not a scientific dualism, but one with a religious origin:

> Christianity viewed all individuals as persons, made in the image and likeness of their creator. But they are considered as such precisely because they are divided into two natures, one spiritual and the other corporeal, with the latter subordinated to the former. This is how we passed from a functional division between human being and person, as in Roman law, to an ontological division within the human-person composite, between the two substances that form it. (Esposito 2015: 36)

If this is the archaeology of the person, what might its effects be? Could it transform a chimp into a person? Would the chimp's 'own' body have 'rights'? Once made a 'person', would the chimp be in the position of breaking the law? In the first line of their 'Declaration on Great Apes', Cavalieri and Singer write:

> We demand the extension of the community of equals to include all great apes: human beings, chimpanzees, gorillas and orang-utans. 'The community of equals' is the moral community within which we accept certain basic moral principles or rights as governing our relations with each other and enforceable at law. (1994: 4)

Immediately after this, in the second point of the declaration, the problem we just discussed appears: 'the detention of those who have not been convicted of any crime, or of those who are not criminally liable, should be allowed only where it can be shown to be for their own good, or necessary to protect the public from a member of the community who would clearly be a danger to others if at liberty' (1994: 4). How can a chimp commit a crime? We would be going back in time to the trial of the pig. Perhaps, then, those laws were not so absurd – maybe they were even more advanced – since the 'community of equals' included insects and pigs, and not just the animals we believe to be closest to us (often on the basis of unconscious prejudices; see Cimatti and Vallortigara 2015). Here we discern the link between the question of animality and biopolitics, that is to say the sum total of administrative and scientific practices that have as their object the control of a living being. For example, in *The History of Sexuality* Foucault explained that 'sex' is a *creation* of those forms of discourse that have as their object the sexed body: 'It is this deployment that enables something called "sexuality" to embody the truth of sex and its pleasures' (1978: 68). Sex is to the subject/person as the human being is to the ANIMAL. 'Sex' – *qua* political and scientific object – is used to make the body more controllable, and to put it at the State's and the person's service: 'sex is the most speculative, most ideal, and most internal element in a deployment of sexuality organized by power in its grip on bodies and their materiality, their forces, energies, sensations, and pleasures' (Foucault 1978: 155). Similarly, to turn a chimp into a person means, whether or not this is our intention, dragging it into this enormous biopolitical machinery – made of religion, jurisprudence, science and economy – that has no other purpose but to enslave the living body. The conclusion of the second point of Cavalieri and Singer's declaration demonstrates how what is at stake in their discourse is legal rights: 'members of the community of equals must have the right to appeal, either directly or, if they lack the relevant capacity, through an advocate, to a judicial tribunal' (1994: 4). What begins with an animal life ends in a tribunal – but where judges and lawyers begin, there life ends. What is at stake for a philosophy of animality, then, is not just a defence of animal rights but rather a way to think a world without persons, and therefore without laws, judges, economists and policemen. It is not a matter of personalising the world, but rather of depersonalising life.

There is, therefore, a less than evident link – which *Unbecoming Human* purports to reveal – between the question of the animal and biopolitics. The problem is that the question of animality is not that of animal rights, nor a demand for the equal standing of all forms of life. The point is that the subordination of the animal is a problem

10

that pertains not only to (for example) cows in farms, but also to 'our' own body. There can be a police dog only because there is a policeman – the subject/person – who keeps the recalcitrant body, the living body, the rule-less body of the human animal, under control, exactly as he controls 'his' own dog. This is why the question of animality mostly pertains to *human* animality; indeed, the question of animality is probably the most relevant philosophical issue we can face. For example, until the mind/body dualism – i.e., the biopolitical dualism between subject/person and subjugated body – has been overcome, the ecological problem cannot even begin to be addressed, since the human animal treats the natural environment in the same exact way as he treats his or her 'own' body: as a resource to be exploited. As long as the human body is considered as the *animal* of the subject, like the neutered cat purring on our lap, neither the farm animals nor the plants, nor the seas, nor the very atmosphere of planet Earth will be 'freed'. The hotly debated question of the Anthropocene (Crutzen and Brauch 2016) is nothing but the ecological side of the question of animality.

Let us go back to the subject/person, because the book you are now reading is concerned with this figure and how to leave it behind. A living body becomes properly a person only when it becomes capable of self-representing itself as an 'I', that is, able to *say* about itself that it *is* an 'I'. This also entails the alienating ability to take a stance towards ourselves, towards the body we inhabit. This is, once again, both a psychological and a juridical gesture: 'in order for the subject to be able to make a judgment about itself, it must be able to separate from itself, taking on the dual role of the judge and the accused' (Esposito 2015: 43). The 'judge' is the voice declaring itself to be an 'I', while the 'accused' is the body that, from that moment onwards, will be at the subject/person's service.

In a lecture course held at the University of Louvain in 1981, titled *Wrong-doing, Truth-telling: The Function of Avowal in Justice* (*Mal faire, dire vrai. Fonction de l'aveu en justice*), Foucault returned to the nexus between subjectivity and subjugation of the body, i.e., the 'government through truth' over oneself. The 'confession' – that peculiar discursive practice through which the subject speaks the truth about itself – actually plays another and more important function: through confession the living human being institutes itself as a 'subject', as 'someone' who does not coincide with him or herself and, more precisely, as someone who *judges* the body's deeds. A body that is always moved by ungovernable desires and passions. It is

11

the practice of confession itself that institutes the body as the animal within the human. The body in itself, like *Dogman*'s dogs, is neither animalistic nor savage; it is the subject that needs a beast to wrestle, in order to present itself as other than animal. Once again, the animal is an invention, and a leftover, of subjectivity and of juridical/religious discourse. Indeed, Foucault speaks of 'technologies of the subject' – i.e., those 'techniques through which the individual is brought, either by himself or with the help or the direction of another, to transform himself and to modify his relationship to himself' (2014: 24) – rather than of some special 'psychic' substance.

The subject/person is then a machinery producing *separation*: between the self as an 'I' with respect to the body, as well as between different 'I's. Esposito speaks of a 'push for immunity' (2015: 115) as a distinctive feature of the subject/person. Here we encounter another facet of the problem of animality: the political aspect. One of the defining traits of our time, and perhaps the most distinctive, is the pre-eminence of economic neoliberalism (Harvey 2005), presented as inevitable and without alternatives, the final and definitive political order. The subject/person is born as a distancing gesture towards the animal body; the 'I' is nothing but this separation, always repeating itself. Through Foucault and, as we will see (Chapter 5), through Lacan, we have understood how the subject/person controls the body only because it is, in itself, the effect of juridical/discursive practices that are beyond its control. From this point of view the subject/person is the perfect '*homo œconomicus*', i.e., 'someone who is eminently governable' (Foucault 2008: 270). The *homo œconomicus* is nothing but a living being that is destroying the planet, whether it conceives of itself as an ecologist or not. Indeed, it unwillingly destroys the planet (the environmentalist activist needs electric energy as much as the landowner who wants a perfect English lawn in Las Vegas), because to be a subject/person means to be a machinery that produces, as if through its own immune system (Esposito 2011), a separation and a distance between itself and other subjects/persons. The subject, precisely because it is not an animal, produces the exploitation of the environment. This point must be clarified: from nature's standpoint there is no difference between polluting a wellspring to extract shale gas and using the wind's power to spin the blades of a windmill. In both cases, nature is submitted to the will of *Homo sapiens*. An environmentalist is no less neoliberal than a Wall Street broker. Both subjects/persons pursue their own goals, calculate benefits and costs, maximise investments, and plan the future. Sadly, Foucault was right

– perhaps even more than he realised – for *homo œconomicus* is not
a transitory figure, but rather *Homo sapiens'* ultimate incarnation,
the most efficient and ruthless. And so,

> from the point of view of a theory of government, *homo œconomicus*
> is the person who must be let alone. With regard to *homo œconomicus*,
> one must *laisser-faire*; he is the subject or object of *laisser-faire*. ...
> *Homo œconomicus*, that is to say, the person who accepts reality or who
> responds systematically to modifications in the variables of the environ-
> ment, appears precisely as someone manageable. (Foucault 2008: 268)

On the other hand, it is interesting to note the existence of a widespread and marked optimism about a postulated primordial human
intersubjectivity, a positive attitude partially justified from a neurological point of view (considering the epochal discovery of 'mirror
neurons', confirming a primordial empathy between human bodies
(see Gallese 2003)). Still, perhaps this narrative about different 'I's
being in harmony is overly optimistic: when a subject/person says 'I'
he or she is tracing a border. Here I am, and *there* – precisely – you
are. The anthropological function of the subject is that of limiting
the possibilities of other subjects that, like the 'I', want to be in the
position to utter 'I'. Conflict, exploitation, exclusion and segregation
are already implicit in the foundational anthropologic gesture, that
utterance of 'I' which makes the emergence of human subjectivity
possible (Cimatti 2000).

On the contrary, this book aims at delineating the field of a
human individuality not grounded in the 'I', a non-personal and non-
subjective human body. This requires a preliminary rethinking of
the *animality* of the human, that perennially excluded and discarded
part of human life, located in a space that remains unthinkable
(we cannot even imagine a thought without a thinking 'I'), beyond
language. This *beyond* is important: the humanity of the human is
grounded on its ability to speak, and therefore we will never find the
animality of *Homo sapiens* in other animals, those who do not define
themselves through language. In this sense, the title *Unbecoming
Human* indicates a Deleuzian 'line of flight' away from humanity,
an exploration of a possible humanity not grounded in language. An
animality to be built, rather than discovered, which lies ahead of and
not behind us.

To think animality means to imagine a different way of being
human, not divided into mind and body. That is to say, a human life
capable of being completely expressed, without residue, in our lived

existence, the *only* life we can live. This kind of non-subjective human-ity would not be split between the present and a still-unlived future life which perhaps one day will be. The life we are trying to imagine is wholly devoid of transcendence, a life that neither projects itself towards the future, nor extends towards the past. For this reason, to rethink the animality of the human – and therefore its becoming a subjugated body – means to think the theme of immanence: a life that does not need to project itself beyond itself, because 'immanence is a thought of life, not a meditation about death' (Ciccarelli 2008: 19).

Before dealing with human animality, it will be necessary to examine how and why animality has been so tenaciously distanced from the definition of the human (Calarco 2008). As we have seen, the first – and hardest – stage of this inquiry entails accepting the fact that *animals* do not exist. They do not exist because we do not know anything about them – we have never really observed them. And that is because we only know the animals we have invented (Despret 2002). The animals do not exist because there isn't – and there can't be – any extended category that would include *all* living beings, except the human. MAN (not the child or the woman or the elderly) on the one side, and the ANIMAL (singular) on the other, a single huge and confused container, which would contain whales and worms, prions and horses, chickens and chimps. The animal does not exist.

The ANIMAL (and therefore animals in general) does not exist, because whenever we are talking about animals we are actually refer-ring to something completely different. That is because they have always been allegories for the human (and not for themselves): either as exemplary representations of a virtue, or of a vice. Let us consider an illustrious example: *The Book of Beasts: Being a Translation from a Latin Bestiary of the Twelfth Century* (the *Physiologus*), a text originally composed between the second and fourth centuries CE in Alexandria, which enjoyed widespread popularity throughout the Middle Ages, and which still today (silently) informs our way of looking at animals. Let us look at the truly *exemplary* treatment reserved for the beaver:

> This is an animal called CASTOR the Beaver, none more gentle, and his testicles make a capital medicine. For this reason, so Physiologus says, when he notices that he is being pursued by the hunter he removes his own testicles with a bite, and casts them before the sportsman, and thus escapes by flight. What is more, if he should again happen to be chased by a second hunter, he lifts himself up and shows his members to him. And

14

the latter, when he perceives the testicles to be missing, leaves the beaver alone. (White 1960: 28–9)

The tale is rather explicit, but also straightforward: the animal is a sign, not an autonomous entity. The animal is a warning to the human. The beaver is like the pious man, forced to castrate himself in order to be admitted to the kingdom of heaven. Here is the question of animality, but not that of the beaver: rather, of the human.

Philosophy was born when a border was created, between us and the others – the animals. We could even argue – somewhat contentiously – that without animals philosophy itself would not have existed, since there would have been no compulsion to define the human. Who would be concerned with the definition of the human in a hypothetical world solely populated by *Homines sapientes*? As Lévi-Strauss rightly observed: 'natural species are chosen not because they are "good to eat", but because they are "good to think"' (1964: 89). In this sense, as much as today ethologists, philosophers, writers, scientists and poets like to talk about animals, this is always a more or less indirect and perhaps unconscious attempt to talk about us, about the talking animal, about *Homo sapiens*. Moreover, it is often the case that even well-meaning animalism does not properly speak about animals, about *their* lives, but mostly about what *we think* about their lives, their emotions and their mind.

As a matter of fact, every definition of the animal is a *negative* definition, starting from the definition of the human (the animal is the living being that lacks something: language, reason, laughter, opposable thumbs, art, hands, fear of death, and so on). The only animal we know is the one who *lacks* something. In this sense, then, animals do not exist, because it is really odd to deal with living beings only to then ask whether or not they possess, for example, language. A beaver is a complete living being, and to ask ourselves if it is endowed with something that another animal has is meaningless – it would be like asking if *Homo sapiens* has feathers, or gills. And this attitude is certainly not limited to philosophy: it is also common in the sciences. It should suffice to look at the many occasions in which the sciences (comparative psychology, ethology, cognitive science) have changed their minds regarding animals and what they can or cannot do. Today the fashionable thing to say is that animals – and some of them in particular (today bonobos, but before them it was dolphins, and pigeons earlier still) – are essentially like us: they have a mind, reason, language, emotions, morality and so on. They are like us (or

15

almost like us, there is never agreement on where exactly to draw the boundary). *Like us*. So, we are the problem, not the animals, who are often forced to endure absurd, often cruel, or sometimes utterly meaningless experiments in order to establish *how* close they are to us. It is curious to note how animalism does not understand this, fairly evident, point: to claim that animals have rights because they are like us is just a way to ignore them. Why would these rights be assigned only to those creatures we (arbitrarily) consider as being *like* humans? Is being human so important, such that we take ourselves to be the yardstick for all living beings?

This is not, therefore, yet another book about animals: there are a lot of those, including a few very good ones (as long as you remember that they are actually about the *animot*). No, this book is about the human animal, *Homo sapiens*: the only animal – and this, granted, is a unique characteristic of our species – that is primarily concerned with setting itself apart from all other living beings. As I have already tried to argue, there is no more urgent task today, in the age of humanity's failure – an ecological failure first, but also a political and ethical one – to keep in contact with the animality that it embodies or, as we should probably say, that it could embody. I would like, in the pages that follow, to discern the echo of a dialogue by Paul Valéry, the *Dialogue of the Tree*. This work has two main characters: Tityrus, a shepherd leaning against a huge and majestic beech, and the poet Lucretius:

> But *you* profess to understand things: you dream you know much more about this beech than it could know itself if it had a thought which induced it to believe it could grasp itself. . . . *I* only wish to know my happy moments. Today my soul is making itself into a tree. Yesterday I felt it to be a spring. Tomorrow? Shall I rise with the smoke from an altar, or soar above the plains with the sense of power of the vulture on its slow wings – how do I know? (Valéry 1989: 154)

In the course of the editorial process that eventually led to the publication of this book (an extended revision of *Filosofia dell'Animalità* published in Italy by Laterza) a reviewer required the addition of some personal information, towards the end of the Introduction, in order to explain to a foreign reader, unfamiliar with a certain kind of philosophical training, why an Italian philosopher would be interested in the theme of animality. In particular, the request was to 'add some detail on your background and how you ended up dedicating your career to studying human language from an unusual perspective'. I can answer this question in at least two ways, from a personal perspective and from a more general one. I got my BA in Philosophy in 1983 at the University of Rome 'La Sapienza' under the supervision of Tullio De Mauro, arguably the most pre-eminent Italian philosopher of language, linguist and historian of languages of that decade. My dissertation was titled *Animal Languages* and was co-supervised by Alberto Oliverio, a psychobiologist. In this dissertation I discussed, from a philosophical standpoint, the scientific literature on animal language. In those years the volume *Approaches to Animal Communication*, edited by the semiologist Thomas Sebeok, was an object of vigorous interest: in it, several cases of 'animal communication' (i.e., nonhuman communication) were presented, composing that set of phenomena known as *zoosemiotics*. My dissertation was aimed at demonstrating how nonhuman animals' linguistic abilities – although very different from those of humans – could however be comparable to human language. The central argument insisted on the 'creative' features of animal languages. What I had done was try to apply the concept of linguistic 'creativity' (which De Mauro explored in several texts, like *Introduzione alla Semantica* (1999) and *Minisemantica dei linguaggi non verbali e delle lingue* (2018)) to zoosemantics. De Mauro's concept of 'creativity' was related to another similar, yet more wide-ranging one elaborated by another Italian philosopher, Emilio Garroni (then a colleague of De Mauro at *La Sapienza*), in his *Estetica ed Epistemologia: Riflessioni sulla Critica del Giudizio* (2003) and *Senso e Paradosso. L'estetica, filosofia non speciale* (1995).

In this first phase of my career my interest in animality was, therefore, very circumscribed, and mediated by the linguistic and semiotic research of De Mauro. For De Mauro, there is no radical difference between verbal language and animal languages, and my dissertation followed this general approach. However, if, on the one hand, I tried to criticise those defending a neat separation between the linguistic competence of *Homo sapiens* and that of other animals, on the other I failed to problematise the very legitimacy of a comparison between different animal species. In fact, the blind spot of my dissertation consisted in the implicit presupposition according to which, in order to study the semiotic (and cognitive) capacities of nonhuman animals, it would be necessary to take the human as an exemplary paradigm. Although I did defend some theses that were 'favourable' to animals, I was still unwittingly under the influence of an anthropocentric bias. Later, I published two books on these topics:

Mente e linguaggio negli animali. Introduzione alla zoosemiotica cognitiva (2002b) and *La mente silenziosa: come pensano gli animali non umani* (2002a). In these texts I attempted to demonstrate how animal behaviour is cognitively sophisticated, particularly when it comes to their communicative abilities. These are books written by a philosopher, but a philosopher informed by the scientific literature on the topic. In fact, it is impossible to talk about animals without having an idea of how they behave and live. A particularly good example – although his analysis is controversial – is that of Martin Heidegger, who in his 1929–30 lecture course on *The Fundamental Concepts of Metaphysics: World, Finitude, Solitude* competently discussed the work of Jakob von Uexküll, at the time the greatest zoologist in Europe. After the publication of my *Mente silenziosa* (a book announcing its thesis in the title itself: animal thought is non-linguistic and non-semiotic, since I was already becoming aware that what makes animals interesting are their differences, not their similarities to us), I started working primarily on questions of philosophical anthropology. In particular, I wanted to explore how language has an impact on the human body, how it can change it and make it capable of behaviours that would be impossible without language. From this point of view, I kept following the scientific literature on animals, yet always with a focus on human behaviour. At the same time, my experience with zoosemiotics has bequeathed me, so to speak, a naturalistic approach to the humanity of the human (as expressed in my *La scimmia che parla. Linguaggio, autocoscienza, e libertà nell'animale umano* (2000)).

In 2006 the problem of animality was powerfully returned to my attention thanks to Jacques Derrida's book, *The Animal That Therefore I Am* (2008). This book literally reversed my perspective: all of a sudden, I realised that everything I had read and written on the animal was based on an unacknowledged anthropocentric prejudice. Faithful to Morgan's Canon – '[i]n no case is an animal activity to be interpreted in terms of higher psychological processes if it can be fairly interpreted in terms of processes which stand lower in the scale of psychological evolution and development' (1903: 59) – I had always criticised other people's anthropomorphism, while being blind to my own anthropocentrism. I now realised that my discussions of animals and animal behaviour said more about me – about my fears and my desires – than they revealed about animals, about cats and moles. From that moment on, I returned to the theme of animality, but as a general philosophical topic rather than simply

18

(or primarily) as an exploration of the cognitive and communicative skills of animals. For me the problem is no longer (for example) 'how does a dolphin think?', but rather 'why am I interested in comparing a human with a dolphin?' Once again, the problem of language is central: it is evident that language is the primary anthropologic device, i.e., the mechanism that transforms a mammal not unlike all other mammals into a *human* animal, capable of thinking about itself as an 'I'. Everything else – religion, politics, science and art – would be impossible without the appearance, on the worldly stage, of that linguistic creature that is the subject/person.

If I used to look at zoosemiotics as a means to understand animals, I now became interested in that peculiar zoosemiotic system that is verbal language, in order to understand how this retroacts onto the human body, how it modifies its animal body/mind. *Unbecoming Human* is the result of this radical change of perspective. In fact, many of the examples and authors discussed in this book have already been examined in my previous works; however, I now consider them, so to speak, from the other side. I now see what was left in the background, because I understand that, when we are observing animality, what we leave in the background is more interesting than that which takes centre stage. This is why, in this book, I try to let the animals speak for themselves. This – I am well aware – is not simply an impossible task, but a misguided one at that, because the animal has its good reasons not to speak, and to force it to do so is a presumptuous act of violence. I tried to look at things from the other side. This is my personal answer to the reviewer's query, explaining how I came to examine human language starting from animality.

There is also another possible answer, one that pertains to the issue of animality in contemporary Italian philosophy and literature (Amberson and Past 2014). I will limit myself to two examples: Giorgio Agamben and Roberto Esposito. Before examining these two thinkers, it is necessary to account for the insular specificity of this tradition of thought, which both isolated it from mainstream philosophical movements and allowed it to avoid the *aporias* into which these eventually fell. This specificity has been discussed by Esposito in his *Living Thought: The Origins and Actuality of Italian Philosophy* (2012a). The Italian tradition never adhered to the 'linguistic turn', and this implied that – at least in its principal outline – it was never a philosophy of the 'subject'. Relatively unencumbered by the presence of a 'subject', Italian thought is able, at least in principle, to explore the theme of animality, and in general all that which eludes the grasp of language.

Moving on from Foucault's work, Esposito has been exploring, at least since *Bios: Biopolitics and Philosophy* (2008), the effects of the biopolitical apparatus on human life. The theoretically most interesting – and all too often misunderstood – point of this inquiry is that the biopolitical apparatus, such as the 'person' machinery pertaining to how we become human, is not a historically recent phenomenon. In *Persons and Things* (2015), for example, Esposito shows how the ostensibly 'neutral' and 'obvious' distinction between things on the one hand and persons on the other is, in its origin, a juridical-religious one. Even if Esposito still hasn't directly tackled the theme of animality (although in his *Living Thought* some very interesting pages are dedicated to the presence of nature in Italian philosophy), it implicitly emerges from his philosophy: what else is the 'affirmative politics' discussed in *Politica e negazione* (2018) if not an attempt to imagine a politics able to escape from the biopolitical trap? It is no coincidence that, in this latest book, Esposito explicitly examines language, that machinery through which the power of the negative is introduced into life, opposing its affirmative vital power. This is not quite the issue of animality, but if human animality is understood as the condition in which biopolitical death drives are neutralised, it would not be mistaken to locate this problem in Esposito's thought.

In Agamben's case the question of animality is even more central to his theoretical work, as well as the object of one of his monographs (*The Open: Man and Animal* (2004)). Starting with *Homo Sacer: Sovereign Power and Bare Life* (1998), Agamben argued for the necessity of rethinking the binary oppositions into which Western metaphysics inevitably falls (and indeed metaphysics is nothing but the never-ending fall into these dualisms) – in particular, the distinction between legal right/language on the one hand and 'bare life' on the other. The originality of Agamben's thought consists precisely in its ability to show the myriad ways in which this dualism presents itself time and again. This dualism cannot be avoided, as it is constantly repeated by choosing one of its – inseparable and interdependent – poles. To choose the body, for example, as phenomenology sometimes seems to do, simply means to 'remove' the subjective/linguistic pole, without which the body cannot exist. Here the case of animality is exemplary: the *open*, where the animal lives, is not simply a material world opposed to the 'spiritual' world inhabited by the human. In fact, the *open* is the place – an utterly unthinkable place for the human (since *Homo sapiens* is by definition unable to stay in the open) – where the distinction between legal right/language and 'bare life' implodes. Agamben has often attempted to describe a human life that would go beyond this primordial distinction; for example, in his *The Use of Bodies* (2016), where he imagines an impersonal and non-subjective human life. Such a life would not be properly human, since only a body shaped by the anthropologic and biopolitical machinery of language can be human (*Language and Death: The Place of Negativity* (2006)). In this sense it would be a human life, but one located beyond the human; better yet, it would be an inhuman way to be human. It would therefore be a life both human and animal. In the last few years Agamben, in a series of very interesting (and ever more impersonally 'personal') books, has attempted to describe these forms of human life located beyond the human, as for example in his *The Highest Poverty: Monastic Rules and Form-of-Life* (2013), *Pulcinella or Entertainment for Children* (2018a) and *Autoritratto nello studio* (2017b). Ultimately, human animality lies just beyond the horizon. Neither Esposito nor Agamben have, so far, explicitly faced the problem of human animality – and yet this theme is recurrent in their thought, as a sort of 'natural' outcome of their theoretical outlook.

Note

1. Egalitarianism attempts, at least in part, to elude this contradiction (Holtug and Lippert-Rasmussen 2007). This is an ethical perspective based on the intuition that, all other things being equal, the best result is obtained where 'happiness' is equally redistributed. In the case of nonhuman animals, egalitarianism holds that it would be necessary to establish the conditions for 'happiness' to be extended to the largest possible number of animals, not just those to whom we can plausibly attribute an inner life and interests: 'egalitarianism implies that we should reject speciesism (the discrimination against those who don't belong to a certain species, which is commonly directed against nonhuman animals) and animal exploitation. Moreover, it entails that the defense of nonhuman animals must be a priority for us, since they are worse off than human beings. This means that we must not only abstain from harming nonhuman animals, but also work actively for them' (Horta 2016: 111). On the practical level, this position has the clear advantage of being able to overcome anthropocentric speciesism, yet it does not question the unexamined juridical presupposition according to which to be a 'person' is better than to be a 'thing'. Horta himself argues that 'according to

most current legal systems, nonhuman animals are considered things; they have the legal status of property. Egalitarians can reject this and advocate the granting of legal rights to nonhuman animals because legal protection of the interests of individuals is carried out by means of legal rights' (2016: 132–3). Respect for the nonhuman animal is subordinated to its acknowledgment of its status as a 'non-thing', i.e., a person. But the subject/person is, by definition, the human being. Ultimately, it appears that egalitarianism does not consider the animal *qua* animal, as something other than a person/subject. This problem is intrinsic to any ethical perspective, since ethics presupposes and implies the presence of a subject/person. The paradox we have already encountered rears its head again: it seems to be impossible to treat animals in a way that is neither anthropocentric nor anthropomorphic.

Another, more general, question needs answering: how far can egalitarianism be extended? Why stop at animals? 'If I see a rock on the ground as a potentially powerful person, my relation to it will be unique to that perspective. My perception of the rock, according to phenomenology, is fundamental and not determined by my awareness of its personhood, but my receptivity to these perceptions is blocked by limitations in thinking about the rock's possible personhood. One's approach to experience shifts in a world in which categories of animate and inanimate don't exist' (Oriel 2014: 52). The rock would be a 'powerful person'. The point is that the concept of 'person' is not ontologically neutral, but is inseparably linked to a human religious and juridical perspective. If a rock is a 'person', it follows that it is not a rock. After all, when this ethical stance is taken to its extreme, it interestingly seems to encourage yet another worldview of complete human control over nature: indeed, since 'nonhuman animals are worse off with respect to humans', then, '[a]ccording to egalitarianism, this means we have strong reasons to change the situation in which they currently are'. A sinister conclusion follows: 'as for animals living in the wild, we should prevent or reduce the harms that they naturally endure. Thus, egalitarianism implies positively assisting nonhuman animals when they are in need, whether it be because of human beings or because of nature' (Faria 2014: 234). One strategy for overcoming this problem is Rosi Braidotti's zoe-centrism, focused on the principle that 'the relational capacity of the posthuman subject is not confined within our species, but it includes all nonanthropomorphic elements, starting from the air we breathe. Living matter – including embodied human flesh – is intelligent and self-organizing' (2017: 33). The core problem is precisely this 'posthuman subject': 'we may yet overcome anthropocentrism by becoming anthropomorphic bodies without organs that are still finding out what they are capable of becoming' (Braidotti 2017: 35). It remains to be seen just how 'subjectivised' such a body could be, since the 'subject' is the principal problem for a philosophy of human animality. To pay attention to animality means (or should have meant) paying attention to the nonhuman world, a world ever more threatened by the incursions of *Homo sapiens*. If to save nature means to transform it, in order to make it 'better' than it actually is (for example, by freeing it from the suffering it imposes on living beings), then nothing *animal* would be left in animality. What is natural in a nature humanised according to ethical considerations?

1

Animal?

A main cause of philosophical disease – a one-sided diet: one nourishes one's thinking with only one kind of example.

(Wittgenstein 2009: I, § 593)

The Missing Animal

A cat looks at us. We begin with a common animal, one that even a city dweller, not particularly fond of animals, might know. Like our aunt's cat, or the neighbours' dog. When we step into its house, the cat might come to greet us, brushing its tail against our legs; or it may ignore us, resting in its preferred spot, its armchair, or under a bed. Either way, the cat's life will proceed. That is because the cat's life is different than ours, often so different to be beyond our imagination – yet a life nonetheless. This is the point: it is an unimaginable life. It cannot be imagined because an abyss separates it from ours. The cat, sure enough, eats, sleeps, plays, has sexual appetites, dreams (perhaps), and finally dies – just like us, and like any other living being. But these similarities are too generic, and cannot help us imagine what living a cat's life might really mean.

The problem is not simply that the cat incarnates a unique point of view on the world (Nagel 1974), for that is obvious, and the same separation of standpoints obtains between different human beings. In fact, what assurance can we have that the person next to us feels exactly what we are feeling? The cat effectively represents a completely different way of living, of perceiving and of thinking than that of the human (Cimatti 2002a). This book explores this absolute difference – a radical difference that has only rarely, in the history of philosophy and of science, been thoroughly thought through. This difference – and now we begin to understand the difficulty of properly articulating the problem – does not simply highlight a divergence between the cat's world and the human world. This framing of the problem, which is the traditional way of looking at things, presupposes two categories: on the one hand the human, on the other the animal, each time exemplified by a different species – in this case, the cat. Now, the problem is that the cat, like the HUMAN, does not exist. There is no CAT, there is only *this* cat, this particular living body. But if the cat does not exist, the animal does not exist either – this strange being supposedly containing the characters of all nonhuman living beings (plants excluded, as well as those 'unfortunate' beings that we cannot classify as either plants or animals): from prions to viruses, from amoebae to whales, from eels to chimps. And yet, as we will see, philosophy talks (almost) always about the *animal*, strictly singular.

The animal is radical *difference*, not simply with respect to human beings, but in itself. Before elaborating this point, however, it is necessary to address those who believe that the discovery of so-called 'mirror neurons' (Rizzolatti et al. 1999) has allegedly proven the existence of an empathic common ground between living beings, particularly mammals (Huber et al. 2009). What did this discovery amount to, precisely? Let us consider this scenario: an ape sees another ape reaching out for an apple with its hand. In the brain of the observing ape, neurons in the motor cortex fire up, the same neurons that control the movement of its own arm. In this sense, the ape sees the gesture of the other animal and 'comprehends' that it too can perform it. Ultimately, it is a kind of resonance. But this does not at all mean that the observed ape has somehow become 'transparent' with respect to the observing ape's gaze. The grasping gesture does not express its own 'meaning'. Is it an explorative gesture? Is it motivated by hunger? Or perhaps the ape is simply taking the apple before the other has the chance to snatch it first. Either way, their sharing a common neurological basis does not entail that the animals we are observing are any less 'mysterious' than they are. And in the case of a human dealing with a nonhuman animal there is a further complication: if two human beings do not understand each other, they can *speak* of this lack of understanding, and try to use their *words* to explain their intention, even if they speak a different language. In the case of a nonhuman animal – or indeed an infant – this is not possible. The *other*, in this case, is mute, in the radical sense of being *before* language. Even if many so-called animal lovers claim that it is 'as if' 'their' pets could speak, that remains untrue. They actually have no truck with language. This is one of those cases when anthropocentric anthropomorphism plays tricks on us (Wynne 2007).

The most interesting theoretical point here is that the animal embodies a *difference in itself*, and not with respect to something else. The animal – and in particular the nonhuman, non-linguistic animal – therefore embodies the Deleuzian concept of 'difference in itself' (Deleuze 2001a: 28). A difference in itself is not established with respect to a model, such as when we recognise the difference between two shades of the same colour: in this case we do not grasp a colour in itself, but only with respect to another shade of the 'same', a reference point, a standard chromatic model. Deleuze rather invites us to pay attention to difference in itself, and animality can be discovered through this gesture: '[t]here is a crucial experience of difference . . . [i]t presupposes a swarm of differences, a pluralism of free, wild or untamed differences; a properly differential and original space and time; all of which persist alongside the simplifications of limitation and opposition' (2001a: 50). Rather than beginning with the ANIMAL, it is then necessary to begin with this radical and absolute animal difference, unthinkable and unsayable, because *'without identity'* (2001a: 57).

For this reason, the animal cannot be represented and, therefore, the human – the living being defined by language and representation – is unprepared for the appearance of the animal. *Homo sapiens* can only think the animal as a living being more or less similar to itself, i.e., only in an anthropocentric and anthropomorphic manner: the human only sees the animal as something that either *is* or *isn't* like itself. On the contrary, to think animality means seeing the animal – and animality itself, not limited to that of the animal – as a vital *affirmation* that implies no negation: '[i]n its essence, difference is the object of affirmation or affirmation itself. In its essence, affirmation is itself difference' (Deleuze 2001a: 52). To think, for a human being, means to begin with a model and then evaluate how much a singular example approaches and/or deviates from it. In such a schema, the animal disappears, turning into a mere particular *exemplar* of a species. So, our thought always proceeds from an original negation, for example 'this is not that', or 'this is similar to that'. But difference, Deleuze argues, is primordial, and presupposes nothing: 'difference is primary: it affirms difference and distance' (2001a: 54) – distance, that is, from any taxonomical principle. Ultimately, 'difference is affirmation' (2001a: 55), an affirmation that negates nothing and simply 'affirms' its own absolute difference. This difference is 'creation' precisely because it lacks any presupposition. But what are these differences in themselves? They are *'impersonal individuations and pre-individual singularities'* (2001a: 277). In order to be *something*, it is not necessary to be a 'person' nor to be individuated and

26

recognisable. The animal is this difference in itself, and *animality* is the ontological status of everything that exists without being – or aspiring to be – a person or an individual. This is why *Homo sapiens*, the personal animal *par excellence*, is not an animal.

What is, properly speaking, the animal? We know everything about the animal, even before having actually met one, as we will see. This is the destiny of animals: to be known and to always have been known by us. In particular, we know that the animal – or better yet, the ANIMAL – is a living being with many characteristics, some of which are shared with us. But most of all we know that the animal, as similar to us as it might be, is always *lacking* something. The animal is, by definition, the living being that lacks something: language, for example, is the feature that is traditionally said to be lacking in animals – setting them apart from human beings. *The animal is lacking*: this is the philosophical essence of animality. Virtually every definition of the animal follows this schema: on the one hand the human being (typically, *man*), on the other the animal, which lacks some human characteristics. It should be noted that this schema is also employed by those – today a large group – who claim that the animal possesses more or less *all* of the human's characteristics. Let us consider the case of someone who, upon reading Darwin, comes to the conclusion that chimps possess all (or nearly all, in an under-developed form) of the cognitive and behavioural characteristics of the human.

Compared to the conception of the animal as a lack, this stance might seem revolutionary, and yet it follows the same pattern of thought. That is because those who consider the chimp an almost-human are actually considering the animal only as compared to the human model: the chimp speaks, thinks, hopes, feels empathy, possesses a sense of justice and so on. It is clear that we are not talking about the chimp, but we are always and only considering the human animal as the standard against which to evaluate all forms of life. The problem, then, is not to understand the chimp's peculiar kind of life, but rather to see how close its life is to *ours*. Paradoxically, we do not care at all about the chimp's life. Even the most zealous animal rights activist still looks down on the animal from the human stand-point. Consider the bioethical debate regarding nonhuman animals' experience of pain (Safran Foer 2009; Bermond 1997; Sneddon et al. 2014), particularly those killed in industrial farming. In order to establish whether or not these animals feel pain, human suffering is used as a standard, taking into consideration how close their nervous system (if they have one) is to our own. It could be objected that a starting point is necessary, and it is only natural to begin from that which we know best: ourselves. But this is precisely the problem: we always begin from ourselves. The yardstick is *always* the human animal. So, if an animal's nervous system can be compared to ours, some rights will be assigned to it – but not if it doesn't. In order to be acknowledged, animals need to be like us. This is why this book will not engage with the doubtlessly urgent and extremely important problem of the extension to nonhuman animals of at least some rights recognised for human beings (Singer 1975; Regan 1983). This book will rather examine a problem that precedes the question of rights (and is, in some ways, even more fundamental): what is *human* animality? I believe that the problem is not how to formulate yet another definition of the animality of animals; on the contrary, it is necessary to look for the animality of the living being that seems to be uniquely concerned with setting itself apart from all other life forms. The problem is not 'what is a cat?', but rather 'which animality is possible for *Homo sapiens?*'

'World' and 'Environment'

What does the animal lack? The most explicit answer given to this question can be found in a short book written by the Estonian zoologist and philosopher Jakob von Uexküll: *A Foray into the Worlds of Animals and Humans*. This text has exercised a powerful influence on many philosophers, and still does to this day. Martin Heidegger was particularly inspired by von Uexküll's work for the construction of his theory of animality and of the human (Agamben 2004; Wolfe 2003; Buchanan 2008; Brentari 2015). Von Uexküll's premise is anti-Cartesian: animals are not machines, and they must no longer be conceived 'merely as objects but also as subjects, whose essential activities consist in perception and production of effects' (2010: 42). Here we encounter again the ambiguity intrinsic to the human gaze directed towards animals, when the human is once again taken as a fixed reference point (Mäekivi and Maran 2016): if the animal is not a machine, as Descartes argued, what is it? It is a living being with its own *subjectivity*. But subjectivity is, by definition, *human* subjectivity, because *Homo sapiens*, since time immemorial, has defined itself as a self-conscious being. The animal, then, is not a machine but a kind of human being, albeit different and somewhat inferior in grade. It seems that the definition of the animal cannot but go through that of the human. We have already encountered this impasse, this impossibility of thinking the animal outside of human categories. The critique of those who, like Descartes, have exaggerated the difference between animals and humans resolves in the impossibility of grasping animality *qua* animality, rather than simply as an inferior humanity.

What is the animal environment? Von Uexküll writes that 'everything a subject perceives belongs to its *perception world* [*Merkwelt*], and everything it produces, to its *effect world* [*Wirkwelt*]. These two worlds, of perception and production of effects, form one closed unit, the *environment* [*Umwelt*]' (2010: 42). Von Uexküll appears to assign some freedom to the animal (since it is no longer a machine), but in fact this very freedom is reversed into its opposite. The animal – and we will soon see which particular living being is the model for this theoretical structure – can only perceive, in the natural world, what is biologically meaningful from its point of view. This aspect, the 'perception world', triggers a series of actions that become adaptive behaviours: this is the 'effect world' composed by the actions that allow the animal to survive. According to von Uexküll, the most characteristic aspect of the animal's environment is its *closure*: the animal perceives only that which is necessary for survival, while the rest is biologically meaningless, and therefore unworthy of any attention. This is why the environment is closed, because in the *Umwelt* of an animal only that which is biologically meaningful can appear. Von Uexküll uses the example of a butterfly gliding over grass: from our point of view – and this will prove to be a crucial caveat, since the introduction of the human gaze abruptly introduces a hierarchy between animals, with the human on top – that vernal grassland is sprinkled with many different colours, smells and shapes. From the butterfly's standpoint, on the other hand, there are only shapes that signify sources of food or occasions for mating. Ultimately, the sensible richness of nature is inaccessible to the butterfly:

> We begin such a stroll on a sunny day before a flowering meadow in which insects buzz and butterflies flutter, and we make a bubble around each of the animals living in the meadow. The bubble represents each animal's environment and contains all the features accessible to the subject. As soon as we enter into one such bubble, the previous surroundings of the subject are completely reconfigured. Many qualities of the colorful meadow vanish completely, others lose their coherence with one another, and new connections are created. (von Uexküll 2010: 43)

Every animal lives within such an invisible 'bubble', within which only what is biologically meaningful for the animal presents itself. In this world there is no freedom, every perception is necessarily accompanied by an action, and vice versa: no disinterested gaze is possible, nor any casual gesture. There seems to be no space, within this bubble, for an aesthetic gaze, observing something for the pure pleasure of doing so. Then there are the 'surroundings' (*Umgebung*): a theoretically crucial concept, although biologically ambiguous. Let us imagine being the butterfly, trapped within its (to it) invisible bubble: the animal within its own 'bubble' is like a prisoner who cannot perceive the walls and the bars of the cage; this means that it is impossible for the animal to have information about the 'surroundings' – that which lies outside of the bubble. For the butterfly, only the living environment exists, with its perceptual marks – for example a certain colour indicating that a flower is rich in nectar – to which specific operational marks correspond, like the action of flying towards that coloured flower in order to drink its nectar:

> Figuratively speaking, every animal subject attacks its objects in a pincer movement – with one perceptive and one effective arm. With the first, it imparts each object a perception mark [*Merkmal*] and with the second an effect mark. Certain qualities of the object become thereby carriers of perception marks and others carriers of effect marks. (von Uexküll 2010: 48–9)

For the butterfly there is only the environment and there cannot be any trace of the surroundings. How can we speak of surroundings then? Who or what can perceive them? So far our discussion seems to concern biology, but here again metaphysics appears on the scene, in the form of the opposition between the human and the animal. That is because the 'surroundings' can only be perceived – or better, thought – by the human animal. Once again, a hierarchy is formed, inevitable whenever we talk about animality.

But which animal serves as a model for von Uexküll's thought? Which animal bears the responsibility of representing the endless crowd of all existing living beings? This is always the case: when we talk about animality we are actually thinking about a specific animal. In von Uexküll's case, it is the tick. The tiny arthropod's life is described as a 'functional cycle' each step of which is triggered by a specific 'perceptual mark', which in turn is translated into a specific operation. It should be noted that '[t]he effect mark extinguishes the perception mark' (2010: 49); the tick perceives a certain object through a specific 'perceptual mark' – a peculiar smell, for example – which in turn releases a specific action. The tick can only perceive, of the object, that which triggers the action; after that, the object literally disappears from the perceptual/cognitive horizon of the animal. Never, during the tick's life, does a perceived object exists autonomously, i.e., independently from the actions it prompts. If it exists, it triggers a biologically vital action, and once this action gets underway the object ceases to exist. To exist, for the tick, is to be perceived, and only that which is relevant for survival can be perceived – a Berkeleyan biology. Hence, the animal's environment is closed, because nothing can escape from this structure: there cannot be objects perceived without some significance for life, just as there cannot be disinterested actions. So von Uexküll argues that '[a]ll animal subjects' – and this 'all' should be flagged, since the tick is now standing for the entire animal kingdom – 'from the simplest to the most complex, are inserted into their environments to the same degree of perfection', since, von Uexküll insists, '[t]he schema [representing the functional cycle] shows how subject and object are interconnected with each other and form an orderly whole' (2010: 50, 49).

Let us follow closely this famous example – turning the tick into a model for many other philosophical animals. The cycle begins with the animal waiting. That is because when the vital mechanism is not active the animal remains still, inert, waiting, despite the fact that von Uexküll is firm in considering it a 'subjectivity'. Yet the tick is not actually 'waiting' for anything since, until the functional cycle that will lead to reproduction gets activated, the tick is within *another* functional cycle. And between two successive cycles there seems to be, for the tick, a radical separation – or at least this is how von Uexküll describes the life of this being. To wait, on the other hand, means to have some kind of expectation about the awaited event: we will see later how much of the problem of human animality hinges on this question of temporality. The tick, then, sits still, hidden in a bush among the foliage; it will remain still until a mammal enters in its perceptual space (if ever): '[t]he mammal's skin glands comprise the feature carriers of the first cycle, since the stimulus of the butyric acid sets off certain perception signs in the [tick's] perception organ, and these signs are transposed outward as olfactory features' (2010: 50). A mammal, a dog for example, walks by the tick's hiding place; butyric acid secreted by the dog's skin reaches the tick's specialised receptors, and now the tick's cycle can begin:

The processes in the perception organ bring about corresponding impulses by induction (we do not know what that is) in the [tick's] effect organ which then bring about the releasing of the legs and falling. The falling tick imparts to the mammal's hairs, on which it lands, the effect mark 'collision,' which then activates a tactile feature which, in its turn, extinguishes the olfactory feature 'butyric acid'. (2010: 50)

Every perceptual moment triggers an operational step which, in turn, triggers a new perceptual moment, and so on. Each step of the way, the tick is either guided by a stimulus coming from the external environment, or by the internal effects of such a stimulus. It is therefore in a state of complete *abandonment* with respect to its environment; once again, the subjectivity that von Uexküll assigns to the tick (and by extension to animals in general) is very peculiar, insofar as it is a subjectivity free from expectations and projects, regrets and desires. The tick is completely *dependent* on its environmental status. It has now landed on the mammal's body, and it can finally reach its skin: '[t]he new feature activates the tick's running about, until this feature is in turn extinguished at the first bare patch of skin by the feature "warmth", and the drilling can begin' (2010: 50). A new operational cycle begins, since the blood sucked from the mammal's body will allow the tick to complete its reproductive process. Once the cycle is completed, the animal can let itself die, since the eggs it has deposed will give rise to a new vital cycle.

What is the tick lacking, then? On the grassland that served as a stage for this tale of life and death there are a large number of perceptual stimuli, but all this richness and beauty is foreclosed to von Uexküll's tick – and to his animals in general. Unable to perceive it, it is as if the richness of the world literally did not exist for the tick: '[f]rom the enormous world surrounding the tick, three stimuli glow like signal lights in the darkness and serve as directional signs that lead the tick surely to its target' (2010: 51). Everything else remains dark and invisible. This is what the tick, and every other animal, lacks: it can only inhabit a limited and closed *environment*, within which only entities that play a biological role can appear: '[t]he whole rich world surrounding the tick is constricted and transformed into an impoverished structure that, most importantly of all, consists only of three features and three effect marks – the tick's environment' (2010: 51). A different animal, like a chimp – today very fashionable among both ethologists and philosophers – will have a richer environment, i.e., one populated by more 'perception marks' and corresponding 'operational marks'. Yet this does not change its intrinsic nature: the environment of the chimp, like that of the tick, is a closed and essentially static space composed by pertinent stimuli and by the actions triggered by these stimuli. The animal is a subjectivity, and yet it lacks the ability to freely move in its environment; paradoxically, the animal is only free to do that which its environment compels it to do. So, the butterfly will only see the flower as a source of food, the tick will only perceive the heat of dog – signalling its blood flow – and the chimp will consider a fruit merely as an object to sink its teeth into.

Von Uexküll considers the human condition to be a wholly different affair. While the tick's environment is closed, the human one isn't (this is the distinction that Heidegger codifies in his opposition between animal 'environment' and human 'world', which I will explore in the next section). The problem is not a biological but an epistemic one: how can we know that the tick lives in an environment composed 'only of three features and three effect marks' (2010: 51)? From the tick's point of view, due to the organisation of its perceptual apparatus, it is meaningless to say that its environment is closed, because there is nothing else to perceive other than what it actually perceives. *Who* can reveal to the tick that there is much more to be perceived in its environment? A human being, naturally, the only being capable of perceiving that which goes beyond the biological boundaries of any given environment: '[t]he animal's environment . . . is only a piece cut out of its surroundings, which we see stretching out on all sides around the animal – and these surroundings are nothing else but our own, human environment' (2010: 53). Jakob von Uexküll seems unable to grasp all the consequences of the radical difference – a difference he has established himself – between the tick's environment and that of the human. The human world, to use Heidegger's terminology, is not simply more extended than the tick's: it is constitutively open, since it contains entities and properties – like the flowers and their beauty – that have (or seem to have) no biological value while still being perceivable. The human animal's relationship with the world does not exhaust itself in those functional cycles in which the tick is trapped. While the tick is 'governed directly by Nature's plan' (2010: 88), this bind does not in fact apply to the human animal, who lives in the 'surroundings' of other living species. But why is it that the human animal, alone among all living beings, can see what other animals cannot see – the 'surroundings' of various animal 'environments'? Is the distinction between 'environment' and 'surroundings' a biological one, or is it something imposed by the human, *qua* animal without a natural 'environment' but dwelling in 'surroundings'? Is von Uexküll a zoologist or a metaphysician? And, crucially, we should ask the most disquieting question: is there a way to distinguish between these two?

According to von Uexküll the human animal too lives in an 'environment', but the way in which he describes it sets it radically apart from that of all other animals. The human being represents a kind of absolute gaze cast upon the various animal environments: it inhabits a world that the tick can neither perceive nor imagine itself unable to perceive. Although von Uexküll does not want to explicitly place the human outside of the natural world, in fact he reinforces – with new and subtler arguments – the traditional conception of a separation between the human and animality. *Homo sapiens* is the animal species that is able to discern the animality of other animals and therefore – as proven by the very existence of a book like *A Foray into the Worlds of Animals and Humans* – able to distance itself from its own animality, since it can see what lies beyond its 'environment'. This is the intrinsic theoretical tension explored by von Uexküll's book: on the one hand it aims to describe animal environments (including the human one); on the other, it aspires to be a *general* theory of animal environments. This twin ambition is self-contradicting. Every environment, von Uexküll argues, is enclosed within an invisible 'bubble'. This means that the tick is unaware that it lives in a bubble – indeed, it means that the tick is convinced that no other environment exists. For the tick it is meaningless to speak of environments in the plural: only its own environment can exist. Now, if it is true that both humans and animals live in a 'bubble that encloses each and every one of us on all sides' (2010: 70), how is it possible to write a book like von Uexküll's, purporting to describe *all* animal environments, including the human's? Who wrote this book, and how (Nagel 1986)? This confirms the privileged position that is still assigned to the human, or to be precise to MAN. Insofar as the human is able to move across various animal environments – traversing their 'surroundings' – its exceptionality with respect to the rest of the animal world is restored. The tick lives its life: good or bad, it is the only life it can live. The human, conversely, can both see the life it is living and (most importantly) can distance itself from it. The human is indeed able to relativise its point of view, and to take it as an object of reflection. The 'world' as Heidegger calls it, is precisely this capacity of non-adherence to one's own life, i.e., one's natural 'environment'. Indeed, for Heidegger the question of the 'world' is directly connected to the fundamental idea that '*man is world-forming*' (1995: 335). While the animal cannot be separated from its environment, in the case of the human the 'world' depends on, and is subordinated to, the human being itself: '[w]e are deliberately employing the expression "world-formation" in an ambiguous manner. The Dasein in man forms world: [1.] it brings it forth; [2.] it gives an image or view of the world, it sets it forth; [3.] it constitutes the World, contains and embraces it' (1995: 285). The 'world', then, is human and uniquely human.

However, the very existence of a book like von Uexküll's attests to this constitutive split between lived life and thought-of life, between animal and human life. After all, the human being is a tick who knows it is a tick, thus ceasing to be one. This is why the animal is always lacking something: it can only live in the 'environment' it happens to live in, and any access to the 'world' is foreclosed to it. Any other lack that has been attributed to the animal, starting with the fundamental absence of a language (de Fontenay 1998; Timofeeva 2018), is nothing but a consequence of this primordial absence: the animal lives a bare life, while the human does not fully coincide with the life it lives. The animal lacks the ability to see its own life (but, it should be asked, is this really a lack?). This is the happy stupidity of animals. To rethink this essential separation of the human from itself is the stake of animality.

According to Agamben, the main theme of the 'coming philosophy' (1999: 220) will be that of immanence. Immanence is the condition of a life, a generic life, coinciding with its own living, without gaps, self-reflection or consciousness. The life of immanence is completely free of transcendence. But who does, or better yet who *can*, live such a life? The tick trapped in its 'environment', or the human being, thrown into the 'world'? Von Uexküll still provokes us. Since the human has constructed itself around its own self-distancing – the separation from its own animality – it becomes necessary to imagine what a heretofore unexperienced human animality could be. The aim of a philosophy of animality is not that of 'personalising' the whole living world. On the contrary, its focus is the becoming-tick of the human animal. As we have seen, the paradox of the animal rights movement is that of trying to humanise – and, most crucially, *subjectivise* – the animal. That is because not even this movement can imagine a non-subjective, non-personal and non-interior life:

Subjects-of-a-life not only are in the world, they are aware of it and aware, too, of what transpires 'on the inside', in the lives that goes [*sic*] on behind their eyes. As such, subjects-of-a-life are something more than animate matter, something different from plants that live and die; subjects-of-a-life are the experiencing center of their lives, individuals who have lives that fare experientially better or worse for themselves, logically independently of whether they are valued by others. At least in the case of mammals and birds, then, the conclusion we reach is simple: as a matter of fact, these animals, as is true in our case, are subjects-of-a-life. (Regan 2003: 93)

In the final analysis, Regan here is simply shifting the boundary traced by Heidegger between 'man' and 'animal', so that now the latter becomes included within the 'subjective' world. Regan, like Heidegger, considers the non-animal world to be less 'meaningful' from an ethical point of view. But the point is not to transform a tick into a 'subject-of-life'; rather we need to be able to see the animal as a plant, absorbing sunlight and emitting life, a being that dies and becomes soil, pure relation, pure immanence (McCracken 2012: 90). Here it is important to highlight the theme of the 'becoming-tick' of the human. This does not indicate a transformation into a tick – an impossible and useless act, since the tick already exists. Becoming-tick means to dwell in the space of indeterminacy between 'environment' and 'world', where the living being is neither a tick nor a human, neither a subject nor an object: 'God is in every thing as the place in which every thing is, or rather as the determination and the "topia" of every entity. The transcendent, therefore, is not a supreme entity above all things; rather, *the pure transcendent is the taking-place of every thing*' (Agamben 2007: 14–15).

A Bestial Life

Humanism places the human in a peculiar position vis-à-vis the rest of the living world. According to a famous definition: 'man is not only that which he conceives himself to be, but that which he wills himself to be, and since he conceives of himself only after he exists, just as he wills himself to be after being thrown into existence, man is nothing other than what he makes of himself' (Sartre 2007: 22). The existence of the human animal precedes its essence, and therefore the human is the being who *decides* what to be. Since, going back to von Uexküll, the tick does not decide what to be (remember that the actions that the animal can perform are all foreshadowed by its 'environment'; they are as closed as the 'environment' is), we could say that, for Sartre, the human is *human* precisely because it is *not* a tick. But what makes a human being so different from a tick? Its 'subjectivity'. So, Sartre explains that 'man is indeed a project that has a subjective existence, rather unlike that of a patch of moss, a spreading fungus, or a cauliflower' (2007: 23). But there is really nothing animalistic in such a life. Rather, a life is a human one precisely insofar as it is not that of an animal, because it is a life perpetually dissatisfied with what it is, a life of transcendence. Humanism, then, means that

> man is always beyond himself, and it is in projecting and losing himself beyond himself that man is realized; and, on the other hand, it is in pursuing transcendent goals that he is able to exist. Since man is transcendence ... he is himself the core and focus of this transcendence. The only universe that exists is the human one – the universe of human subjectivity. (Sartre 2007: 52–3)

Humanism, transcendence, subjectivity. What is at stake in the pursuit of animality is not simply their negation, but rather the discovery of an escape route from within: because the animal always escapes.

Although humanism is not necessarily speciesist, it is always anthropocentric (Calarco 2008) and, paradoxically, anthropophobic. The humanist project – grounded on the adult, self-conscious subject gifted with *logos* – was shattered at Auschwitz. That self-conscious subject/person was incapable of avoiding the tragedy of humanism. This project is largely based on the separation, in the human, between its rational part and its vital and animal parts: '"person" qualifies that which, in a human being, is other than and beyond body' (Esposito 2012b: 76). Auschwitz was possible precisely because, at the core of this project, lies a machinery that produces a two-tiered exclusion: 1) *Homo sapiens* is constituted by the tracing of a boundary separating those who belong to humanity and those who do not, i.e., animals and things; 2) the subject can say 'I' only because through this very act of affirmation of its own self it excludes others. I am an 'I' because you are not. In the end, one becomes human only by condemning someone else to inhumanity, to the condition of the silent moss Sartre talked about. There is a direct link between humanism and antihumanism, like two facets of the very same concept: '[p]olitical activity is whatever shifts a body from the place assigned to it or changes a place's destination. It makes visible what had no business being seen, and makes heard a discourse where once there was only place for noise' (Rancière 1999:

30). Politics is grounded on the basic disagreement between human beings, since '[a]ny subjectification is a disidentification, removal from the naturalness of a place' (Rancière 1999: 36). In this sense Auschwitz was, and still functions as, the omnipresent human temptation, because every subjectivity is paradoxically constituted at the expense of other subjectivities. Agamben's 'coming philosophy' is precisely the attempt to conceive a way out from humanism.

How does the human represent this double exclusion? The central figure for the problem of humanism is Martin Heidegger. It is indicative that Agamben, in his essay 'Absolute Immanence' (in Agamben 1999), is unable to place the German philosopher vis-à-vis the theme of immanence: is Heidegger in the camp of the philosophers of transcendence, from Kant to Derrida, or on the side of the philosophers of immanence, from Spinoza to Deleuze? On the one hand, Heidegger is the philosopher who, in his 'Letter on Humanism', aimed at abandoning the stifling 'metaphysical subjectivism' (Heidegger 1993: 248). On the other, he is the philosopher who sanctioned the definitive separation of the human from its '*animalitas*' (1993: 227). The human being can finally become fully human – what Heidegger describes as exiting from the 'oblivion of Being' (1993: 248) – only by abandoning its position as owner of the natural world and recognising that 'Man is not the lord of beings. Man is the shepherd of Being' (1993: 245). For Heidegger, this crucial shift can occur only if the human is drastically separated from the animal. Agamben's difficulties in identifying Heidegger's position are explained: on the one hand he reminds us that it is necessary to escape from the humanism of a metaphysical subject, responsible for the 'oblivion of Being'; but, on the other, he tells us that in order to perform this epochal transition it is necessary to radically de-animalise the human. Reaching a proximity with Being presupposes a distancing from oneself and one's own animality. An exclusion – that of the human from Being – is overcome by means of another exclusion, that of the human animal from nonhuman animality, and ultimately from the natural world itself:

> Of all the beings that are, presumably the most difficult to think about are living creatures, because on the one hand they are in a certain way most closely akin to us, and on the other are at the same time separated from our ek-sistent essence by an abyss. However, it might also seem as though the essence of divinity is closer to us than what is so alien in other living creatures, closer, namely, in an essential distance which, however distant, is nonetheless more familiar to our ek-sistent essence than is our

scarcely conceivable, abysmal bodily kinship with the beast. (Heidegger 1993: 230)

The divine – that which is most remote from us, a transcendence both unreachable and unthinkable – is still closer to us than the animal is. That is to say: it is easier to think of ourselves as close to God than to a cat or an earthworm. This is a sincere and very profound admission on Heidegger's part. But the path he suggests we follow in order to overcome the humanist project – and the arrogant metaphysical subject along with it – immediately takes an unexpected turn: it does not proceed towards animality, the body and nature; it rather goes in the opposite direction, abandoning them once and for all. It is hard to imagine how this road could lead towards immanence, the coincidence of life with itself. The escape route out of humanism and its consequences increases, rather than reduces, the distance between the human and animality:

> Above and beyond everything else, however, it finally remains to ask whether the essence of man primordially and most decisively lies in the dimension of *animalitas* at all. Are we really on the right track toward the essence of man as long as we set him off as one living creature among others in contrast to plants, beasts, and God? We can proceed in that way; we can in such fashion locate man within being as one being among others. We will thereby always be able to state something correct about man. But we must be clear on this point, that when we do this we abandon man to the essential realm of *animalitas* even if we do not equate him with beasts but attribute a specific difference to him. In principle we are still thinking of *homo animalis* – even when *anima* [soul] is posited as *animus sive mens* [spirit or mind], and this in turn is later posited as subject, person, or spirit [*Geist*]. (Heidegger 1993: 227)

What is at stake is the *decision* (which, as we have seen, Sartre considers to be the very essence of humanism) between *homo humanus* and *homo animalis*. For Heidegger, the difference between *humanitas* and *animalitas* is represented by language, which allows the human to access 'the clearing of Being' (1993: 228), i.e., allows it to grasp Being *qua* Being (not as this or that concrete being). On the other hand, other living beings – like the tick on the dog's skin – can only come in contact with particular *beings*. Only the human can relate itself with the 'surroundings' that span across the limitless space beyond the closed animal 'environments'. Thus, language sets us free from the identity of perception and action, the fundamental biological characteristic of the animal and of its relationship with the environment. The animal, again like the tick, can see in its 'environment' only that which immediately corresponds to a functional action, something that increases its evolutionary fitness.[1] We now understand why Heidegger considered the separation from animality to be the condition for our access to Being: '[m]etaphysics thinks of man on the basis of *animalitas* and does not think in the direction of his *humanitas*' (1993: 227). If the human being was thought of as an animal among others, it wouldn't be able to escape the 'bubble' of its environment; only particular entities show up in an environment, and no Being is presented. In order to break out of this environmental 'bubble' one must have access to the 'surroundings', the space of Being (in the 'surroundings' there are no beings, since it is the space *between* beings). But how can the space of the 'surroundings' be grasped if it is not itself a being? Language allows us to move from beings to Being, because it is not limited by the expression of this or that being, but rather open to the possibility of *any* being. For this reason, 'language is the house of Being in which man ek-sists by dwelling, in that he belongs to the truth of Being, guarding it' (1993: 237).

I began, with Agamben, from the problem of a 'coming philosophy', i.e., the question of immanence, of a life without transcendence that coincides without residue with life itself. On this path we met Heidegger, the philosopher who first – and perhaps better than anyone else – grasped the crisis of subjectivity at the core of the humanist project. And yet Heidegger's solution does not overcome the separation between subjectivity and mind, the first and most fundamental schism of our existence. If we want to find immanence and animality, the first division to be recomposed needs to be precisely that between subjectivity and corporeality, between *homo humanus* and *homo animalis*, a split that makes the mind transcendent with respect to the body: *Homo sapiens* is nothing but such a relentless splitting. The crisis point is to be found in language. To be the linguistic animal means being the animal who can have a relation with the world only through the mediation of the word: there can be no 'world' – as opposed to a mere animal 'environment' – without a language: 'λόγος, *language, and world* stand in an intrinsic connectedness' (Heidegger 1995: 306). To excise *animalitas* from the human means to preserve the separation of body and mind, of subjectivity and life, of transcendence and immanence. Heidegger clarifies that what is at stake when talking about animality is the *human body*, not that of the mouse or the chimp:

40

The human body is something essentially other than an animal organism. Nor is the error of biologism overcome by adjoining a soul to the human body, a mind to the soul, and the existentiell to the mind, and then louder than before singing the praises of the mind – only to let everything relapse into 'life-experience,' with a warning that thinking by its inflexible concepts disrupts the flow of life and that thought of Being distorts existence. (Heidegger 1993: 228)

The human body is not – nor should it be – merely an animal body. The human is not a human entity because of its animal body, the animality of its body is human *notwithstanding*. This is Heidegger's final determination with regards to human animality. The objective of his philosophical work was that of recomposing the relation between the human and Being, and for that to be possible the metaphysical/humanist notion of a subject – a self-conscious 'I' with will and power, authoritarian and violent – had to be abandoned. It is then necessary to return to the subordination of the human to Being, as the only avenue to develop a different notion of the human than that inherited from the metaphysical tradition. The objective is a recomposition: a goal that Heidegger aims to reach by emphasising the more-than-animal character of the human: '[t]o think the truth of Being at the same time means to think the humanity of *homo humanus*. What counts is *humanitas* in the service of the truth of Being, but without humanism in the metaphysical sense' (1993: 254). That is to say, not a *homo animalis*, but rather a fully *humanus* human, beyond animality. But is this a viable path? Is it really possible to imagine a humanity free from the traps in which the human subject is inevitably doomed to fall, without first rethinking our own animal corporeality?

Note

1. A discussion could (perhaps *should*) be opened here around the 'aesthetic' abilities of nonhuman animals (Watanabe 2012; 2015). In reality, this debate is routinely framed in the wrong way, because what is asked is whether or not animals are capable of appreciating 'beauty'. Since Darwin, however, we know that animal 'beauty', or at least what we consider as beautiful, is functionally motivated: in particular, it helps reproduction (by attracting a sexual partner). But the theoretical point is not whether or not animals 'like' what humans find 'beautiful', because this is yet another variation of the question 'how similar to us are animals?' The point is to ask ourselves whether or not animals are capable of having 'aesthetic experiences', i.e., non-functional and

non-adaptive experiences, not simply meant to maximise evolutionary fitness. Such an experience, going back to von Uexküll, would imply the ability to see (in the case of an animal with eyes, like a bird) the 'environment' – that is, not simply seeing something in particular, but seeing all that lies before the animal's gaze. So not merely seeing a tree, but *seeing that a tree is being seen*. For von Uexküll, this is impossible, and Heidegger shares this opinion. But before wondering about the animal's aesthetic experiences we should ask ourselves if the human is capable of them (Cimatti 2017). We should not ask 'can a mole have aesthetic experiences?', but rather 'can a human being actually have an aesthetic experience?'

2

The Anthropologic Machine

[N]egativity is the human means of having language.

(Agamben 2006: 85)

The Tick and Boredom

The anthropologic procedure through which a still non-linguistic member of the species *Homo sapiens* (an *infans*) becomes fully human consists in the implantation, in his or her flesh, of a machinery (language) that, from that moment onwards, will produce separation and dualism. Hence, it engenders transcendence: *'man is the animal that must recognize itself as human to be human'* (Agamben 2004: 26). For the human to live it does not suffice – as it does for von Uexküll's tick – to have an 'environment' within which resources for survival, or dangers to be avoided, can be found. The human must literally get out of itself: this is the process of self-recognition, that of always-again *declaring* oneself human. The Heideggerian couple 'environment'/'world' illustrates this movement. The tick spends its entire existence in its environment, it lives and dies within its 'invisible bubble'. The human, on the other hand, must *see* itself living in the environment, i.e., it needs to step out into the 'world' (the space *between* the environments, von Uexküll's 'surroundings'), and to affirm its humanity from this eccentric position. It is only through this doubling that the human discovers and institutes itself as a human, a separation that takes it outside of itself, therefore instantiating the schism between a here-and-now corporeality and a transcendent gaze – beyond and outside the body – that allows (or condemns) that incarnation to declare itself human. Agamben, by highlighting the fact of *having* a language, is telling us that, on the one hand, the human *is not* its language while, on the other, that it is possible – although this is a task that exceeds the reach of our thought – to imagine a human *without* a language. To have something implies the possibility of losing it, of being able to do without it. But this thought is also unthinkable in principle, because human thought is linguistic and literally made of linguistic entities (Cimatti 2000). It is therefore unthinkable because, if we need language to think human thoughts, it is impossible to think without language. Yet this does not exclude the existence of a vital field, independent from language. It is a field to be *lived*, not *thought*. The paradox is that only that which is not a tick can think the being-tick of a tick.

Before trying to delimit this vital field, it is necessary to describe in greater detail the machinery that produces humanity. This is the anthropologic machine: a violent and painful operation, perpetually in process. Once again, let us take von Uexküll's tick as an example. What kind of life does it live, within its environment? We are interested in the emotive tone of the relations between the tick and other entities it can encounter. Let us begin with its experience of time: according to von Uexküll the tick can wait many years for a mammal to walk by its hiding place, without either dying or experiencing impatience. It simply sits still, but not because it is waiting for something – because in that case, after many years of frustrated expectations, it would move elsewhere. No, it remains in its place because the environmental stimulus that could trigger a new functional cycle has failed to appear – or such is von Uexküll's story. Should this stimulus never arrive the tick – unaware of its waiting for something – would simply die where it has spent its entire existence. In this sense, then, we can say that the tick is not waiting for anything at all, because in order to wait for something it is necessary to have an idea of something that is lacking, and which one hopes will one day come. Hope is an emotion that takes a body out of itself, projecting it beyond its present condition. The tick, however, cannot expect anything: its entire life, spent clinging to the bush it is hiding in, coincides with that bush. There is nothing else: a complete and perfect congruence of life with itself. It would not even be correct to say that the tick lives in the present because, insofar as it neither expects nor regrets anything, it has no other time to live in: in this sense it does not live in the present *qua* time distinct from past and future. It lives its life, and nothing else. If a life without transcendence exists at all, we should look at the tick's life to find it. From this point of view, this is also a life without boredom, or hope. The tick lives the life's life. If there is a heaven, the life of its blessed inhabitants probably does not differ much from that of the tick.

Such a life, as dangerous as it might be and – from our point of view – lacking events and emotions, is still characterised by an involvement in life itself that seems to be precluded for us human animals. It is hard to even imagine such a life and, for example, the totalising passion that links the tick to the skin of the dog it lands on: a passion without doubt, without hesitation or regret. A *total* passion indeed, meaning that it absorbs the entire vital power of the being that lives it. It would be incorrect to claim that the tick 'has' an experience: the tick *is* that experience. It is not a subject/person, and this excludes the humanist dualism between mind and body, between those who have a feeling and the feeling itself. There is no dualism in the tick, for it is one and the same with the dog's skin (Manzotti 2017). In that moment, it stops being a tick (*Rhipicephalus sanguineus*) and is rather a becoming-dog: 'von Uexküll, in defining animal worlds, looks for the active and passive affects of which the animal is capable in the individuated assemblage of which it is a part' (Deleuze and Guattari 1987: 257). There aren't two separate beings – the tick and the dog – but rather an 'assemblage' (*agencement*) wherein the distinctions between subject and object, agent and receiver, or mind and body collapse. In this sense, animality is not a substance, but rather a 'degree of power' (1987: 257), a determinate capacity – varying from body to body – for participating in an assemblage. It is important to insist on the fact that the tick does not take part in such an assemblage: the tick ceases to exist as an independent and autonomous entity, just like the dog's skin ceases to be something separate from the tick biting it. Hence, 'affects are becomings' (1987: 256). The animal world is not composed of subjects and objects, but only of 'becomings', i.e., of 'affects' (both active and passive) and of 'assemblages'. In all of its forms, animality is this becoming, wherein no one becomes anything.

Ultimately, it is no coincidence that the thinker who best described this animal passion is Heidegger, the same philosopher who intended to clearly set *animalitas* apart from *humanitas*. It is as if Heidegger, by means of the tick's passion, tried to articulate the possibility of a life he thought to be foreclosed to us. We can almost detect a note of regret in the pages of his *The Fundamental Concepts of Metaphysics* where he describes animal behaviour. His analysis starts from the condition – both incomprehensible and intolerable for us humans – of the tick waiting on the bush's branch. In an experiment, so recounts von Uexküll, a tick stayed in this position for eighteen long years. Before even wondering how it survived hunger and thirst, the question that comes naturally to us is: how could it bear the boredom of such a long wait? Indeed, it seems impossible for a human being to lie still, waiting, for such a long time. Not even a hermit could have performed such a feat, considering that a hermit would have spent the time – so to speak – in prayer, or hoping for an approach to God. This is impossible for the tick. Once again, the problem is: who or what can feel boredom? Who or what can get bored? We have seen that the tick is not really *waiting* for the dog onto which – if it ever walked by – it would land to feed on its blood. The tick does not seem to desire anything more than what it already is, its passion coincides with the condition it is *already* experiencing; the tick does not desire to be what it is not. On the contrary it already is all that it can be. For this reason, its passion is total, without residue, thoughts, or desires.

So, what is boredom? It is a condition that can only be accessed by a living being who experiences time – indeed it is the essence of our experience of time. The one who is bored is the one who, in any determinate experience, feels a gap with temporality in general: I am living this particular experience now, but I feel that this is just *an* experience destined to run its course, like everything else, in time. I therefore realise the vacuity of this experience, it being nothing but *an* experience among others, no matter how extraordinary or satisfying it might seem now. All that appears in time is destined to be swallowed by time's indifference. Boredom, then, is the awareness of this unbridgeable gap between the here and now I am living in and the endless immensity of time. I am living this experience, but I am already bored by it because it is nothing but a fleeting instant of temporality. I am bored through the act itself of experiencing it: '[w]hat *bores* us in profound boredom . . . is *temporality in a particular way of its temporalizing*' (Heidegger 1995: 158). Only a living being who experiences temporality can be bored; boredom and temporality are two facets of one and the same phenomenon. But under which condition can this experience be had? It is necessary to grasp oneself in the flux of one's existence, to be able to see oneself within the 'environment', moving from this to the 'world' and back again. Unlike the tick, so absorbed in its passion as to be blind to itself: it is precisely the absoluteness of its passion that makes it impossible for the tick to see itself as having a passion. The tick is the passion-of-the-tick. A tick that could see itself outside of its 'invisible bubble' – i.e., a tick able to displace itself in its 'surroundings' – would be able to be at once itself as a passionate tick and itself as seeing that which excited its passion. The experience of temporality consists in this gap. There is no time in the tick's existence: the tick is pure becoming.

The human animal, on the other hand, can get bored because it is a living being who experiences time, since its existence oscillates between the two poles of 'environment' and 'world'. This oscillation depends on the fact that between the human and what it experiences there is always the screen of language. Between the hand and the thing it grasps, there is always a word denoting the thing; but such denoting can be truthful – in which case the hand-word will indeed grasp the thing – or it can be false, and the hand will grasp nothing. The word *distances* the experience, it opens up a space separating the 'environment' from the 'world'. This could serve as a genuine litmus test for evaluating the humanity of a living being: a being is human if it can get bored. As Heidegger puts it: '[w]hat is boring is . . . *temporality as such*. Yet this temporality does not stand alongside "objects" and "subjects", but constitutes the ground of the possibility of the subjectivity of subjects' (1995: 158). Temporality is the ground of the subject, and therefore of *humanitas*, just as the absence of temporality is the ground of *animalitas*.

It follows that the tick does not get bored simply because it cannot get bored (and this could be a definition of the animal, or of the blessed soul: the being who cannot get bored). It can keep its tenacious grasp on the twig for many years, without getting bored. From the tick's point of view the eighteen years that have elapsed (for us) did not really pass, for it cannot experience time. The tick lives the life it is living. In this tautology – a tautology only from a logical point of view, one that does not apply to a living being trapped in an 'environment' – lies the tick's life power. Considering this radical difference, what is – according to Heidegger – the emotive tone of the tick's life, or of the animal in general? Let us consider another example employed by the German philosopher, that of the forager bee flying from flower to flower over a grassland in springtime, looking for the nectar needed to produce honey. Heidegger is careful to remind us that the bee's flight is not disinterested, but answers to a biological function. Here Heidegger follows von Uexküll closely, arguing that animal 'behaviour' (a human action, for Heidegger, is a 'comportment') is always placed within a functional cycle. The bee is attracted to the flower's scent, because this scent is a 'perception mark' which, in the bee's environment, corresponds to the 'operational mark' of sucking nectar. The outcome is a bee landing on a flower.

How is this 'a flower' for the bee? What kind of entity is this flower? As part of the functional cycle, the flower enters into the bee's experience only *qua* the trigger of the action that will lead to the nectar. The flower, for the bee, exists only as a passage towards something else: it is not perceived as a *flower*, an autonomous entity with properties like a specific colour, shape, texture and scent. These characteristics are only accessible by exiting the bee's environment, and moving in its 'surroundings'. Within the environmental bubble of the *Apis mellifera* the flower only appears as a source of nourishment. Let us imagine this to be a beautiful flower, according to our human criteria: even admitting that a bee could perceive this beauty, from its standpoint this would only be an utterly nonessential characteristic, to which it would pay no attention whatsoever. The bee's flower exists only as a phase of the functional cycle and not in itself – it is not a flower *qua* flower. The flower is its nectar. Heidegger asks himself: 'Is there any evidence that the bee recognizes the presence, or the absence, of honey?' (1995: 241).[1] This is an odd question: why would a bee wonder about this? The life embodied in the bee needs nectar, a flower: the bee is not a scientist, and indeed it is a bee precisely insofar as it does not ask questions about the world, but takes it as it is appears. How does Heidegger reply to the question he raised? He writes:

> Clearly there is. For, attracted by the scent of the flower, the bee stayed on the blossom, began to suck up the honey, and then stopped doing so at a certain point. But does this really prove that the bee recognized the honey as present? Not at all, especially if we can and indeed must interpret the bee's activity as a driven performing and as drivenness, as behaviour – as behaviour rather than comportment on the part of the bee toward the honey which is present or no longer present. (1995: 241)

If we were observing a 'comportment', we would be presented with a situation where the bee chooses to fly here or there, attracted first by a shape and then by a scent. But that of the bee is a 'behaviour', a 'captivation' by the functional cycle of nourishment towards the flower-nectar. This is why the bee's passion is totalising, because it knows no hesitations nor second thoughts: when there is a passion for the flower-nectar no other passion is possible. In that moment, the entirety of the bee's life is the passion-flower-nectar. So absorbing is this passion that the bee flies 'captivated' – to use Heidegger's term – over the grass. A peculiar captivation, a kind of haze, not simply that experienced by someone with concussion, who remains for a few moments unaware of what has happened to him or her, for this is only a temporary state, followed – provided that the concussion was not too severe – by a full regaining of consciousness, and therefore self-presence. The captivation of the animal, on the other hand, is a permanent characteristic of its life. The animal is its own captivation.

Let us go back to the bee, and its graceful and seemingly whimsical flight around the fields. How will it manage, once filled with nectar, to return to its hive? Heidegger argues that:

> If we say that the bee notices the position of the sun, the angles, the distance traversed in flight and so on, we should bear in mind that explicitly noticing something – apart from anything else – always involves noticing something with regard to some end, with intent to something – here with intent to finding the way back to a hive located at a particular place. But the bee knows precisely nothing of all this. (1995: 246)

The bee knows nothing, in the sense that it is neither explicitly nor consciously aware of its position with respect to the sun; the bee follows the 'perception marks' that guide its flight, step by step. The bee *resonates* with the information flux which carries it along (Gibson 1966), beginning with the flower-nectar and ending at the hive. There is almost a trace of envy in Heidegger's words when he describes the bee's state, blindly following the sun to find its way home:

> The bee is *simply given over* to the sun and to the period of its flight *without being able to grasp either of these as such*, without being able to reflect upon them as something thus grasped. The bee can only be given over to things in this way because it is driven by the fundamental drive of foraging. It is precisely because of this *drivenness*, and not on account of any recognition or reflection, that the bee can *be captivated* by what the sun occasions in its behaviour. (1995: 247)

The bee is in love with the sun, and like every living being in love, it wastes no time with any ridiculous 'recognition or reflection' about the object of its love.

We now reach the crucial point of this Heideggerian counter-analysis of the animal: the *animalitas* that he wants to distance the human from is a form of falling in love, the sort of abandonment proper of the lover who does not pose, between itself and the loved one, any filter nor any theoretical reflection. Animality is a passion for assemblages. The lover doesn't appraise anything, it simply loves. Better yet, the lover *is* the love that loves. Here is immanence, the complete adherence of life to itself, the tautology that *humanitas* cannot bear:

> The *captivation* of the animal therefore signifies, in the first place, essentially *having every apprehending of something as something withheld*

from it. And furthermore: in having this withheld from it, the animal is precisely *taken by things*. Thus animal captivation characterizes the specific manner of being in which the animal relates itself to something else even while the possibility is withheld from it – or is taken away from the animal, as we might also say – of comporting and relating itself to something else as such and such at all, *as* something present at hand, *as* a being. And it is precisely because this possibility – apprehending *as* something that to which it relates – is withheld from it that the animal can find itself so utterly taken by something else. (Heidegger 1995: 247, 248)

As Heidegger clearly states, 'captivation is the essence of animality' (1995: 248), by which he means to say that the animal is the living being who can live the fullness of life in a complete and 'absolute' manner. This fullness can be lived because what is experienced is not perceived (or thought of) *qua* determinate object. The bee is a passion for the flower, i.e., it poses no radical distance between itself and the flower, it can lose itself in the flower like it abandons itself to the sun. The bee is not a subject facing an object (the flower, or the sun), rather the bee partakes, along with the flower, in a single flux of energy and life: '[b]ecause of this driven directedness the animal finds itself suspended, as it were, between itself and its environment, even though neither the one nor the other is experienced *as* being' (1995: 248). Ultimately, then, what does the bee not grasp of its 'environment'? According to Agamben, the animal does not grasp its being *thus*, rather than being some other way. For the animal the world has no *thus*-ness, there is only the world as it is. That is because the animal, ultimately, is 'content' with the world there is: the real of the world is sufficient, and the animal does not dream of other possible worlds:

> *Thus*. The meaning of this little word is the most difficult to grasp. 'Hence things stand thus': But would we say of an animal that its world is thus-and-thus? Even if we could exactly describe the animal's world, representing it as the animal sees it (as in the color illustrations of Uexküll's books that depict the world of the bee, the hermit crab, and the fly), certainly that world would still not contain the thus; it would not be *thus* for the animal: It would not be irreparable. (Agamben 2007: 93)

Self-Taming

The problem posed by animality to the human being – the living being who lives in the 'world' but, like Heidegger, laments the loss of the 'environment' – is that of the very peculiar modality of experience encapsulated in the formula of 'being *qua* being'. The bee sees the flower, but not as a determinate, self-differentiated being with a number of independent properties – i.e., not as a *thing*. Rather, it immediately perceives it as the implicit terminus of an action with a biological value. There is no bee on the one hand and flower on the other (a Subject and an Object), separated by the bee's thoughts about the possibilities afforded by that flower: *immediately* there is an energy flux, the assemblage bee-flower-nectar. Neurological research confirms that, in the brain of living beings who possess hands and limbs in general, the sight of a graspable object activates not just the areas dedicated to visual perception, but *at the same time* parts of the motor cortex that control hand movement: 'the sight of a coffee cup', by a monkey for example, 'is nothing but a preliminary form of action, a call to act that, whether it gets answered or not, characterizes it as something *to be grasped* by the handle, with two fingers, etc. thus identifying it according to the motor affordances it contains' (Rizzolatti and Sinigaglia 2006: 47–8). These animals can see with their hands; in other words, the meaning of what is visually perceived is directly and strictly linked with what can be done with it. There is no initial phase of pure perception, in which the object would be neutrally and disinterestedly explored, followed by a motor initiative: seeing and acting proceed in lockstep. We see with our hands and touch with our eyes.

But if objects, in animal environments, are always 'hypotheses for action' (Rizzolatti and Sinigaglia 2006: 75), whence the flower *qua* flower that Heidegger considers as the distinctive characteristic of *humanitas*? To identify a flower *qua* flower means to consider it independently from what can be done with it. The flower '*qua*' flower breaks the perceptual-operational assemblage comprised of eyes-hands-flower. The kind of relation between us and the world entailed by the '*qua*' is a neutral and disinterested one. The existence of a flower *qua* flower presupposes that of a subject qua Subject as well as that of an object *qua* Object; two poles separated by an abyss of 'recognition or reflection' as Heidegger put it. The challenge posed to *humanitas* by animality lies in the unbridgeable gap created by language between the hand and the thing it grasps, which is reflected in the just as unbridgeable distance between the I that says 'I' and its own body.

It is now necessary to take a closer look at the process of anthropogenesis, through which a member of the species *Homo sapiens* can become a subject, an animal body that can refer to itself as an 'I'. It begins with an animal body, a little mammal with cognitive and behavioural capacities which are similar to those of other mammals (Macphail 1998). In effect, anthropogenesis is not a one-off event. On the contrary, the human is such precisely because it never stops becoming human, and therefore it never stops being, in itself, inhuman: 'Homo is a constitutively "anthropomorphous" animal . . . who must recognize himself in a non-man in order to be human' (Agamben 2004: 27). It never ceases to humanise, and therefore to inhumanise, itself because it constantly oscillates between 'environment' and 'surroundings', and it therefore lacks a natural substance: 'Homo sapiens, then, is neither a clearly defined species nor a substance; it is, rather, a machine or device for producing the recognition of the human . . . [an] anthropologic . . . machine' (2004: 26).

The process begins (and never stops beginning) when a human body, born when its brain development is still largely incomplete (Thompson et al. 2003), comes into contact with a particular kind of parental care, going through a semiotic mediation, in particular through the language spoken by the adults who care for a newborn. The first step of this process even precedes birth: a *name* is assigned to the soon-to-be-born baby. From that moment onwards the community into which the little human will be born will refer to him or her using that name (and others that may be assigned later). Thus, before the social life of the baby has even begun, he or she has already been assimilated by the network of language. There is his or her fleshy body, which will receive the care of the adults, but at the same time there is also a symbolic body which accompanies his or her name, together with all those practices that will leave a mark on it: that body will have to learn to eat, get dressed, walk, sit, smile, make love and so forth. From the beginning, then, the process of anthropogenesis has a double register: a corporeal one and a symbolic one. More specifically, the 'anthropologic machine' produces not just an animal body but rather a body *qua* counterpart of a subject/person. Agamben defines this symbolic body, submitted to the force of law, as 'bare life': '[i]t is important not to confuse bare life with natural life. Through its division and its capture in the apparatus of the exception, life [the life of the *infans*, still *before* language] assumes the form of bare life, which is to say, that of a life that has been cut off and separated from its form' (2016: 263). On the one hand, the 'form', i.e., the subject/person; on the other, the body captured but also expelled from that very form, the 'bare life'. The problem of animality is the problem of this primordial separation, which never stops widening and deepening.

The decisive step in this process takes place when the young human being begins to impose upon him- or herself those symbolic and linguistic practices which he or she first learnt to employ with others. Let us imagine this scenario: a little boy, already able to speak, is in the company of the house cat. The cat, standing on a chair, gingerly puts its paw on the kitchen table. The boy, imitating what he has heard many times from his parents, says to the cat 'no! you cannot climb on the table!' He is repeating what he learnt from the adults – using language as a form of power – to forbid something to another body, that of the cat (this means that through this gesture the cat is reduced to the condition of feline 'bare life'). On another occasion, the child is hungry and knows that there is ice cream in the fridge. There are no adults around and, if he is quick about it, nobody will notice him eating it. But he also knows that his mother does not want him to eat before dinner, because otherwise he will not finish his meal, and she will be cross. There is hunger, and the ice cream. But there is also that 'no' which, having heard it used many times before to stop his actions, he has now learnt to use himself with the cat. The boy is about to open the fridge when that 'no' occurs to him; in fact there is no need for him to imagine it, since it resounds in the sudden hesitation in his actions. In the end, after a protracted uncertainty, the boy gives up, and the ice cream remains in the fridge (such a 'no' is operative even if the child ends up opening the fridge: in this case the 'yes' to the ice cream desire has passed through the negation of the first 'no'. From this point of view any 'yes' to life is in fact a 'not-no'). Language spoke for him even though no adult was heard: now there is no need for an adult to utter that 'no' for it to be commanding, for the boy can use it himself. Language, now, *speaks for itself*. The 'no' does not merely control the cat's body, it now controls his own body, like his parents used to: their presence is unnecessary to forbid him something, for he's now able to stop himself. The baby has, in the end, become his own guardian. He has learnt to control himself, to control the body that he is and that, from this moment onwards, he *has*, because the human body is at the subject/person's disposal. It is now 'bare life', and therefore an object that is available to any power able to control it.

It should be highlighted that the linguistic gesture of the 'no' is precisely what splits in two the corporeality of the child (Virno 2013), since from now on there will always be a 'no' ready to forbid something, or a 'yes' to allow it. Through the 'yes' and the 'no' the child has definitively abandoned his natural 'environment' – wherein perception was always immediately accompanied by action – and has stepped into the 'world' (indeed, *Homo sapiens* means nothing but an interminable farewell to the environment). To impose on the body now a 'yes' and then a 'no' means to be detached from corporeality, being now able to observe one's own body from the outside; the child who says 'no' to himself has moved to the 'surroundings' of his original environment, and in virtue of his being outside of it he can now evaluate it, accept it, or refuse it. Now the child really *has* a body, because it is at his disposal. In the process of anthropogenesis, this is a point of no return: *animalitas* means *being* the body that one is, with nothing beyond it (the immanence of the body to itself). *Humanitas*, on the other hand, precisely consists in this doubling: the body that one once was now becomes the body one owns, a thing-body ('bare life') fully at the mercy of that strange conscious function that can say 'I' (the transcendence of the subject over the body). The Lacanian psychoanalyst Jacques-Alain Miller observes that: '[i]f we can identify being and body for the animal, we cannot do the same for the human species. As far as the speaking body is concerned, it does not emerge from being but from having' (2001: 15).

To *be* a body is to be unaware of being one, as in the case of the tick and its 'invisible bubble'. It means that seeing an object is already an attempt to grasp it, that the body is always in action – a body-affect – and that it is impossible to be out of sync (before or after) with one's own body. This is the tick body then, or that of the bee that surrenders itself to the warmth of the sun: the captivated body that simply is what it is. When the child in our example learns how to talk to himself, he is not simply learning a new and more complex use of language: he is modifying his own bodily nature. To say 'yes' or 'no' to oneself means creating an unbridgeable distance from the body, and to change its status: it now becomes something at our disposal. This coincides with the acquisition of the capacity to turn the power and the normalising violence of language upon oneself; a passage that signals how the child has become his or her own adult, or guardian (in this sense, the guardian angel is a policeman that needs no baton). Just as Heidegger understood, without a language there can be no oscillation between 'environment' and 'world'. This is why the turning point is not the simple acquisition of language, for only when language becomes self-control does the young human leave *animalitas* to enter into *humanitas*: 'the subject, from the moment in which it is subject of the signifier, cannot identify itself as its body, and it is precisely from there that its affection for the image of its body proceeds. The enormous narcissistic bombast, characteristic of the species, proceeds from this lack of subjective identification with the body' (Miller 2001: 16).

A 'narcissistic' bubble comes now to replace the tick's environmental 'bubble'. In this new bubble lives the subject who says 'I'. This is the bubble that accompanies the living being in the 'world': such a being does not know where its place is, nor how to be there, precisely because it lacks an 'environment'. To live in a 'world' means to have nobody to tell us what should be done, and why (indeed, for the tick, 'environment' means: 'having nothing to worry about'). So, this 'I', at once despotic (since it can only preserve itself as an I through the control it exercises on the body) and fragile (since the absence of a closed environment deprives it of any certain reference point to guide its choices and actions) has no other way to keep itself alive than to seek refuge in a 'narcissistic' bubble. It is only by admiring itself in a mirror that this 'I' can try to recognise itself; not being a body it tries to have one, but the only body it can possess is the imaginary one constituted by the other's gaze. And so, transcendence rears its head, since a body that says 'I' can find itself only within the other: outside and beyond itself. The other, however, is unreachable since the fissure carved by language into the human body cannot be recomposed, it is a wound that cannot heal, and the very essence of the human is traversed by this 'lack of . . . identification between being and body' (Miller 2001: 16).

Lacan, careful reader of Heidegger's work, has drawn the ultimate consequences of this anthropological premise: the human subject is born as the effect of a fracture, between the 'I' and the body, between *humanitas* and an *animalitas* that discovers itself as *animalitas* (this is what *humanitas* really amounts to). Transcendence appears, in human life, only as an effect of language upon the body: alienating the subject from the body, since to say 'I' means to leave the body behind, accessing the possibility (which is precluded to the tick) of seeing itself as *external* to the body. Lacan highlights how this operation implies the assumption of the gaze of the other in order to discover itself; to see oneself from the outside means to adopt the other's point of view, just like the child who says 'no' to his desires is using his parents' words, so that his talking is always a ventriloquising: '[t]he Other is the one who sees me' (Lacan 2014: 23). With Lacan we locate this fracture, this 'lack' as he calls it, within human subjectivity itself: *Homo sapiens* is nothing but this lack. This is the paradox of the animal who refers to itself as an 'I', the only being who, unsatisfied with the mere incarnation of its own individuality, is brave and foolish enough to affirm it. Yet this very gesture condemns it to immediately lose the 'I' it just proudly proclaimed: the body that says 'I' loses it at once, because the 'I' really depends on the 'desire of the Other' (2014: 22). The passage from *animalitas* to *humanitas* entails that the 'I', as Freud famously put it, 'is not even a master in its own house' ('A Difficulty in the Path of Psycho-Analysis', 1917). This is a curious claim, because the 'I' still dwells in its own house, although one within which it has no mastery. This means that that the 'I' is that strange entity which lives in a house that belongs to it while being owned by others. To be a *Homo sapiens* means to possess a house to call one's own – but in that very act something malignant lurks, forcing us to accept the fact that someone else owns our house. To renounce ownership of your house is the condition of owning one. The paradox of anthropogenesis lies in this double movement: at once receiving and losing. An exemplary analysis of this achievement, which amounts to a loss, is offered by Lacan by means of the mirror predicament – nothing but another instance of an 'anthropologic machine':

> Already, just in the exemplary little image with which the demonstration of the mirror stage begins, the moment that is said to be jubilatory when the child, grasping himself in the inaugural experience of recognition in the mirror, comes to terms with himself as a totality functioning as such in his specular image, haven't I always insisted on the movement that the infant makes? This movement is so frequent, constant I'd say, that each and every one of you may have some recollection of it. Namely, he turns round, I noted, to the one supporting him who's there behind him. If we force ourselves to assume the content of the infant's experience and to reconstruct the sense of this movement, we shall say that, with this rotating movement of the head, which turns towards the adult as if to call upon his assent, and then back to the image, he seems to be asking the one supporting him, and who here represents the big Other, to ratify the value of this image. (Lacan 2014: 32)

In the End, There Is The I

On the one hand we have the *infans*, looking at her own mirror image; but on the other hand, in order for the *infans* to recognise herself in that image, the presence of an adult who explains what she is seeing (a child), and how to see it (as herself), is necessary. The 'I' is outside of itself, the 'I' is what others say it is. Anthropogenesis is the process that leads a living being to utter 'I', and therefore step outside of itself and of the flux of its own living, in order to see itself from the outside.[2] Ostensibly, there is always only one body, both acting in the 'environment' and saying 'I'. In truth, the animal corporeality is split in two, mind ('I') and body ('bare life'). The nostalgia and desire for immanence begin here. But what connotation does the pronoun 'I' have? Let us return to the child we have already met, who hesitantly steps into his *humanitas* – where the need for another flesh and blood person to control him disappears – because he has now internalised this guardian, and is thus able to control himself. Until this point his life was like that of the tick – in some ways richer, in others poorer, but still a life of power and passion. That child lived in an 'environment' where he could find food, warmth, pain and tenderness, i.e., affects and 'assemblages'. This is a full 'environment' in which his body (a body he is still unaware of having, and is still merely 'being') occupied a central position, while being unaware of the existence of other possible positions. Then comes the word of language. Not just any word, because there is a kind of language that fits in the 'environment': like the bees' dance, expressing where and how far away the flowers can be found. This is a language as full as the tick's environment. Indeed, this language makes it impossible to lie, to produce a false statement (Hauser and Konishi 1999). But if the false cannot be stated, neither can the truth. An animal language cannot say the world otherwise than it actually is.

In the child's language, on the other hand, there are some particular expressions – like the pronouns 'I' and 'you' – that have no fixed referent. First the mother speaks, and says 'I'; the father then intervenes, and he is the one, now, to say 'I'. Not only that, but the mother addressed him with a 'you', while the father did the same when referring to her. This is a first, not quite reassuring, discovery for the child: 'I' and 'you' are not like names, which remain attached to their owners (it is well-known how children insist that things should have one name, and only one). *Who* is 'I', then? The child too becomes a 'you' in other people's utterances. Eventually, one day he too becomes an 'I': simply, and without great fanfare, he begins to talk. Here lies a big surprise: in order to become an 'I', one must simply talk. Nothing more is necessary, we become an 'I' – and others a 'you' – just by virtue of talking. But the excitement is short-lived, because as soon as the child pauses his speech, immediately the 'you' he was addressing becomes an 'I' once again. What is the meaning of this strange and elusive word? '[w]hat then is the reality to which *I* or *you* refers? It is solely a "reality of discourse," and this is a very strange thing. *I* cannot be defined except in terms of "locution," not in terms of objects as a nominal sign is. *I* signifies "the person who is uttering the present instance of the discourse containing *I*"' (Benveniste 1971: 218). 'I' is the person who speaks, and therefore it does not refer to a specific object; on the contrary, 'I' refers to itself, to its own uttering. While a normal 'nominal sign' indicates a particular object (or class of objects), 'I' is a linguistic sign that folds upon itself, referring to the very same body who utters it. In this sense, we can say that there are as many 'I's as there are speakers, because this sign is available to all those who can participate in language. But then what is the I, really?

> It is in the instance of discourse in which I designates the speaker that the speaker proclaims himself as the 'subject.' And so it is literally true that the basis of subjectivity is in the exercise of language. If one really thinks about it, one will see that there is no other objective testimony to the identity of the subject except that which he himself thus gives about himself. (Benveniste 1971: 226)

The disheartening conclusion, then, is that the child becomes an I because it says 'I'. As soon as he experiences the thrill of being an 'I', the child has the immediate, sobering realisation of being just one 'I' amongst many. Until that moment, like von Uexküll's tick, he had experienced his existence without problems – he just lived, and that was it. Now he discovers that, beyond living, there is also a (kind of) possible life located next to his former, unproblematic existence. For example, he discovers that if he is hungry, he can say 'I am hungry'. By saying that he is hungry he is discovering his hunger – this is the passage from *being* a body to *having* one. Having now discovered his hunger, he also notices that he can decide to postpone his afternoon snack, because he would rather keep playing with his friends, or that it is really not a good idea to eat more chocolate because one day, when he ate too much of it, he felt sick. Becoming an 'I' adds an additional factor to his life, something which – as long as, like the tick, he was content living his bare life – he never perceived as an absence. This discovery comes with the realisation that it is impossible to return to the previous condition: even if he was to stop using that word the discovery has already been made, and he is now an 'I'. And when one finds out one has a body it is impossible to ignore it. We will later see how the problem of immanence pivots on this issue: how can a condition of immanence be imagined from the standpoint of transcendence? How can a subject/person *be* a body?

The 'I' is the denotation of the very linguistic act that contains the pronoun 'I'. But this self-reference is not a declaration of autonomy. Because an 'I' can exist only if there is a 'you' that confirms and 'ratifies', as Lacan put it, the 'I's being. But this also means that the gesture by means of which the body declares itself an 'I' is not a sovereign one: without another who accepts being the temporary 'you' for a body who declares itself an 'I', such self-proclamation would be invalid. 'I' am *me* only because *you* confirm it. The newly acquired subjectivity of the body, now able to identify itself as an 'I', had to traverse the body of another – of a 'you' – without which the child's speech act would remain meaningless. But both 'you' and 'I' are 'linguistic forms' (Benveniste 1971: 227); subjectivity is made out of nothing but a chain of linguistic acts. This 'I' will endure as long as the self-referential act is repeated. The word, then, not only breaks the fullness of the primordial experience of the 'environment' (the *infans*-tick vanishes as soon as it announces itself an 'I'), but also leaves the newly formed subjectivity in a state of perennial vulnerability: it is enough for 'you' to stop acknowledging my right to say 'I' for this 'I' to crumble, precisely because it cannot sustain itself on its own.

The transcendence that language introduced into *humanitas* is now tainted by violence, because the lure of *animalitas'* immanence – the temptation of a fullness completely homogeneous with life (which the human, the animal who speaks, never knew, since its linguistic history pre-dates its own by means of the name it gets assigned at birth – there is no human before anthropogenesis) – always needs to be fought against. In this perspective, it is instructive to consider how Lev S. Vygotsky – the greatest psychologist of the 1900s – compared those that today we know as nothing more than *animots*: the 'ape', the so-called 'primitive man' and the 'child' (the very idea of such a comparison is both terrifying and enlightening). His book *Studies on the History of Behavior: Ape, Primitive, and Child* tries to describe the differences between the natural intelligence of the apes – of chimps in particular – and that of human animals. Vygotsky argues that the passage from one form of intelligence to the other is marked by the acquisition of language, not merely as an instrument of communication – since chimps too can use such a language – but as an instrument of behavioural self-control. The human, according to the guiding idea of Vygotsky's book, is the animal that, through the use of language as interiorised command (the child saying 'no' to himself), manages to domesticate itself. On the contrary: 'thinking in a chimpanzee is absolutely independent of speech' (Vygotsky and Luria 1993: 73). This is what is at stake: the relationship between body and language, and therefore between 'bare life' and person/subject.

According to Vygotsky and Luria, the emergence of language produces, for the first time in human history, a 'second line of development' (1993: 37). On the one hand there is the 'organic' line, which we can find in other animals (even, in a certain measure, in the tick). While this still applies to humans, another 'cultural' line of development is unique to them, and goes through '[l]abor and, connected with it, the development of human speech and other psychological signs used by primitive man to gain control over behavior' (1993: 37). The main function of language, for *Homo sapiens*, would not be communication but rather one's own 'mastery'. What is at stake is the control of one's immediate reactions, i.e., the control of the body: it always boils down to killing the tick. Vygotsky and Luria use an example (taken from a book by the German psychologist Wolfgang Köhler), that of a hungry chimp who has to resolve a problem, or at least what a psychologist (someone who has utterly forgotten how they once lived like a tick) has trained it to consider a problem (Despret 2009): in a corner of the room, outside of the cage where the chimp is kept, there is a piece of fruit, while in the other corner there is a stick. The chimp cannot reach the fruit from the cage, but can get the stick. The psychologist thinks (hopes?) that it will occur to the chimp to use the stick to get the fruit closer to the cage. The chimp is not of the same persuasion though: having tried, without success, to stretch its arm and get the fruit, it gives up and grumpily sits down in the back of its cage. Today, we have a neurological explanation for this behaviour (Rizzolatti and Sinigaglia 2006): animals envision possible actions, and not objects (the chimp, Heidegger would say, does not see the fruit *qua* fruit). The chimp tried to get to the fruit in vain, for the experiment was designed to render this spontaneous reaction futile and indeed frustrating:

> One interesting thing found in [this experiment] was that the task could be accomplished only when both the fruit and the stick were so close to each other that they were in the same visual field and the animal saw them

simultaneously. But whenever the stick was placed far enough away so that the ape could not take in at one glance both the tool and the goal, the solution of the task turned out to be either impossible or very difficult. (Vygotsky and Luria 1993: 47–8)

Actually, the experiment shows that the gaze-action that is so effective in an animal 'environment' is utterly useless in a human 'world'; in order to resolve the 'problem' (and here is another definition of the human: the living being who transforms nature into a series of *problems* to be resolved), the chimp should have controlled its spontaneous reaction, the natural gesture of reaching out to grasp the fruit. Here is the inaugural moment of *humanitas*: to *stop* the body and to *delay* the action. The chimp should then have looked around, searching for a way to solve the 'problem'. This is why the psychologist, with some malice, had left the stick on the floor. But the psychologist's stick is not the *same* as the chimp's stick: for the chimp, the stick is something that can be grasped but that, in this predicament, is useless, and is indeed ignored. For the psychologist, on the other hand, the stick is an instrument, a *sign* for something else, a means to the end of reaching the fruit. Here we witness the clash of two, radically different, ways of being a body: the body of the animal abandoned to the fullness of the perceptual flux, and that of one who sees the 'world' as a kind of workshop, as transformation, as 'labour'. This is the fundamental difference: the psychologist – here representing the human being in general, and its *always* utilitarian relationship with the natural world – uses her eyes to *work*, not quite to see. We understand how violent this transformation must be: the chimp's 'captivated' body must literally be restructured in order to fathom this change, to stop seeing through the eyes/hands and become a vigilant, reflexive and analytical body:

> in the area of man's psychological development from the moment of the acquisition and use of signs, which allow man to gain control over his own processes of behavior, the history of behavioral development, to a significant degree, transforms into the history of the development of artificial, auxiliary 'means of behavior' – into the history of man's mastering his own behavior. (Vygotsky and Luria 1993: 77)

The history of language, then, is the history of 'man's' mastering of his own 'behavior'. This explains our treatment of animals and of their *animalitas*, because they passively experience this mastery as heteronomous violence, and not as a free choice to be reinforced and celebrated day after day.

Notes

1. Heidegger here uses the term 'honey' to refer to the nectar in the flower.
2. The ethologist and philosopher Roberto Marchesini defends a more gradualistic position on the relationship between language and *humanitas*. In particular, Marchesini holds that 'the most controversial aspect in assuming language as an anthropogenetic principle is that it makes the emergence of language itself inexplicable, as in any self-grounding claim one is always condemned to a *regressio ad infinitum*. If, however, we treat language as one of the many cultural expressions of the human – capable of educating the human being, but not an autopoietic and emanative product of the human – we can set language within the decentrative experience inaugurated by animal epiphany' (2017: 44). There are at least two points worth stressing about this position: 1) the fact that the usual Darwinian accounts are still unable to explain the emergence of language does not imply that language is 'inexplicable'; explicable is not synonymous with gradual. 2) The so-called 'animal epiphany' can only take place when someone sees an animal as something different from a prey or a sexual partner, that is, as a 'bearer' of a further and invisible 'meaning'. Such a possibility already presupposes a linguistic mind, that is, a mind that is able to see the 'meaning' of an object when beholding said object. An 'animal epiphany' can only occur in a mind that is already capable of mastering the basic linguistic difference between 'signified' and 'signifier'.

3

Rage and Envy

---

*Ora, se la vita è cosa più perfetta che il suo contrario, almeno nelle crea-
ture viventi; e se perciò la maggior copia di vita è maggiore perfezione;
anche per questo modo seguita che la natura degli uccelli sia più perfetta.*
[Now, if life is something nearer perfection than its opposite, at least in
living creatures, and if therefore abundance of life is greater perfection, in
this respect too it follows that the nature of birds is more perfect.]

(Leopardi 1976: 185)

Why Them, and Not Us?

What is unthinkable, about the animal, is that it could live by simply
living. To construct oneself through the anthropologic machine
means, as we have just seen, turning the 'environment' into a 'world'.
In the 'environment' what is perceived is always already an action
– think of the seagull's reckless confidence, jumping down from its
nest on a high cliff, towards the void and the sea below. Between
eyes and wings, to use this example, there is no thought-interval,
and therefore neither hesitation nor fear. This means that there is no
mental space – so infinitely wide a space for us humans – separating
a plan from its realisation, the space that distances the eye from the
hand and that, for the human, never stops widening, since *Homo
sapiens* precisely means that the hand is always farther away from
the eyes. The 'environment' cannot even be considered as the 'house'
of the animal, since that would imply a hostile outdoors. We often
consider the den or the nest as a kind of animal home. In truth,
that is an incorrect – and anthropocentric – conception. It is the
human who needs to feel at home somewhere, even if just within the
nomad's tent. That is because the human is the animal without an
'environment', forever lost in the 'world'. There can be the necessity
of a home only because one is lost in a 'world'. On the contrary,
the animal lives in an 'environment' that, as dangerous as it might
be, is 'predictable' – as when the gazelle's hooves 'announce' the
savannah, the seagull's wings 'announce' the sky, or the tick's mouth

'announces' the warm and smelly skin of the dog. The den is not a house, but rather the becoming-soil of the mole, or the becoming-chick of the swallow. The den is a becoming while the house is, on the contrary, both an interruption and a fear of becoming. The walls that cross many lands on our planet – like the one between Mexico and the United States, or the watery administrative wall that separates North Africa from Southern Europe – are nothing but the extreme, yet coherent and inevitable, development of the walls that separate our homes from the rest of the 'world', unknown and hostile. In this sense *Homo sapiens* represents a continuous 'territorialising' temptation: that of drawing borders, raising walls and watchtowers. Animality, on the other hand, embodies the opposite vector, aiming towards an inexhaustible 'deterritorialisation'. This is the core theme of Deleuze and Guattari's *Kafka: Toward a Minor Literature*:

> There is no longer anything but movements, vibrations, thresholds in a deserted matter: animals, mice, dogs, apes, cockroaches are distinguished only by this or that threshold, this or that vibration, by the particular underground tunnel in the rhizome or the burrow. Because these tunnels are underground intensities. In the becoming-mouse, it is a whistling that pulls the music and the meaning from the words. In the becoming-ape, it is a coughing that 'sound[s] dangerous but mean[s] nothing' (to become a tuberculoid ape). In the becoming-insect, it is a mournful whining that carries along the voice and blurs the resonance of words. Gregor becomes a cockroach not to flee his father but rather to find an escape where his father didn't know to find one, in order to flee the director, the business, and the bureaucrats, to reach that region where the voice no longer does anything but hum: '"Did you hear him? It was an animal's voice," said the chief clerk.' (1986: 13)

The internal/external dualism, just like the opposition between familiar and foreigner, friend or foe, can only be applied to the 'world', and not to the 'environment'. The 'world' thus becomes both a burden and a reason for pride: this is the humanist presumption, because only the human 'has' the world at its disposal while – in Heidegger's simplified and rather superficial description, which indeed completely ignores plants[1] – 'the stone (material object) is *worldless*' and 'the animal is *poor in world*' (1995: 177).

Reading his account of stones, which, in this simplistic confrontation between animality and humanity appears only as a way to somehow bridge the otherwise enormous gap that separates them, it is clear what Heidegger is aiming at:

The stone is lying on the path, for example. We can say that the stone is exerting a certain pressure upon the surface of the earth. It is 'touching' the earth. But what we call 'touching' here is not a form of touching at all in the stronger sense of the word. It is not at all like *that* relationship which the lizard has to the stone on which it lies basking in the sun. And the touching implied in both these cases is above all not the same as *that* touch which we experience when we rest our hand upon the head of another human being. (1995: 196)

The examples used here are bizarre to say the least. The sun we have already encountered in Heidegger's text makes a comeback: the lizard basks in this sun, like the bee abandoned itself to its warmth to find its way back to the hive. It seems that all this basking in the sun bothers Heidegger: for animality the sun is first of all (and immediately) warmth. Then there is a hand touching another person's head. It seems to be more a paternalist than an innocent gesture, one establishing a hierarchy: our hand resting on the head of someone who cannot refuse this contact. The 'world', then, is something made, since we know that 'man is world-forming' (1995: 196). The difference between humans and animals and stones (and this is a very odd comparison indeed, using stones and lizards to affirm the special nature of the human) is here: for the stone, the world is already there and it requires no intervention, for it is adequate as it is:

it lies upon the earth but does not touch it. The earth is *not given* for the stone as an underlying support which bears it, let alone given as earth. Nor of course can the stone ever sense this earth as such, even as it lies upon it. The stone lies on the path. If we throw it into the meadow then it will lie wherever it falls. We can cast it into a ditch filled with water. It sinks and ends up lying on the bottom. In each case according to circumstance the stone crops up here or there, amongst and amidst a host of other things, but always in such a way that everything present around it remains essentially *inaccessible* to the stone itself. Because in its being a stone it has no possible access to anything else around it, anything that it might attain or possess as such, it cannot possibly be said to be deprived of anything either. The stone is, i.e., it is such and such, and as such turns up here or there or is simply not present. (Heidegger 1995: 197)

What is wrong with the stone? It lies there peacefully, it endures without complaint being tossed in the water-filled ditch (it looks like Heidegger really cannot stand the stone's strange passivity, since a stone is, strictly speaking, neither active nor passive), and it remains close to the other stones it rolled next to. Most importantly (and this is something I have already highlighted in the case of the bee who abandons itself to the sun without 'recognition or reflection'; it seems that for Heidegger philosophers cannot possibly enjoy lying in the sun), the stone has no need to 'ever sense this earth as such'. The stone is in the world, just like that – there is little to explain or to debate. This is why *humanitas* begrudges the stone and its way of being in the world, with no need to make an issue of it, simply being. This is so unbearable for *humanitas* – since it represents an utterly alien kind of existence from that produced by the anthropologic machine – that, in this case, a nonhuman animal's life is preferred to it: that of a plain and humble reptile. Indeed, Heidegger explains:

> The lizard basking in the sun on its warm stone does not merely crop up in the world. It has sought out this stone and is accustomed to doing so. If we now remove the lizard from its stone, it does not simply lie wherever we have put it but starts looking for its stone again, irrespective of whether or not it actually finds it. The lizard basks in the sun. At least this is how we describe what it is doing, although it is doubtful whether it really comports itself in the same way as we do when we lie out in the sun, i.e., whether the sun is accessible to it *as* sun, whether the lizard is capable of experiencing the rock *as* rock. (1995: 197)

The lizard seeks the warmth of the sun and – unlike the stone which, when tossed in the shade, does not move – follows its light as it moves. But the lizard too does not know its environment, since it simply exploits the opportunities offered by it (in truth, all living beings modify their 'environment'; see Odling-Smee et al. 2003). Both the stone and the lizard are in their present environment, and do not need a world that is not here yet. This is why Heidegger is keen to specify that the lizard's sun is not the sun *qua* sun, it is not an autonomous entity: like a star, a physical object with its own properties. Rather the lizard's sun is *simply* and *immediately* – without 'recognition or reflection' – light and warmth.

On the contrary, the human animal's 'world' is an ensemble of beings *qua* beings at its disposal, precisely because it is not an 'environment'. For the human, the sun is not immediately light and heat, but is first of all a material (astronomical, religious, ecological and so on) entity. Only a being which is thought of as an independent entity can be considered for purposes different from those that are immediately presented upon perceiving it. Consider the chimp analysed by Vygotsky and mentioned in the previous chapter, and its inability to use the stick to reach the fruit. That task is impossible for the chimp precisely because it cannot see the stick *as a stick*, as a long and thin tool; rather, it sees it as something that can be grasped but that, in the context of its present predicament, has no use and is therefore not worthy of attention. The animal is 'poor in world' precisely because it is *not interested* in beings *qua* beings. So for the lizard the 'rock on which [it] lies is not given for [it] as rock, in such a way that it could inquire into its mineralogical constitution for example', just like 'the sun in which it is basking is not given for the lizard as sun, in such a way that it could ask questions of astrophysics about it and expect to find the answers' (Heidegger 1995: 197–8). The point is that the problem of human animality could be entirely encapsulated in this simple question: why would a living body ask 'questions of astrophysics', while its sole interest is that of getting warm? There is a vast disproportion between the lizard's elementary action – that of lying in the sun – and the conditions that it would be necessary for a human to meet in order to indulge in the same action. The human is the living being for which the sun is *not* simply the sun.

There is a kind of resentment at work here, aimed towards the immediacy of animal life precisely because animals *can* bask in the sun without asking questions: the sun is something that warms you, and this is all there is to know. When Heidegger observes that

> The blade of grass that the beetle crawls up, for example, is not a blade of grass for it at all; it is not something possibly destined to become part of the bundle of hay with which the peasant will feed his cow. The blade of grass is simply a beetle-path on which the beetle specifically seeks beetle-nourishment, and not just any edible matter in general. (1995: 198)

One feels like asking: why would the beetle ask so many questions about the blade of grass? Why cannot it be enough for it to search for food? On the contrary, the human being who desires to be warmed by the sun is forced to go through the artificial yet inevitable mediation about its own condition of 'world-forming' being. I feel cold, and I would like to warm myself up in the sun; but when I finally lie down to soak up its warmth, there persists even in this context the obscure and irritating awareness of the fact that the sun is a being *qua* being about which (if perhaps not immediately, because I am really too cold) I could ask 'questions of astrophysics'. Thus, even the simple and direct pleasure of feeling my body warmed up by the sun is disturbed by my awareness that the sun is always a being *qua* being. *Humanitas* never *ever* leaves me alone.

The feeling of fatigue which is part of the human condition produces then a kind of inversion, making it impossible for us to be in the world like a stone lies on the ground. Isn't the human animal trapped in the cage of the '*qua*'? Isn't this unseen prison – made of language and of the 'I' – a far more stifling cage than the 'invisible bubble' of the animal's 'environment'? No, Heidegger insists, on the contrary '[t]hroughout the course of its life the animal is confined to its environmental world, immured as it were within a fixed sphere that is incapable of further expansion or contraction' (1995: 198). This claim is, from Heidegger's own standpoint, wholly unjustified (and one should add that this 'fixed sphere' is a human creation; see Patterson 2002). That is because the 'environment' is not perceived, by those who inhabit it, as something closed. The tick is in an 'environment' precisely because the tick utterly ignores the fact that it lives 'in' an environment among many others. But then, if the animal lives within this invisible bubble, the tick cannot be aware of it. It is only from Heidegger's standpoint that the animal can be said to be 'confined' anywhere. Only from within a prison can there be a desire to escape, and if the animal does not feel imprisoned, it has no need to escape. Indeed, if there is a truly free living being, that is the animal. Heidegger seems to be projecting, and attributing his own state of mind to something else: he is the one in prison, not the tick – and certainly not the lizard, happily basking in the sun.

It often happens that, when talking about animality, the human's point of view is coloured, more or less indirectly, by a vague shade of loss, even of nostalgia. Vygotsky, the Marxist psychologist, recounts, with the optimism of a revolutionary, the historical process that language triggers in the animal human body:

> having the specific function of retrograde effect, it [language] transfers the mental operations into higher and qualitatively new forms and allows man to control his own behavior from outside with the aid of external stimuli. The use of the sign, being simultaneously a means of autostimulation, results in a completely new and specific structure of behavior in man, a structure that breaks with the traditions of natural behavior and creates for the first time a new form of cultural-psychological behaviour. (Rieber and Carton 1999: 47)[2]

What is at stake – and this is the fundamental core of the humanist project – is, quite simply, mastery over nature on the one hand, and over the human itself (and its body) on the other. But if the animal is utterly incapable of self-domestication, what happens to the child, so dangerously suspended between *animalitas* and *humanitas*, the child whose 'perceptions . . . are still primitive and distinctive' (Vygotsky

68

and Luria 1993: 146)? According to Vygotsky the child's world – but we should probably say the child's 'environment' – is characterised by the very same fullness and immanence that we have already encountered in the cases of the tick, the lizard, the beetle and the bee: the 'external world' is 'seen in a primitive way, it is perceived usually as something near at hand, within the child's reach, touch, grasp, or groping, that is, all these primitive forms of possession' (1993: 147). This child, like the lizard lying still in the sun, or perhaps even like the stone lying inert on the ground, is captivated by a world that can be felt, touched, swallowed and grasped. Such a world is not constituted by beings *qua* beings, but by graspable beings, squeezable beings, lickable beings and swallowable beings. This world is as alive as the child is, who perceives it 'with unusual brightness. In these images external impressions are mixed with and corrected by the images preserved from previous experience' (1993: 148).

But historical-social development brings the party to an end, when '[n]ew "adult" cultural forms of behavior gradually replace primitive childhood ones' (1993: 168). Interestingly, among all possible examples to illustrate this transition Vygotsky chooses that of a stone, the same stone that for Heidegger is 'worldless': '[t]he industrial and cultural environment gradually changes them and . . . every human being we know today is a stone repeatedly cut and altered under the influence of the industrial and cultural environment' (1993: 170). It was as if the stone, the lizard and the human were sitting in a circle, so that the first would touch the last, thus making it a little more like itself (the human would be partially 'stonified', the stone partially 'humanised'). Indeed, for Vygotsky, the human treats itself like a dull stone to be sharpened, in order to construct a perfect tool, sharp and dangerous. But how does this process, leading the child to become a 'world-forming' human, properly unfold? And, in particular, what does the child lose and what does he earn in this epochal transition from *animalitas* to *humanitas*? As Vygotsky describes it,

> the child's entire behavior becomes reconstructed; the child develops the habit of *refraining* from immediate satisfaction of his needs and drives and of *retarding* immediate reactions to external stimuli, so that by using indirect ways and acquiring the necessary cultural skills he could gain easier and better control over the situation. It is this *inhibition* of the primitive functions and the development of complex forms of adaptation that constitute the transition from primitive forms of child behavior to adult forms. (1993: 171; emphasis added)

The Unhappy Animal

It is clear now that the human animal is the living being that, in order to become a 'world-forming' human, has self-domesticated itself (Theofanopoulou et al. 2017). In order to have a 'world' the human animal had to renounce its environment, to expel itself from its own body, thus transforming it into a 'bare life'. The point is that *Homo sapiens* is nothing but this unbroken process of loss of an 'environment' that actually *never* was. For this reason, it is correct to say that, actually, *Homo sapiens* was never an animal, and its fascination for animality is a longing for what was never known. Let us go back to Vygotsky's text by means of Nietzsche: a description becomes a diagnosis. In *The Gay Science*, in the paragraph dedicated to '*the genius of the species*' (Nietzsche 2001: 211, §354), Nietzsche tackles the problem of consciousness, and in particular of how the human animal becomes 'conscious of something'. What is at stake here is not merely consciousness, which is common to all the living world, but *self-consciousness*, the ability to control oneself. The transition from consciousness to self-consciousness is tantamount to that from 'environment' to 'world', from *animalitas* to *humanitas*. It is clear that, for Nietzsche, one can very well live without self-consciousness: '[f]or we could think, feel, will, remember, and also "act" in every sense of the term, and yet none of all this would have to "enter our consciousness" (as one says figuratively)' (2001: 212). Indeed, this expression is not used figuratively because the 'voice of consciousness', which is the sensible manifestation of self-consciousness, is originally the adult's discourse (Perrone-Bertolotti et al. 2014; Alderson-Day and Fernyhough 2015). And indeed, that discourse *enters* the human body through the ears. Thus, self-consciousness is literally *implanted* in a human body which could very well survive without it, since '[a]ll of life would be possible without, as it were, seeing itself in the mirror' (Nietzsche 2001: 212). It is interesting to note how Nietzsche employs the same example used by Lacan, that of the mirror. Self-consciousness is the introjection of an external reflected image. This introjection is aided by the fundamental role of the adult, who *says* to the young human being that she is the one out there, in the mirror. Nietzsche has no doubt that self-consciousness is a linguistic phenomenon: 'it seems to me that the subtlety and strength of consciousness is always related to a person's (or animal's) ability to communicate' (2001: 212). Self-consciousness is, in practice, the introjection of the other's external discourse. One's intimate states are wholly exposed

to the light of day, because without communication with another –
external to me – there could be no self-consciousness:

> The sign-inventing person is also the one who becomes ever more acutely
> conscious of himself; for only as a social animal did man learn to become
> conscious of himself – he is still doing it, and he is doing it more and
> more. My idea is clearly that consciousness actually belongs not to man's
> existence as an individual but rather to the community. (2001: 213)

Therefore, and we will often return to this conclusion in later chapters, 'each of us, even with the best will in the world to understand
ourselves as individually as possible, "to know ourselves", will
always bring to consciousness precisely that in ourselves which is
"nonindividual", that which is "average"' (2001: 213).

Nietzsche highlights how the process described by Vygotsky as
an accomplishment – as indeed it is – amounts also to a radical loss,
which the human being keeps undergoing. That is to say that the
price to pay for the achievement of *humanitas*, or self-consciousness,
is the loss of one's absolute and unutterable singularity: '[a]t bottom,
all our actions are incomparably and utterly personal, unique, and
boundlessly individual, there is no doubt; but as soon as we translate
them into consciousness, *they no longer seem to be*' (2001: 213).
The conclusion of Nietzsche's reasoning casts a sinister light on self-
consciousness, especially considering what, only a few decades later,
would happen to human consciousness, including the revolutionary self-consciousness Vygotsky was so proud of: '[i]n the end, the
growing consciousness is a danger . . . it is a sickness' (2001: 214).
Indeed, 'the solitary and predatory person would not have needed
it' (2001: 213). I will return to this link between animality and
impersonal singularity in the last two chapters, but for now it should
be clear how, for Nietzsche, the animal condition is not something
that the human has left behind but, on the contrary, it is a vector
of development (see Acampora and Acampora 2004; Lemm 2009).
Nietzsche is the philosopher of the becoming-animal.

Let us return to the animal, then: the crow perched on the lamp-
post, the dog barking behind a gate, the cat that casts a quick glance
at its surroundings before darting under the cover of a parked car.
What is the animal? The animal stands as a reminder that a different
life than ours is not only possible, but is in fact practised and lived
in front of our eyes, right here and right now. The 'world-forming'
human being can exist only thanks to the presence of the animal. For
the same reason, the animal – the philosophical animal in particular

– says very little about its life, and rather reveals much about the philosopher who speaks of it (de Fontenay 1998; Khandker 2014). Better yet, it reveals what kind of human life a philosopher – who is ostensibly referring to animals – is vouching for. In this perspective, one of the most interesting philosophical animals is the Hegelian one. For Hegel the animal is an 'organic individuality' which 'exists as subjectivity in so far as the externality proper to shape is idealized into members, and the organism in its process outwards preserves inwardly the unity of the self' (Hegel 2004: 351; §350). Here again appears the very close relationship, which we have already encountered in the previous chapter, between individuality and voice/language. For Hegel the animal – being, in the Aristotelian manner, a subjectivity – has a 'voice'. However, this voice will never be turned towards the animal itself, as a voice of consciousness, of an 'I': indeed, animality is an individuality completely absorbed in its relationship with the world. The animal's subjectivity can only exist as a counterpart of the objectivity of the world that faces it: '[t]he self-feeling of the individuality is also directly exclusive and in a state of tension with a non-organic nature' (Hegel 2004: 380; §357).

What relation is there then between this subjectivity and its 'environment'? Here Hegel introduces a new and different consideration as compared to what we have examined so far, particularly when it comes to the perfection that, for von Uexküll, would characterise the relationship between 'perception marks' and 'operational marks'. So far, the 'invisible bubble' of the animal environment has been presented without gaps: there is no separation, for example, between the eye that sees and the claw that grasps. But for Hegel this state of completeness is precluded for animality because, on the contrary, only a self-conscious subjectivity can achieve this condition. And so, a gap is introduced in the 'environment': '[o]nly what is living feels a *lack* . . . [b]ut it is a *lack* only in so far as the lack's overcoming is equally present in the same thing, and contradiction is, as such, immanent and explicitly present in that thing' (2004: 385; §359). The contradiction lies within the living organism itself, carving this 'lack' on the inside: for example, hunger as a lack (and therefore a need) of food. To be hungry means that the organism is incomplete, that it needs something external, a need that, in turn, triggers a search for that which can satisfy it. Hegel describes this lack as something that overcomes the living being; but this means introducing a form of natural transcendence within animality itself. Indeed, Hegel's 'lack' goes beyond mere physiological need, like hunger or cold:

according to him animality is intrinsically lacking, and therefore projected towards transcendence. So far, we have always considered *animalitas* as an occasion to think immanence; Hegel, for his part, does not want to renounce transcendence, but rather intends to merge it into the life of spirit, thus making natural life an existence oriented towards transcendence. The animal features only as a step in the progression towards the human, a necessary step like any other, but one to be overcome as soon as possible. And yet, to feel hunger does not necessarily mean to be overcome by something external, and superior, to lived existence, and to be pushed back towards transcendence. Hunger drives the beetle to climb the blade of grass, but this does not mean that the beetle experiences its condition as lacking something: the beetle is hungry, just like the lizard is cold and thus moves towards a source of heat.

Locating 'lack' in animality allows Hegel to spiritualise the tick's behaviour: lacking something implies the ability to represent this lack, and eventually to long for it – if it was once possessed – or to desire it, if it was never experienced. But this means banishing the animal from its 'environment' and condemning it to wander, forlorn, in the 'world'. Indeed, only from this new standpoint could the tick see its actions and their objects as distinct entities. But the tick would then cease to be a tick, because the condition of animality is the impossibility of leaving one's environment. What does the animal lack, precisely? It lacks something insofar as it is nothing more than an animal, it suffers its being *merely* an animal. This intrinsic limit of animality emerges when the animal falls sick, when it internally comes into contact with the possibility of death (in this case, the death caused by another animal, like a fish eating a smaller fish, does not apply: this would be an accidental death, while the fact of dying is not):

> Its organism, as a determinate existence, has a certain quantitative strength and is, indeed, capable of overcoming its dividedness; but . . . in overcoming and ridding itself of particular inadequacies, [the animal] does not put an end to the general inadequacy which is inherent in it, namely, that its Idea is only the immediate Idea, that, as animal, it stands *within Nature*, and its subjectivity is only *implicitly* the Notion but is not *for its own self the Notion*. The inner universality therefore remains opposed to the natural singularity of the living being as the *negative* power from which the animal suffers violence and perishes, because natural existence (*Dasein*) as such does not itself contain this universality and is not therefore the reality which corresponds to it. (Hegel 2004: 440; §374)

The animal is condemned by its own animal nature to remain incomplete. To be an animal, indeed, means to live a life trapped within the limits of this life itself ('its Idea [i.e., its essence] is only the immediate Idea ... *within Nature*'), without seeking anything external to it, because such a beyond (e.g., for a tick) simply does not exist. Hegel agrees that this is the character of animal life, but for this very reason it is a constitutively incomplete life, precisely because it ignores the possibility of overcoming itself, transitioning to the life of spirit. Therefore, subverting the perspective we have followed so far (yet actually confirming it, since Hegel's theoretical work recognises, in animality, the experience of immanence – although he considers this to be the poorest and saddest form of experience): '[t]he disparity between [the animal's] finitude and universality is its *original disease* and the inborn *germ of death*' (Hegel 2004: 441; §375).

Animality is destined to death; this is the 'inborn *germ*' that condemns it. Dying, nothing remains of the life that once was. This is the animal's radical disparity between finitude and universality, i.e., the tritely immanent life of *animalitas*, wholly concentrated on its own living, here and now (hence inadequate to the universal). This is a life that does not tend towards something that would overcome itself; on the contrary, it is completely exhausted, without residues or regrets, in itself. Therefore, and coherently with his outlook, by privileging transcendence over immanence Hegel overturns the description of the 'environment' offered by von Uexküll: this is not a place of perfection but, on the contrary, 'contains factors which are almost wholly alien; it exercises a perpetual violence and threat of dangers on the animals' feeling which is an *insecure, anxious*, and *unhappy* one' (2004: 416–17; §370). This is the conclusion Hegel was seeking: *the animal is unhappy*, and therefore – *pace* the animal rights defenders – it is ugly. As he puts it in the *Aesthetics*:

> The real seat of the activities of organic life remains veiled from our vision; we see only the external outlines of the animal's shape, and this again is covered throughout by feathers, scales, hair, pelt, prickles, or shells. Such covering does belong to the animal kingdom, but in animals it has forms drawn from the kingdom of plants. Here at once lies one chief deficiency in the beauty of animal life. (Hegel 1975: 145)

The animal is both unhappy and ugly – not because its existence has been unlucky, as if some other life could be joyous and serene. No, animality is unhappy precisely because it is *animality*, because the possibility of having access to superior, more developed and civilised forms of existence is precluded.

This story has a familiar ending, as we have already seen in Heidegger's case: for Hegel – uninterested in life itself, but rather in the development of Spirit – animality is irrelevant, and indeed it is something to be abandoned as soon as possible: the animal must die, in more than one sense, since only when nature *qua* nature dies is the path of Spirit, culture, history and language finally cleared: the path leading to us, speaking animals, 'world-forming' humans. Thus, anxiety is not the distinguishing characteristic of the human but rather of the tick (and Hegel is perfectly right: it suffices to think about the treatment of nonhuman animals in industrial farming (Patterson 2002)).

Hegel's conclusion is both surprising and enlightening: the 'world' is not a place of insecurity, anxiety and sadness – as Heidegger would argue. The tick – rather than the human, thrown into the 'world' without fixed and reliable reference points (Mazzeo 2009) – is unhappy. This is only partially surprising, since it ultimately amounts to a confirmation of the thesis that animality means immanence – except that, for Hegel, immanence is a condition to be abandoned as soon as possible (and from this point of view we never stopped being Hegelians). Immanence should be left behind, because it can represent a danger for the condition of a 'world-forming' human. The point still stands though: a confrontation with *animalitas* always provokes some envy, regret or, more often, anger. There is that 'inborn *germ of death*' at stake. Ultimately, Hegel tells us that the primordial deficiency of the animal can be found in its simple death, a fact that amounts to its inadequacy to universality. A dog that is run over by a speeding car lies dead on the roadside. It is a sad story, one that neither knows nor expects any redemption. Indeed, as Heidegger knew, the dog does not properly die, but simply *ceases to exist*, because only a human (*Dasein*) can truly die; on the contrary, Heidegger defines 'the ending of that which lives ... "perishing"' (1962: 291). This is the scandal of animality: animals just 'perish', constantly and by the millions, but this death simply puts a definitive end to their existence. They just die, and this inadequacy does not bother anyone, except that particular deceased body. This is the scandal: how is it possible to die like that?

Jacques Lacan – who lived in an era when the belief in the history of Spirit had become impossible, even with the best of intentions – disagreed with Hegel. Anxiety is produced neither by the 'environment' nor by *animalitas*; on the contrary, the 'world' itself is anguishing, not simply due to its complexity, for the tick's environment is complex too, but precisely because it *is* a 'world', because it means *humanitas*: 'you shall see very well what there is to be seen as regards anxiety, namely, that there isn't any safety net. When anxiety is at issue, each piece of the mesh, so to speak, only carries any meaning in so far as it leaves empty the space where anxiety lies' (Lacan 2014: 9). To live in the 'world', as opposed to what happens in the animal 'environment', means having no 'perception marks' that could guide the correspond-ing 'operational marks'. And this means, quite simply, that there is *no right answer* (i.e., a biologically justified one) to any given situation. What should be done then? Well, to live in a 'world' precisely means to lack an answer to this question – not because it is too complex, but rather because *it has no answer*. On the other hand, in the context of an 'environment' there is always a correct answer, even if one fails to formulate it; in an 'environment' every fullness corresponds to a lack, every concave structure to a convex one, and every stimulus to a response. But what happens when we inhabit a world of lacks with no corresponding fullness, and vice versa? Lacan writes: 'should all the norms, that is, that which makes for anomaly just as much as that which makes for lack, happen all of a sudden not to be lacking, that's when the anxiety starts' (Lacan 2014: 42). What truly provokes the envy of *animalitas'* immanence is precisely this absence of anxiety. Animals have many problems, but when we leave them alone they are genuinely immune from anxiety – as long as we leave them be. As Heidegger wrote in *Being and Time*: '[b]eing-anxious discloses, pri-mordially and directly, the world as world. . . . [T]he *world as world* is disclosed first and foremost by anxiety, as a mode of state-of-mind' (1962: 232). Anxiety is the emotive operator which 'discloses' the 'environment', transforming it into a 'world'. Precisely because the 'world' is the human being's dwelling, many humans – motivated by anger, envy, or both – try to also transform the animal environment into a horrible 'world', as in the case of Harry Harlow's infamous experiments (Harlow et al. 1965; Despret 2002; Vicedo 2009). One of his better-known articles opens with a claim both obvious (for who has ever doubted that letting a child grow alone and isolated would be detrimental to her mental health?) and sinister: 'human social isolation is recognized as a problem of vast importance'. Is this a mere assessment, or a threat? Is it science or sadism? Or – the grimmest scenario – is it both? Harlow continues: 'For the past ten years we have studied the effects of partial social isolation by raising monkeys from birth onward in bare wire cages. . . . These monkeys suffer total maternal deprivation and, even more important, have no opportunity to form affectional ties with their peers' (Harlow et al. 1965: 90). Not satisfied with what he has already discovered – that such a life is unbearable – the next scientific step is that of trying to observe the effects of a life 'of total social isolation by housing monkeys from a few hours after birth until 3, 6, or 12 months of age in the stainless-steel chamber' (Harlow et al. 1965: 90). Harlow does not realise it (or perhaps he realises it all too well), but what he is engineering in his laboratory is a forced transition (even in nature a little monkey can lose its parents, but that is a limit situation, which still belongs to the realm of possibilities of an 'environment') from an 'environment' to a 'world'. Indeed, after the experiment ran its course, the animals displayed all the symptoms of anxiety:

> the findings of the various total-isolation and semi-isolation studies of the monkeys suggest that sufficiently severe and enduring early isolation reduces these animals to a social-emotional level in which the primary social responsiveness is fear. Twelve months of total social isolation is apparently sufficient to achieve this result consistently in rhesus monkeys. (Harlow et al. 1965: 96)

Harlow's formulation is ambiguous, since it is not clear if this effect was merely observed, or if it was indeed the experiment's desired result. Either way, the experiment's outcome is anxiety, even though the scientist uses more neutral terms: when released from their condition of total isolation the animals are 'generally fearful or fearless, generally hostile or without aggression, or selectively fearful or selectively hostile' (Harlow et al. 1965: 96). These experiments have been rightly criticised from an ethical standpoint (Gluck 1997), but perhaps what makes them most (abhorrently) relevant is something else: Harlow's account demonstrates the inextricable tangle of feelings provoked by animals in human beings. Indeed, these experiments seem to have been motivated by envy, anger, but also by an odd form of preoccupation with animals themselves. Harlow is keen to let his readers know that the state of isolation was never too long, that the animals ultimately managed to overcome the trauma, and that no specimen died while in isolation (although several died after having been 'freed'). This is another way to interpret Heidegger's anxiety: *Homo sapiens* is anxious about the animal's lack of anxiety. They therefore need to be punished, because not feeling anxiety ultimately means to be unafraid of death:

The animal doesn't know how to 'let be,' let the thing be such as it is. It always has a relation of utility, of putting-in-perspective; it doesn't let the thing be what it is, appear as such without a project guided by a narrow 'sphere' of drives, of desires. One of the questions to be raised, therefore, would be to know whether man does that. . . . For that is the relation to the being as such, that is to say, the relation to what is inasmuch as one lets it be what it is, that is to say, that one doesn't approach it or apprehend it from our own perspective, from our own design. In order to have a relation to the sun as it is, it is necessary that, in a certain way, I relate to the sun such as it is in my absence, and it is in effect like that that objectivity is constituted, starting from death. (Derrida 2008: 159, 160)

'Siegfried and the Salmon'

Derrida highlights the fundamental nexus linking the humanistic project (of a subjectivity that says 'I'), on the one hand, and death – and therefore anxiety – on the other. We have seen that a subjectivity that refers to itself as an 'I' does so by demarcating its position with respect to another: in order to exist, an 'I' needs to place the other in the position of a 'You'. Of course, the 'I's' position is interchangeable with the 'You's' – however, no 'I' can exist without carving its own space at the expense of a 'You'. The founding gesture of subjectivity at once includes and excludes. Most of all, though, it excludes that which is by definition 'without words' – the body of the speaking subject, the *spoken-of* body – by means of an 'exclusive inclusion' (Agamben 1998: 8) of bare life. The paradox implicit in this gesture is that the 'I' can die – as an *I* – only because it says 'I'. It is only because I have withdrawn myself from the world – this is what being/saying 'I' means – that I can be left aside, that I can die. 'I' means, resorting again to the Heideggerian strategy, that *I* exist *qua* 'I' only because I have self-delimited myself as an I. The operation through which we affirm the autonomous existence of the 'I' is wholly analogous to that used to single out the sun *qua* 'sun'. The lizard, just as it lacks a relationship with the sun *qua* 'sun', cannot have a relationship with itself *qua* 'I'. Considered as a purely objective entity, as if nobody could see it (or if only God could) the sun is, as Derrida would put it, just as it would be in my absence. This sun is unseen by me only when I am dead. The same goes for the 'I': to see myself *qua* 'I' means having an outside-in perspective, to be external to my body and looking inwards, as if I was observing someone else – as if I was gone, or dead. The objectivity and the autonomy of the 'I' go hand in hand with its replaceability, with its mortality.

Temporality enters into human experience through our declaration of the 'I'. To speak means to occupy a position in the linguistic field, like planting a flag in an unknown territory: here, and now, *I* am with this flag, being the one who fixed my position through this gesture: '*here* and *now* delimit the spatial and temporal instance coextensive and contemporary with the present instance of discourse containing *I*' (Benveniste 1971: 219). To utter 'I' constitutes the speaker as an 'I' capable of saying 'I'. The same applies to spatial and temporal linguistic expressions: *here* and *now* do not indicate pre-existing positions which would precede, in time and space, the enunciative act. On the contrary, they define the reference points with respect to which time and space can be thought and organised. 'Here' allows us to distinguish 'near' and 'far', just like 'now' introduces a differentiation between a before (past) and a not-yet (future): 'it is a fact both original and fundamental that these "pronominal" forms do not refer to "reality" or to "objective" positions in space or time but to the utterance, unique each time, that contains them, and thus they reflect their proper use' (Benveniste 1971: 219). The anthropologic machine produces a subject – insofar as it can utter 'I' – and at the same time it places it in time and space. As soon as it comes to exist in the world, the 'I' becomes temporal, and therefore mortal. This is the price we pay to say 'I', to *have* a body, and to partake in *humanitas* – and no one had warned us of just how high this price would be.

It is here that perhaps we can look for an explanation for the anger that (together with envy) is addressed to *animalitas*. The animal, its gaze unable to grasp the '*qua*' (if we follow Heidegger), looks at us – when it observes us – as a body, as a mere part of the environment in which it lives: a part now annoying, now dangerous (as in the terrified look in the eyes of the monkeys in Harlow's experiment video tapes), now indifferent. The animal sees the appearance of the body we are. It sees nothing else, for there is nothing else to see. While that body is an 'I', the animal's gaze delivers it back to the condition of a mere body. The 'I' cannot stand this gaze, for it provokes too many miserable memories that it would rather not remember. In Curzio Malaparte's wonderful novel *Kaputt*,[3] in the chapter titled 'Siegfried and the Salmon', there is an episode that precisely recounts this human passion for the annihilation of animals (truly, the whole book is a tale of relations between humans and animals). The scene is set in Finland, during the Second World War, along the river Juutuanjoki which flows in the northern part of the country, near the border with the USSR. The morbid atmosphere of the tale is introduced by a dialogue between the writer and some German army officials, on the topic of using human skin to make armchairs: '"I wonder how many hundreds of thousands of armchairs could be covered with the human skins of Jews whom you have killed during this war?" I asked. "Millions!" Georg Beandasch said' (Malaparte 1948: 321). The Jew is a *Jew*, akin to an animal, an entity *qua* entity epitomising, in a supreme abstraction, the whole of Jewish humanity – like the animal epitomises *all* nonhuman living beings. The *animot* exists because Auschwitz exists, and vice versa. It is no coincidence that this tale begins by shifting life away from the plane of vital evidence to that of abstraction, of the linguistic being. That is because the animal does not exist, just like the Jew does not exist. And yet, there is a thread linking the primordial gesture of a body that says 'I' to the creation of imaginary entities, like the ANIMAL or the JEW. As we have seen, the 'I' is not the name of some pre-existing psychological entity, but is a gesture that both includes and excludes. The first elision in this process of exclusion is that of the body and, along with it, of *animalitas*. 'I' *qua* producer (and necessary producer) of always new '*qua*'s', and therefore new inclusions/exclusions. Within the anthropologic machine itself there is a reason for both the slaughterhouse and the extermination camp. In the boreal night, the tale goes on, the writer walks within the woods near the front line. The war is close – both friends and foes, the stranger and the patriot – but just then a pack of animals, looking like dogs with fur 'the colour of rusty iron', quickly and fearlessly crosses the woods:

> 'The wolves,' the soldiers said.
> They passed close to us and looked at us with their red glistening eyes. They seemed to have no fear, no suspicion of us. There was something in their confidence that was not only peaceful, but detached – a kind of sad and noble indifference. They ran noiselessly, fleet and light, with their long, nimble, soft gait. There was nothing of the beast in them, but a kind of noble shyness, a kind of proud and most cruel tameness. (Malaparte 1948: 324)

The war rages on, but the wolves stride next to soldiers and cannons with 'a kind of sad and noble indifference'. This is the indifference proper of *animalitas*, which disturbs and worries *humanitas*, always ready to take itself far too seriously (there is no pride without an 'I', and there is no more prideful 'I' than one wearing a uniform). A soldier, with an almost unconscious reflex, raises his rifle to shoot a few of them, but a fellow soldier stops him, 'as if in those inhuman solitudes, even man found no other means of expressing his humanity, except by acknowledging a sad and tame wildness' (Malaparte 1948: 324). A respectful gesture, but not one expressing equality: it is rather a magnanimous gesture, because when addressing animals (as with any *body*) any gesture is always paternalistic. Even petting a cat is an imposition of power, because that hand could just as well kill it. The hand that beckons always reminds the animal that it could reject it – there is always a hierarchy of power, of life and death, at work.

After the wolves pass by the soldiers – *animalitas* is uninterested in warring *humanitas* – the salmon appears in the narration: this most elusive of animals, with a keen but inscrutable gaze. Had Levinas taken the fish as an example of a *face*, his philosophy would have been profoundly different. Indeed, as Calarco argues:

> the face of the Other cannot be delimited a priori to the realm of the human; . . . animals of various sorts might have a face, which is to say, animals might call upon and obligate me in ways that I cannot fully anticipate. 'The question of the animal' is thus a question deriving from an animal who faces me, an interruption deriving from a 'singular' animal, an animal whom I face and by whom I am faced and who calls my mode of existence into question. (2008: 5)

As Derrida already noted, it is novelists – rather than philosophers or scientists – who are able to let themselves be questioned by the animal gaze. Malaparte writes: '"For some days," Georg Beandasch said, "General von Heunert has been beside himself. He cannot catch a salmon. All the strategy of German generals is powerless against the salmon"' (1948: 324). This is the challenge: the general and the salmon, man and beast, *humanitas* against *animalitas*. This is, naturally, an uneven challenge, since the salmon lives in the river – where salmons have always lived – without provoking the human. It is only General von Heunert who perceives this existence as a challenge. And what is at stake? The honour of the general as an 'I', because a German and Nazi general cannot be bested by anyone, least of all a fish. But what is this *honour* if not the gaze of the Other? The 'I' cannot stand alone, it always needs – like the child, turning around after having seen herself in the mirror to be confirmed by the adult holding her – to be 'ratified', as Lacan put it, by the Other. Without this passage, the 'I' would remain a meaningless noise. This is the anthropological meaning of the challenge to the salmon: there is an 'I' that needs to be reminded of its being so, and wants everyone who witnesses its actions – like the troops deployed along the river banks to protect and acknowledge the 'I's value – to confirm it.

So, the general rises to the challenge: specifically for this fishing goal he summons a captain, an expert fisherman and a trout specialist:

> 'Of the trout. Why not?' General von Heunert said. 'Captain Springenschmid, who is well known throughout the Tyrol as a specialist in trout fishing, maintains that the Tyrolean trout has the same temperament as the Lapp salmon. Isn't it so, Captain Springenschmid?'
>
> 'Jawohl!' Captain Springenschmid replied with a bow. (Malaparte 1948: 335)

It makes little difference whether it is trout or salmon. They are still fish, animals, and we know everything about animals: we *always* know everything about *animalitas*. The narrator asks:

> 'Yes, trout,' I said. 'But what about salmon?'
>
> 'Salmon are like trout,' Captain Springenschmid said with a smile. 'The trout is not a patient animal; it becomes tired of waiting and rushes into danger. As soon as it bites, it is lost. Gently, delicately it is reeled in by the fisherman. It is child's play. Trout–
>
> 'Yes, trout,' I said. 'But what about salmon?'
>
> 'Salmon,' Captain Springenschmid said, 'is only a larger trout.' (Malaparte 1948: 335)

Here we have it: the trout is a salmon, and the salmon is a trout, no point in beating around the bush – in the end, they both pertain to the FISH category. And yet, in Malaparte's novel, the salmon that lives in the Juutuanjoki river is a peculiar fish, *that* specific salmon, perhaps not even properly a salmon (*Salmo salar*), but simply an organism living in that particular place. And yet, once captured by the net of language this animal – unbeknownst to it, since to be an animal means being unaware of what humans know about you – immediately becomes an abstraction, a generic salmon *qua* salmon.

> 'It looks,' General von Heunert said, 'as if my salmon were the finest specimen ever seen in these rivers. It's a huge beast, extraordinarily plucky. Just think, the other day it almost knocked its snout against my knees!'
>
> 'It's an insolent salmon!' I said. 'It deserves to be punished.'
>
> 'It's a damnable salmon,' General von Heunert said. (Malaparte 1948: 335)

This living being now incarnates a challenge, because it has punctured the honour of a German general: it has now become a property, it is *his* salmon and for this reason it has lost all of its specificity, merely transformed into 'the finest specimen ever seen in these rivers'. The animal is always a 'specimen' of some category. Biopolitics is older than both State and Science, and indeed it begins with the act of nomination – of enclosure – of a living being within a name. After all, as Deleuze and Guattari put it '[l]anguage is not life; it gives life orders' (1987: 7). There is an absolute and unbridgeable gap between life – this life, the life of *this* fish – and the language that turns it into an abstraction. Two linguistic beings are clashing on the Juutuanjoki river: an 'I' and an 'animal'. Such a clash can only take place in the 'world'; for in an environment there would only be two bodies struggling for a specific reason, like food, shelter or reproduction. Immanence, unaware of transcendence, knows nothing of either honour or pride:

> the struggle had already lasted about three hours with varying success, when I perceived ironic smiles rising on the yellow wrinkled faces of Pekka and of the other Lapps who were huddled together, their clay pipes between their teeth. Then I looked at the General. There he was in the centre of the river, in full battle dress, his big Mauser dangling from his belt, wrapped in the folds of a large mosquito net. The wide reddish stripes on his general's trousers glistened in the dead reflection of the nocturnal sun. Something was rising in him; I could feel it. I sensed it in his impatient gestures, in his hungry face, in the voice in which from time to time he shouted '*Achtung!*' – a voice with overtones of wounded pride, of a subtle and troubled fear. (Malaparte 1948: 338–9)

The fish, the salmon, turns out to be more stubborn than General von Heunert, and refuses to be removed from the river it has always lived in. Both are fighting, but while the Nazi general is fighting against shame (the death of the subject), the fish is fighting for survival (the life of the body). Because the salmon is struggling against the death brought about by the termination of life, and that hook is pulling it towards a place it wants to avoid. Its life, quite simply, is in the river's water. The general, on the other hand, does not fear physical death (at least not yet), since the salmon poses no threat. He rather fears the death of the 'I' because, should he fail to capture the salmon, he will become a laughing stock, thus losing the gaze of the Other. At stake there is, on the one hand, a death in immanence (the death of a body), while on the other a death in transcendence (the death of an 'I'). But the 'I' cannot die, and therefore the animal must die; the salmon was already doomed before the fight with the general even started. The animal must die because its death grants the survival of the subject who refers to itself as an 'I'. The realm of transcendence – *humanitas* – has no space for immanence, for *animalitas*:

> General von Heunert suddenly turned to Beandasch and shouted in a hoarse voice:
> 'Genugf Erschiesst ihn'
> 'Jawohl!' replied Georg Beandasch, and he moved forward. He walked downstream with long, slow, hard steps: when he was close to the salmon that struggled in the foaming water pulling the General downstream, he stopped, drew his pistol from its holster, bent over the brave salmon and fired two shots point blank into its head. (Malaparte 1948: 339)

Notes

1. Indeed, in *The Fundamental Concepts of Metaphysics*, Heidegger only considers three possibilities for his fundamental ontological tripartition: the human 'subject', the animal and the stone as a generic representative of all 'inanimate' beings. The entire plant world is excluded, which is really surprising considering Heidegger's fondness for forests (McWhorter and Stenstad 2009; Moyle 2017). The 'philosophical' problem (Marder 2013) of the plant world is directly linked to the general theme of *animality*, especially if one considers animality as something that does not merely pertain to sardines and dogs, but to the living world and the 'natural' world in general. From this standpoint a philosophy of animality is more generally a philosophy of 'assemblages' – whether or not they are, strictly speaking, animal ones. Indeed, if we want to overcome the anthropocentric prejudice, the animal-centric prejudice should also be abandoned. On the one hand, what was already clear to Aristotle is becoming ever more obvious: in his *De Anima*, he spoke of a *nutritive soul* (θρεπτικὴ ψυχὴ) common to *all* living beings:

   > we must first speak about nourishment and reproduction; for the nutritive soul belongs also to the other living things and is the first and most commonly possessed potentiality of the soul, in virtue of which they all have life. Its functions are reproduction and the use of food; for it is the most natural function in living things, such as are perfect and not mutilated or do not have spontaneous generation, to produce another thing like themselves. (Aristotle 1993: 17)

   For Aristotle, 'sensibility' is not solely an animal feature, and contemporary research confirms this intuition (van Duijn et al. 2006; Garzón and Keijzer 2011; Trewavas 2014; Calvo 2016). However, a neurocentric prejudice is still widespread (Alpi et al. 2007): the substantialist idea according to which there is intelligence and cognition only where neurons and brains are present. But it is not necessary to identify intelligence with neuronal activity. The great conceptual achievement brought about by cognitive science and artificial intelligence research is that intelligence is not dependent on a material substratum, but rather should be sought in the functioning of such a substance (Turing 1950). There is therefore no reason to deny sensibility, movement and intelligence to the plant world (Coccia 2018). However, some want to interpret the plant world according to the subject/person paradigm (Hall 2011). But, as I have already observed in the Introduction, this approach does not question the anthropocentric and anthropomorphic paradigms – on the contrary, it extends them to the natural world as a whole. The challenge is not that of transforming a daisy into a kind of juridical 'person'; the point is rather to see the 'person' as a kind of daisy. We should not aim to see the world through the biopolitical lenses of law and ethics, but to see natural beings as such, without further qualifications. The adjective 'natural' is itself metaphysically laden (language is nothing but an ever-active machine, unwittingly producing 'metaphysics'). We should endeavour to see the natural world with as little anthropocentric baggage as possible. The problem, as we are well aware, is that this ambition clashes with an insurmountable limit: the fact that it is always a (clearly anthropocentric) human being who talks and thinks. Yet, we can at least *try* to de-centre our gaze. This is the challenge of so-called panpsychism (Strawson 2006): 'panpsychism is the thesis that even rocks have minds' (Shaviro 2015: 19), a position with a long and often unacknowledged history (Skrbina 2017). According to Shaviro, panpsychism is 'kind of countertendency to the anthropocentrism, and the hierarchical ontologies, of dominant philosophical dogmas. Panpsychism offers a rebuke both to extravagant idealism on the one hand, and to reductionism and eliminativism on the other' (2015: 20). However, it is unclear how panpsychism could represent a viable way out of the mind/body dualism (and, consequently, out of the animal/body dualism). Every dualism is grounded on an opposition. The mind/body dualism holds that the mind (whatever that might be conceived to be) is separate and distinct from the body. There are two traditional ways to escape this dualism: either denying the existence of mind (eliminative materialism) or that of matter (idealism). However, it should not be forgotten that the notion of 'mind' at work in the mind/body dualism cannot be separated from the correlative and contrary notion of a 'body'. We could not have any conception of a 'mind' without a 'body', and vice versa. The problem with panpsychism, then, is that it assumes the existence of 'mind' as something self-evident:

> evidently, I have no proof of the inner life of a neutrino. But strictly speaking, I also have no proof of the inner life of a bat or a cat, or indeed of another human being. This absence of proof is unavoidable, given the spectral nature of inner, private experience. But because I nevertheless do acknowledge and respect the inner lives and values of other human beings, I can potentially

do the same with other entities of all sorts. What's needed, perhaps, is an extension of sympathy. (Shaviro 2015: 40)

Shaviro does not detect the blind spot in his argument: the problem is not that of the neutrino's 'inner life' but of Shaviro's own. How can he, along with other panpsychists, be so sure he has an inner life? The mind/body dualism pivots precisely on the presupposition of the existence of an inner life, as opposed to a bodily existence. But this is far from being factually evident, and indeed it is an effect of the mind/body dualism itself, in turn a product of the 'anthropologic machine', i.e., of the effect of language on human life. Once again, it is not a matter of choosing this or that pole of the dualism (mind over body, or body over mind), but rather of defusing the metaphysical machinery that produces such dualisms. From this point of view, panpsychism is as unsatisfactory as eliminative materialism. A properly 'philosophical' work on materialism entails the attempt to elaborate notions that would not be 'compromised' with the very same dualism one aims at overcoming. Let us consider the case of Bergson's *Matter and Memory*, a book that endeavours to establish a new monist ontology capable of eluding the traps of dualism. The world, according to Bergson, is made neither of minds nor of things, as dualism forces us to think. Dualism's conceptual impasse, for Bergson, depends on 'the conception, now realistic, now idealistic, which philosophers have of matter'. On the contrary, he argues, the world is made of non-psychological 'images': '[m]atter, in our view, is an aggregate of "images". And by "image" we mean a certain existence which is more than that which the idealist calls a representation, but less than that which the realist calls a thing – an existence placed halfway between the "thing" and the "representation"' (Bergson 1991: 9). An image, then, is not a *representation*. We are beyond dualism, leaving behind us both materialism and panpsychism.

2. Recently, the authenticity of many of Vygotsky's texts has come under scrutiny (Yasnitsky and van der Veer 2016); however, the theses considered in this book are very similar to others that can be found in texts the authorship of which is undisputed.

3. Curzio Malaparte was the pseudonym of the Italian journalist and writer Curzio Suckert (Prato 1898–Rome 1957). Malaparte was a multifaceted personality, independent and controversial; after an early participation in fascism, he switched to anti-fascism (which cost him confinement in 1933), and later subscribed to communist ideas. He wrote acute political-literary texts, including *Italia barbara* (1925), and novels such as *Kaputt* (1944) and *La pelle* (1950), extraordinary first-hand accounts of the atrocities of war.

4

To Be Seen

Dimmi, occhio di topo
schiacciato sul selciato, dimmi:
chi guardi?
[Tell me, squashed eye of a mouse
crushed on the cobblestones, tell me
who are you looking at?]

('Occhio di topo', Marcoaldi 2006)

The Wolves are Watching Us

I dreamed that it is night and I am lying in my bed. . . . Suddenly the window opens of its own accord and terrified I see that there are a number of white wolves sitting in the big walnut tree outside the window. There were six or seven of them. The wolves were white all over, and looked more like foxes or sheepdogs because they had big tails like foxes and their ears were prickled up like dogs watching something. Obviously fearful that the wolves were going to gobble me up I screamed and woke up. . . . The only action in the dream was the opening of the window, for the wolves were sitting quite still in the branches of the tree, to the right and left of the tree trunk, not moving at all, and looking right at me. It looked as if they turned their full attention on me – I think it was my first anxiety-dream. (Freud 2002: 227)

This is one of the most famous dreams in the history of psychoanalysis, known as the Wolfman dream. Freud – after long years unsuccessfully trying to break through his patient's resistances – finally interpreted it as the disguised return of the primal scene: a sexual relation between the patient's parents, which he would have witnessed around one and a half years of age. The dream's analysis – developed by Freud in painstaking detail, down to the time of day when the alleged sexual act would have taken place (five o'clock in the afternoon) – is extraordinary, but here I am only interested in one aspect of this dream to which, paradoxically, Freud pays no particular attention: the *animality* of the wolves observing the dreamer. Freud's patient, Sergej Costantinovič Pankejeff, dreamt of some animals, either wolves or dogs. Though Freud talks of wolves, he never really considers them as such, but treats them as 'symbols' of something else (animals often appear in Freud's writings (see Stone 1992; Genosko 1993; Sauret 2005; Cimatti 2016), yet always as symbols). Psychoanalysis has often been unable to appreciate the transformational power of our relationship with *animal* animality. For psychoanalysis, animality is always *allegoric*. As Deleuze and Guattari observed:

> We wish to make a simple point about psychoanalysis: from the begin- ning, it has often encountered the question of the becomings-animal of the human being: in children, who continually undergo becomings of this kind; in fetishism and in particular masochism, which continually con- front this problem. The least that can be said is that the psychoanalysts, even Jung, did not understand, or did not want to understand. They killed becoming-animal, in the adult as in the child. They saw nothing. They see the animal as a representative of drives, or a representation of the parents. They do not see the reality of a becoming-animal, that it is affect in itself, the drive in person, and represents nothing. (1987: 259)

In Sergej's dream the wolves are observing him, quietly perched on a large tree. But first, the window of the room where he is sleeping swings open. Let us take the dream quite literally, for what it appears to show. There is a double movement of gazes: from the wolves in the tree towards Sergej lying on his bed, and then from Sergej to the wolves in the tree. These gazes meet and produce anxiety (rather than terror, since the wolves do not seem aggressive). If we keep our interpretation on this literal level the dream's most meaningful moment is precisely that of the window's opening. In order to see the wolves, one must first be seen by them. And to be seen, to be able to see what is watching us, it is necessary to be exposed to their gaze. The wolves' gaze challenges transcendence, because their attention is turned towards a body, and nothing more. For example, when a wolf is looking at a sheep, it *only* sees a sheep. The same happens to Sergej, who therefore feels anxious on account of his being observed as a body and not as a little boy, or as the boss's son, or as his mother's love. That is all gone, and Sergej is just an animal body facing another animal body. That of the wolf is not our gaze being returned by the mirror, that says 'I' because it is ratified by the Other (see Chapter 2). The wolf's gaze belongs to *that wolf-body* that is observing Sergej, and nothing more is taking place. This gaze strips Sergej naked of the subjectivity assigned to him by the Other (the adult who *calls* him Sergej, through linguistic intersubjectivity and the pronoun 'I' itself), and makes him radically exposed to the eyes of another body. Here we encounter the anxiety for animality, which precedes the fear of the wild beast: the wolf does not threaten little Sergej's life, but rather his ability to refer to himself as an 'I'. And we have seen, through Heidegger, how without an 'I' it is strictly speaking impossible to die. Sergej does not fear death, but to be – or better to become – a mere animal. Hence, as Deleuze and Guattari write, the psychoanalytic animal is not a sign of something else, but rather a vector of change, the omnipresent temptation of becoming-animal, i.e., of the dissolution of subjectivity.

On the contrary, psychoanalysis's symbolisation of the animal is a strategy to neutralise this threat, because there seems to be no possibility of psychoanalysis without an 'I' to analyse. This threat must be defused, and the animal should be placed in a completely different space: letting it talk in order to be introduced into the circuit of subjectivity and of consciousness. Here again we encounter the familiar distinction between human 'world' and animal 'environment'. In his 'zeroeth' Seminar, dedicated precisely to the Wolfman, Lacan asks: 'is it not futile to ask what is history? Do animals have a history? Is history not a properly human dimension?' (Lacan 1952a: n.p.). The answer is obvious: history cannot but pertain only to the animal of subjectivity: '[h]istory is a truth with this property: the subject that assumes it depends upon it, in its very constitution as a subject; analogously, history too depends on the subject, because the latter thinks it again and again in its own way'. The animal is outside of history. According to Lacan, Sergej is not fully integrated in the symbolic function: 'the Wolfman does not assume his own life, and his very instinctual life is included, and enclosed like a cyst. Within him, everything belonging to the instinctual order erupts like a tsunami.' Where does Sergej stand then? In the symbolic order (and therefore in the human one), or still in the hesitant, tentative realm of animality? Going back to the window through which the wolves can stare at Sergej, Lacan comments that 'the open window is the other side of the veil that envelops the subject, i.e., a mirror in which the subject sees itself staring at itself, in the form of the animals observing it'. A Deleuze and Guattari-inspired reading would suggest that the window represents a line of flight, of deterritorialisation of *humanitas* towards *animalitas*; but for Lacan – or at least for the 'early' Lacan, still focused on the symbolic – the window is really a narcissistic mirror. After all, in the same text Lacan describes Sergej's psychoanalysis thus: 'for years this man has not talked nor contributed at all, he did nothing but contemplate himself in a mirror, constituted by he who listens to him – Freud in this case'. For Lacan, then, the wolf staring at Sergej is really Freud himself. The result is a thorough reterritorialisation of the wolf – that is to say, the animal is transformed into a human being. But then the wolves' presence in Sergej's dream loses any proper significance. If, on the one hand, as Lacan argues, it is only through the mediation of the Other that the human can have a relation with itself and another human (and with the Other in general), it is also the case that the human always has a compulsion to get rid of the Other, of language and of the subject. But according to Lacan the question raised by the wolves can be reduced, in a rather sterile manner, to the analytic situation: 'the analysis of the Wolf man was influenced by Freud's research on the reality, or non-reality, of the primal scene, and even in this case we can see the strict relationship between transference and counter-transference'. And yet Lacan himself observes how 'the core of the question is "his" proper understanding [the distinctive meaning of the Wolfman], that is, the wolves'. So, what is the role of the wolves in Sergej's dream? It is necessary to accept the unthinkable possibility of the becoming-animal, an always available – and yet always repressed – option:

> To become animal is to participate in movement, to stake out the path of escape in all its positivity, to cross a threshold, to reach a continuum of intensities that are valuable only in themselves, to find a world of pure intensities where all forms come undone, as do all the significations, signifiers, and signifieds, to the benefit of an unformed matter of deterritorialized flux, of nonsignifying signs. (Deleuze and Guattari 1986: 13)

The animal of psychoanalysis is the becoming-animal of the subject. Reducing it to a symbol – and so ultimately to language and the subject – means instead to reterritorialise it, therefore missing the opportunity of animality. Going back to Lacan's analysis of Sergej's dream, the French psychoanalyst writes that:

> Freud teaches the subject how to interpret his own dream, translated to a delirium. In order to translate it, it is sufficient to reverse it: *the wolves stare at me, still and calm, while I am witnessing the scene with great agitation. One could add: these wolves have big tails – look at mine!* This dream leads us back to the reconstructed reality, which is then assumed by the subject. (Lacan 1952a: n.p.)

When Lacan wrote this seminar (around 1952/53) it still hadn't occurred to him (see Chapter 7) how the presence of wolves in the dream could be taken seriously, how to try and imagine an escape route from alienation in the Other (and therefore in language). For Lacan, as well as for Freud (and for most philosophy, unable to take animality seriously), the wolf is not a wolf, but a delirium, a puzzle to solve, a sign. So, the wolf in the dream, Freud argues, was nothing but a 'father-substitute' (2002: 267). The same goes for a 'giant snail', appearing in another dream that, like the wolf, is not an animal since '[t]he snail, an exquisite symbol of female sexuality, stood for the woman' (2002: 268), and, later on, for a 'lovely big butterfly with yellow stripes' (2002: 288) that, needless to say, is for Freud the representation of a woman.

This is the anthropocentric problem posed by the dream of wolves (the dream of a child, it should be remembered): the animals should not be dissolved through an allegorical interpretation, considering them as representing the father or the fear of castration. Rather, we should interpret them as an occasion to put into question the transcendent outcomes of the anthropologic machine. Freud himself indirectly touches on this point when asking himself whether a real contact with one's own experience is actually possible (and here Freud is explicitly Kantian). Discussing the Oedipus complex and how this contributes to the constitution of human subjectivity, he observes how 'the schema takes precedence over individual experience' (2002: 317). Shortly thereafter, he makes even more explicit what the nature of the phenomenon he is describing could be: 'some kind of knowledge' for which 'the only analogy available to us is the excellent analogy with the largely *instinctive* knowledge found in animals' (2002: 318). Here a still unsolved question is opened (and *Homo sapiens* is nothing but the very impossibility of a solution): what happens to this 'instinctive knowledge' once the *infans* becomes an adult, once it has been processed by the anthropologic machine? Freud answers that '[t]his instinctive knowledge would form the core of the unconscious, a primitive intellectual activity later dethroned by human reason when this is acquired and overlaid by it, but often, perhaps always, retaining the strength to drag higher inner processes down to its own level' (2002: 318). Freud's hypothesis, coherently with his Darwinian background assumptions, concerns the existence of a primitive 'core of the unconscious': he is referring to nothing more than the animality of the human. And yet, the question remains whether this animal core lies behind the human or beyond its horizon. But really, if the anthropologic machine is always operational – since 'humanity' *means* this anthropologic machine – then a properly 'primitive' human has never existed (Tattersall 1998). This does not mean that Freud's problem is not very relevant today, for the point is that if the human has never really been an animal, then the objective should not be that of recuperating an 'instinctive knowledge' that never was but, on the contrary, to move towards the *construction* of something like a human instinct. In this sense Freud's 'schema' is Lacan's *Other*, the eccentric movement of transcendence that pushes the immanence of bodies away. Sergej will spend the entirety of his tormented life trying to grasp the wholly terrestrial and immanent value of the wolves' gaze, without ever managing to evade the 'schema' in which the anthropologic machine has trapped him.

The problem raised by Lacan's last theoretical teachings is that of escaping from the symbolic, in order to reach what he calls the 'real unconscious' (Miller 2017) – which is not structured like a language, and is therefore inseparable from the Symbolic and the Other. In this context, the question of animality re-emerges, as an extraordinary biological experiment of an immanent life. In his *Seminar in Caracas* (1980), Lacan, by then near the end of his life, returns to the question of animality, but from a completely different perspective than the one we encountered in his analysis of the Wolfman. Now Lacan does not adopt the position of the Other but, on the contrary, looks at the situation by considering what the human body *loses* when enveloped in the network of language. In particular, Lacan refers to number, as the supreme exemplification of the power of language, because there can be no arithmetic without language and vice versa (Hauser et al. 2002). Number should not be interpreted as a simple counting ability, for it really is a device used to make the world countable. Indeed, to say that something is one means to declare it a separate, distinct – and therefore countable – entity. Essentially, it means to transform the world into an enormous set of things, each separate from the other. The point is that something becomes countable only when assimilated by the machinery of the number, i.e., of language. From this point of view, the numerical abilities of nonhuman animals (Hyde 2011) cannot be, strictly speaking, defined as *numerical* – i.e., grounded on the (symbolic) manipulation of numbers. Animals perceive and evaluate quantities in a holistic manner, whereas humans *count*, i.e., they divide the perceptual continuum into discrete parts. *Animalitas*, for Lacan – and in particular animal sexuality – is possible precisely because it is not hindered by numbers: the sex life of animals would not be thought, by animals themselves, as an encounter between two subjects, but rather as a (non-numerical) bodily movement, what Lacan calls 'sexual peace'. On the contrary, human sexuality is encumbered by the subject and its needs (love, for example):

> Why not admit that the sexual peace of animals – if we just take the one that is said to be their king, the lion – is down to the fact that number is not introduced into their language, whatever it may be. Doubtless, training animals can produce something that looks like it, but it's just appearance. Sexual peace means that one knows what to do with the Other's body. But who knows what to do with a *parlêtre*'s body? Except to hold it more or less closely? What does the Other manage to say, and then only when he really wants to? He says, *hold me tight.* Copulation, easy as pie. Anyone can do better than that. I say anyone – a frog for instance. There's a painting that's been lingering in my mind for a long while now. I've remembered its author's name, not without the difficulties one meets at my age. The painting is by Bramantino. [Lacan here refers to Bramantino's *The Madonna Enthroned with Saint Ambrose and Saint Michael*, where a strange human-sized frog lies at the feet of the Virgin Mary]. Well, this painting vouches very well for the regret that a woman is not a frog. She's been put there, on her back, in the foreground of the picture. (Lacan 2011: 19)

A 'speaking subject' (*parlêtre*) is a human body as shaped by language, the product of the anthropologic machine. This particular living being, like Sergej the Wolfman, cannot really touch another body, precisely because the Other is always in the way. The best that can be hoped for is that this body, still distant, might ask 'hold me tight'. Yet the distance separating them is not spatial, but logical, for language always lies between them. The frog, on the other hand, or the lion (it is frustrating how animals are always referred to in allegories), can know this bodily intimacy, precisely because 'number is not introduced into their language'. Number brings with it a kind of curse, because the body we are holding – if considered as a countable specimen – is nothing but *one* body, after which a second will come, and then a third, and so forth to infinity. On the contrary, a body that is not individuated by language – and is therefore uncountable – like a frog's body, cannot be trapped by this centrifugal process. For a 'speaking subject', the situation is reversed: '[h]ence my mathemes, which stem from the fact that the symbolic is the locus of the Other, though there is no Other of the Other' (Lacan 2011: 19): the Other is the symbolic, i.e., language, and once we are within it (once we are a 'speaking subject') there is no way out ('there is no Other of the Other'). 'It follows', Lacan continues, 'that the best thing *lalangue*

can do is to demonstrate how it is in the service of the death instinct':
only an 'I' can die, and since there is no 'I' without language, then it
is literally true that the anthropologic machine is 'in the service of the
death instinct'.

'Seen seen *by the animal*'

What is really at stake in the conflict between the anthropologic
machine and animality, then, is the intrinsic link between language
and the death drive. It is through language – i.e., the machinery
allowing the emergence of the 'I' and its specific form of temporality
– that the experience of death enters into human life. Indeed, how
can Heidegger distinguish between the death of human beings and
other organisms' mere ceasing to exist? This is not a strictly biological distinction, since both clearly stop living – it rather pertains to the
fact that the living being that says 'I' is present to itself in the 'world'.
Therefore, upon death it is not just the body it *has* that dies, but also
the subjectivity it *is*. The living being in an 'environment' is wholly
projected towards, and immersed within, the experience of a life it
lives without any residue. For this reason, that which dies is not so
much a determinate individuality, rather there is a particular vital
organism-environment relationship that ceases to be. This is why the
animal does not die: because it never existed as a separate individuality, independent from its relation with the environment. It will not be
surprising, then, that when adopting this new point of view – turning
the animal into a subject – a new border between animal and non-
animal is created, where the first 'dies' while the second simply ceases
to live. This happens in Tom Regan's work, which considers animals
as gifted with a kind of subjectivity:

> we [human and nonhuman animals] are not only in the world, we are
> aware of it, and aware, too, of what transpires 'on the inside', so to speak,
> in the realm of our feelings, beliefs, and desires. In these respects, we are
> something more than animate matter, something different from plants;
> we are the experiencing *subjects-of-a-life*, beings with a biography, not
> merely a biology. We are *somebodies*, not *somethings*. (Regan 2003: 80)

In the end, the same fear always rears its head: that of being simple
(living) entities, of being just *something*. Humanism endures, even
when disguised as animalism.

Let us go back, for the moment, to the relation between language
and the experience of death. By affirming itself as an 'I', the talking

animal distances itself from the 'environment', thus establishing itself as an autonomous subjectivity: this is why this living being can properly die, because what ceases to be is an individuated subjectivity. There exists, then, a very close link between subjectivity, language and death:

> To consent to language signifies to act in such a way that, in the abysmal experience of the taking place of language, in the removal of the voice, another Voice is disclosed to man, and along with this are also disclosed the dimension of being and the mortal risk of nothingness. To consent to the taking place of language, to listen to the Voice, signifies, thus, to consent also to death, to be capable of dying (*sterben*) rather than simply deceasing (*ableben*). (Agamben 2006: 87)

Animality is the mode of existence that, being excluded from the anthropologic machine, remains untouched by this form of mortality: it passes away, but cannot die. Moreover, as Derrida observes, the sadness of the animal (also pondered by Hegel, see Chapter 3) is not a consequence of this inclusion, as if the animal would have a confused awareness of its lack of consciousness, and suffer for it. On the contrary, it is the effect of another inclusion: the animal is sad when it receives a name, when it is dragged into language. Because to be inside language means to be into death, to partake in the human way of dying:

> What, for so long now, has been making [nature] sad and as a result has deprived the mourner of its words, what forbids words, is not a muteness and the experience of a powerlessness, an inability ever to name; it is, in the first place, the fact of receiving one's name. This is a startling intuition . . . even when the one who names is equal to the gods, happy and blessed, being named . . . or seeing oneself given one's proper name is something like being invaded by sadness, by sadness *itself* (a sadness whose origin would therefore always be this passivity of being named, this impossibility of reappropriating one's own name), or at least by a sort of obscure foreshadowing of sadness. One should rather say a *foreshadowing of mourning*. A foreshadowing of mourning because it seems to me that every case of naming involves announcing a death to come in the surviving of a ghost, the longevity of a name that survives whoever carries that name. Whoever receives a name feels mortal or dying, precisely because the name seeks to save him, to call him and thus assure his survival. Being called, hearing oneself being named, receiving a name for the first time involves something like the knowledge of being mortal and even the feeling that one is dying. To have already died of being promised to death: dying. (Derrida 2008: 19–20)

The assignment of a name is what opens a living being to the possibility of death, because every name is a 'foreshadowing of death': every name declares, simply through the merciless fact of its existence, that a being has been individuated, and all that exists now will sooner or later cease to be. The same goes, in an even more cruel fashion, for the 'I' that, in virtue of its very individuality, will also cease to be. This is an 'I' thrown into time (properly speaking, *time* is nothing but such a throwing), and inevitably doomed to disappear. It is now easier to understand the source of the Wolfman's anxiety. When exposed to the wolves' gaze, we are exposed to death. Not the death caused by the wolves' attack – for this is an egalitarian kind of death that affects everyone: humans and nonhumans, subjects and non-subjects, animals and plants. The death that produces anxiety is the end of the subject, of the 'I'. The wolf stares at us like it would look at any other object in the world: like a visible thing, something (not someone) existing before its eyes, which can be an object of interest only insofar as it enters into its vital flux as either prey or friend, danger or playmate, life or death. The wolf sees a body facing it, and nothing more. To be exposed to its gaze means to be placed in this intolerable position, to be seen as a mere body and not as an 'I'. This cannot be tolerated because, for the human animal, the condition of being an 'I' is not an accessory, something that could be taken off as an old dress, and exchanged with another one. One cannot choose to stop being an 'I'. But at the same time this represents an irresistible temptation, because the wolf's gaze holds the only chance of redemption offered to our subjectivity. The wolf staring at Sergej reminds him that a different life is possible: it is there, right in front of him. This is why he is anguished, because he feels the irreducible distance separating what he perceives in those eyes and his own condition as a talking animal, doomed with a 'foreshadowing of death'.

To be exposed to the animal's gaze: this is the first step – both momentous and impractical – in a conceivable path towards the animality of a human *to come*. This is a momentous step because it gestures towards a possible existence, completely different from that of the being who says 'I'.[1] Impractical, because this path cannot be followed, precisely because it is impossible to stop being an 'I' by sheer force of will (only an 'I' can *will* to stop being such; but this makes the condition of 'I' inescapable). In any case, offering oneself to the animal's gaze would be an unusual gesture, for it implies putting oneself in the position of being a mere observable being – a thing. The animal's gaze is not the human's, directed towards another human (the mediated gaze of the Other or the linguistic gaze of an 'I' observing a 'you'). It is rather the undetermined gaze between two living organisms, one in front of the other, a gaze that completely exhausts itself in the sensible evidence of two bodies in their relative positions: 'I often ask myself, just to see, *who I am* – and who I am (following) at the moment when, caught naked, in silence, by the gaze of an animal, for example, the eyes of a cat, I have trouble, yes, a bad time overcoming my embarrassment' (Derrida 2008: 3–4). This 'embarrassment' reminds us of Sergej's anxiety, a feeling difficult to account for because simply prompted by a cat, and one does not feel ashamed before a cat, just as cats do not feel ashamed before us (like when, for example, they mate in our presence as if we were not there or – and this is an even more disturbing idea – as if our presence would make no difference whatsoever to them). This embarrassment is strengthened when we are naked, our body exposed. The shame about our body is a feeling characteristically reminding us of the gaze of the Other, judging and evaluating us. But the cat is not the Other, it is just a cat: *this cat* we encounter on our way out of the shower, for example. And yet, we experience embarrassment. Clearly then this is not due to the inadequacy of our body – fat, ungracious, worn out by the passage of time: it rather pertains to the very fact that we *have* a body. That's because this body belongs to an 'I' who can say, of it, that it is 'his' or 'her' body. In the cat's gaze, just like the wolves', there is no such distance between the eyes that stare and a subjectivity that would stare at us *through* those eyes. The staring cat is *just* this cat staring at us. Maybe it is precisely this simplicity that we are attempting to grasp when saying, between banality and embarrassment, that animals are beautiful. Yet our radical non-adherence to the body we own is immediately made evident to us: this makes all the more paradoxical the idea that one could escape this contradiction by turning one's full attention to the body, for this behaviour could only occur to an 'I', precisely to the entity that one wants to bracket. The cat (just like young human beings, after all) never worries about its body – there is never any separation between the cat and its body. On the contrary, Derrida's 'embarrassment' demonstrates an absolute separation, revealed by the cat simply staring at us. The singularity of its gaze instead reveals the duplicity of ours. And this, once again, reveals our incapacity to think the animal as *this* animal right here, because the philosopher's embarrassment is still prompted by an allegorical understanding of the cat. The cat stares at me, what should I do? I feel embarrassed, that is to say I think about myself (the omnipresent narcissistic needs, as Lacan would put it, of the 'I'). The cat's gaze is:

> the single, incomparable and original experience of the impropriety that would come from appearing in truth naked, in front of the insistent gaze of the animal, a benevolent or pitiless gaze, surprised or cognizant. The gaze of a seer, a visionary or extra-lucid blind one. It is as if I were ashamed, therefore, naked in front of this cat, but also ashamed for being ashamed. (Derrida 2008: 4)

This gaze *only* sees what can be seen: a body, naked because the body the 'I' owns is always, and necessarily, an artificial one (so that to be naked means to be covered by the absence of clothing). For the cat's eyes, a body is always just a body, whether naked or fully clothed. Hence this double embarrassment is explained: we are ashamed of having a body – comparing ourselves to the absolute unity of body and cat that is staring at us – but we are also embarrassed by this very embarrassment, because the cat is not an 'I', but just a cat, an *animal*, and there is no reason to feel ashamed in front of something that is not an 'I'. If we feel shame in front of a cat, what else? What are we going to feel when facing Heidegger's worldless stone? As Derrida indeed observes, poets are among the very few who have tried to offer a description of the world free from our gaze, or better yet our becoming world – as for example in the extraordinary poem 'Keeping Things Whole', by Mark Strand:

> In a field
> I am the absence
> of field.
> This is
> always the case.
> Wherever I am
> I am what is missing.
>
> When I walk
> I part the air
> and always
> the air moves in
> to fill the spaces
> where my body's been.
>
> We all have reasons
> for moving.
> I move
> to keep things whole. (Strand 2016: 78)

We are now in a position to better understand the anxiety little Sergej experienced during his dream, since he had just entered, as a child, into the violent and irreversible mechanism that separates the 'I' from the body. The wolf casts Sergej in a particular predicament ('in a field'): that of being 'the absence of field'. In the case of an adult, like Derrida, the animal's gaze is less perturbing yet it still provokes unease and embarrassment: and embarrassment to be embarrassed about. To expose oneself to the animal gaze is a danger, but also a continuous temptation, and for this reason Sergej's dream keeps haunting him even – and probably especially – as an adult. In the end, Derrida is like Sergej, but he has shielded himself against that gaze, since philosophy as a whole is a kind of endless attempt to exorcise the very possibility of being exposed to it. To discover this gaze means that the 'environment'/'world' couple – through which we believe we have sterilised the question of animality (as we do with so-called companion animals, in order to make them tamer and less wild, thus divesting them from their animality and turning them into fully humanised creatures, or 'transitional entities' (see Triebenbacher Lookabaugh 1998; Blazina and Kogan 2016)) – is not at all a solution, but rather the problem. The animal does not lack anything, it is the human who holds within itself something that exceeds the body it is, and that makes it mortal:

> The animal is there before me, there next to me, there in front of me – I who am (following) after it. And also, therefore, since it is before me, it is behind me. It surrounds me. And from the vantage of this being-there-before-me it can allow itself to be looked at, no doubt, but also – something that philosophy perhaps forgets, perhaps being this calculated forgetting itself – it can look at me. It has its point of view regarding me. The point of view of the absolute other, and nothing will have ever given me more food for thinking through this absolute alterity of the neighbor or of the next(-door) than these moments when I see myself seen naked under the gaze of a cat. (Derrida 2008: 47)

It needs to be stressed that to talk about an 'absolute other' is not an attempt – as one might think, comparing it to the theme of the 'face' in Levinas's work – to consider the cat as something through which the transcendent might reveal itself. It is decisively not a way to consider the cat as somehow similar to me, as someone who calls me into question ethically, and with respect to whom I should feel responsible: these attitudes towards animality – as necessary and well-intentioned as they might be – do not grasp the extremely simple message (conveyed without words, and before words) of that gaze: the elementary fact that, over there, a living being is looking at me, as it would look at a mouse or a leaf, a gaze with no space for an 'I'. The cat's gaze does not mean to deprive anyone of anything, just like it does not aim to see anything more than what is actually visible: such a gaze, we could say, is stationary – it neither remembers nor announces anything. It is just what it is, a gaze going from a cat to a naked human being, standing outside of a shower. We should also stress – for this point is often overlooked – that the animal gaze pertains to all animals, including those with no eyes. When discussing Derrida's analysis of the encounter with the cat we must be aware of the omnipresent danger of indulging in a saccharine anthropomorphism: the animal's gaze has nothing to do with the eyes, but with the fact that something – something nonhuman or even inhuman – is staring at us, whether or not it has eyes or is a *'subject-of-a-life'* (it is no coincidence that all the examples used in John Berger's highly praised *Why Look at Animals?* (2009) are mammals. Animality will begin only after we learn to overcome our seemingly untameable mammal-centrism. See Parikka 2010; Aloi 2012b; Samuelsson 2013; Bennett 2015).

The greatest challenge posed by the cat's gaze is precisely its radical immanence with respect to itself. Our best efforts notwithstanding, we cannot know the cat – we just know the cat as an *animot*, a linguistic entity that grasps a generic animality, precisely in order to distance ourselves from the determinacy of this cat right here. After all, this is the primordial nature of language: '[i]t is possible to "take the *This*" only if one comes to realize that the significance of the *This* is, in reality, a *Not-this* that it contains; that is, an essential negativity' (Agamben 2006: 14). As I come out of the shower, I want to try to grasp this cat in front of me by means of a word: in order to do so, I use the word 'cat', formed in my mouth by the tongue that thinks itself through me. But the word 'cat' is not *this* cat – on the contrary it is *any* cat, in any place and time. But then the cat standing in front of my eyes ceases to be *this* cat right here, and becomes a generic and indeterminate *animot*: the cat has escaped, for the mesh of the net I have cast to capture it is too large to keep hold of it:

> No, no, my cat, the cat that looks at me in my bedroom or bathroom, this cat that is perhaps not 'my cat' or 'my pussycat,' does not appear here to represent, like an ambassador, the immense symbolic responsibility with which our culture has always charged the feline race, from La Fontaine to Tieck (author of 'Puss in Boots'), from Baudelaire to Rilke, Buber, and

many others. If I say 'it is a real cat' that sees me naked, this is in order to mark its unsubstitutable singularity. When it responds in its name (whatever 'respond' means, and that will be our question), it doesn't do so as the exemplar of a species called 'cat,' even less so of an 'animal' genus or kingdom. It is true that I identify it as a male or female cat. But even before that identification, it comes to me as *this* irreplaceable living being that one day enters my space, into this place where it can encounter me, see me, even see me naked. Nothing can ever rob me of the certainty that what we have here is an existence that refuses to be conceptualized [*rebelle à tout concept*]. And a mortal existence, for from the moment that it has a name, its name survives it. It signs its potential disappearance. (Derrida 2008: 9)

The paradoxical and unbearable condition in which the cat's gaze casts us is here evident. One the one hand, the cat is simply *this* cat looking at me now, and its gaze makes me uneasy, because I realise how it eludes any generalisation, being simply a cat and not an 'I' nor any other abstruse, pre-linguistic or non-linguistic, subjectivity. But, on the other hand, that is still 'my cat' – indeed, if I call it with the name I assigned to it, it meows and comes closer to me, purring. But through this very act – and here is the tangle of language and experience – I am condemning it to die, because 'its name survives it' and 'signs its potential disappearance', since only a being with a name is an individual, the 'you' of an 'I', and only an individual can die.

Keen to escape from this unresolvable tangle, we try not to be surprised by the cat's gaze, since we do not like to be reminded of how thin an 'I' really is. This linguistic act needs to be continuously repeated, because a short interruption – a quick glance from the cat – suffices to put the 'I' into a state of crisis, unable to understand itself. The history of the thought of animality has been written 'by people who have no doubt seen, observed, analyzed, reflected on the animal, but who have never been *seen seen* by the animal' (Derrida 2008: 13). This is the history of a continuously reiterated attempt not to expose ourselves to the animals' gaze:

It is as if the men representing this configuration had seen without being seen, seen the animal without being seen by it, without being seen seen by it; without being seen seen naked by someone who, from deep within a life called animal, and not only by means of the gaze, would have obliged them to recognise, at the moment of address, that this was their affair, their lookout [*que cela les regardait*].

But since I don't believe, deep down, that it has never happened to them, or that it has not in some way been signified, figured, or metonymised, more or less secretly, in the gestures of their discourse, the symptom of this disavowal remains to be deciphered. It could not be the figure of just one disavowal among others. It institutes what is proper to man, the relation to itself of a humanity that is above all anxious about, and jealous of, what is proper to it. (Derrida 2008: 14)

In a 2012 interview, Giovanni Aloi (an art historian with an interest in animalism) took this challenge to heart, arguing that Derrida highlighted it while not drawing out all of its consequences. How can new relations be established with nonhuman – non-subjective but not merely animated – animality? The point is: what remains to be done once the deconstruction of the animal as a simple *animot* has been performed?

> The idea is not so much to understand them as new subjects, creating an animalcentric system in place of the anthropocentric one that has been dismantled, but to produce a rhizomatic network of interconnectedness of which we and animals are both part and that, most importantly, includes plants – the blissfully ignored living beings on which all life on this planet depends. (Aloi 2012b)

The animality Aloi is referring to is explicitly located beyond the *animot*, but also beyond the nonhuman animal, which is nothing but the reverse of the human. It is rather to be sought beyond the animal itself, as a living being opposed to a plant. From this perspective, animality is more than animal (Bennett 2010): it is the possibility of an escape route from biopolitical and biolinguistic territorialisations. Under this broader conception, animality coincides with the attempt to 'to find a way out, to trace a line of escape' (Deleuze and Guattari 1986: 35).

Beyond the Animot

'The animal looks at us, and we are naked before it. Thinking perhaps begins there' (Derrida 2008: 29). But can we think the animal, starting with Derrida's cat, without going through the *animot*? How can we let it be *this cat right here*, and not a CAT? The most important gesture is to offer oneself to the animal's gaze, and this entails two concessions: 1) it is necessary to accept a confrontation with animality based on something other than the '*qua*' operator, i.e., the metaphysical machinery (and language is nothing but this machinery) that arbitrarily extracts portions of the world, isolates them from their 'vital' connections, and transforms them into objects with a name.

102

From this standpoint, the 'ontological difference' is, at its core, the functioning of language itself, used to single out and nominate. The notion of 'referent' (like the object indicated by a name) is a linguistic invention, because it would not exist without the name. The world is not made up of referents waiting for a name. 2) It is also necessary to accept the possibility of a transformation, contained in the animal's gaze, and therefore to accept that the 'I' would not define a substantial entity, immutable through time. To relinquish the '*qua*' entails the impossibility of shielding oneself behind the 'world'/'environment' distinction, along with all of its corollaries.

For example, without this distinction (which underpins that between human and animal) it becomes impossible to tell apart – with the degree of precision necessary to reassure us – the 'reaction' to a stimulus (instinctual and automatic, i.e., animal) from the 'answer' to a question (intelligent and flexible, i.e., human). And again, this means accepting the permeability and mobility of the threshold that allegedly separates the disinterested gaze of a human from that of an animal, dominated by its biological function. It would also mean conceding that it is not just the human being who can die, but that the animal dies too – or conversely that neither does. This is not so much a problem of evolutionary continuity, that of those who argue that *natura non facit saltus* – the point is rather that the living world is crisscrossed with currents of force that push and pull in divergent directions, and with modalities that our metaphysics lacks the courage to imagine (Fusco and Minelli 2010; Minelli 2011, 2016; Gilbert et al. 2012). The other, equally inevitable, waiver – connected to the notion of the '*qua*' – is to the inviolability of the 'I'. In the final analysis, animality exists to allow the 'I' to proclaim its diversity from the rest of the living world. As Derrida put it:

Yes, animal, what a word!
Animal is a word that men have given themselves the right to give. These humans are found giving it to themselves, this word, but as if they had received it as an inheritance. They have given themselves the word in order to corral a large number of living beings within a single concept: 'The Animal,' they say. And they have given it to themselves, this word, at the same time according themselves, reserving for them, for humans, the right to the word, the naming noun [*nom*], the verb, the attribute, to a language of words, in short to the very thing that the others in question would be deprived of, those that are corralled within the grand territory of the beasts: The Animal. All the philosophers . . . say the same thing: the animal is deprived of language. Or, more precisely, of response, of

a response that could be precisely and rigorously distinguished from a reaction; of the right and power to 'respond,' and hence of so many other things that would be proper to man. Men would be first and foremost those living creatures who have given themselves the word that enables them to speak of the animal with a single voice and to designate it as the single being that remains without a response, without a word with which to respond. (2008: 32)

To renounce to such a reassuring distinction – the animal reacts, the human responds (wholly congruent with Heidegger's distinction between human 'comportment' (*Verhalten*) and animal 'behaviour' (*Benehmen*), or with that between biology and history, as well as body and mind) – means to allow the same de-structuring operation brought about by the Wolfman's dream: to open the window, and offer oneself to a space of reciprocal and equal visibility. This is the first and most radical move, since everything else is downstream from this exposition; on the one hand the child, on the other, some wolves: '[t]his abyssal rupture doesn't describe two edges, a unilinear and indivisible line having two edges, Man and the Animal in general' (Derrida 2008: 31). It is well-known what happens when a frontier is broken: invasions, amalgamations, confusion. The 'I' fears this scenario even more than it dreads the death of its body: it fears the impossibility of relying on the anthropologic machine, it fears that the gesture through which itself proclaims itself an 'I' would lose its value, as well as the absence of an Other able to confirm its existence.

What needs stressing here is that only from the point of view of an individual subjectivity can there be the danger of confusion: it is only the 'I' who is in danger in this predicament. But it is precisely the *only* entity that *needs* to be put into question, because the animal exists only to reassure the 'I', as an exception in the natural order – the 'I' is not an animal. To renounce the animal as a nonhuman means also to relinquish that jealous subjectivity that never stops saying 'I' to itself. And what comes *after* the 'I'? 'Beyond the edge of the so-called human' – because it is indeed an edge, unilaterally established, like most such borders, by only one of the groups it divides – 'beyond it but by no means on a single opposing side, rather than "The Animal" or "Animal Life" there is already a heterogeneous multiplicity of the living' (Derrida 2008: 31). Offering oneself to the animal's gaze means opening the door to this 'heterogeneous multiplicity of the living'. The point is that, between these living beings, there occur dynamics, movements and exchanges that cannot be calculated in advance, and that do not arrest their motion when entering the protected reserve of the 'I'. Instead, this 'I' can keep itself alive only insofar as it manages to keep this multiplicity at bay. The buzzing of life knows no 'I', nor any uncrossable border; while the 'I' pre-supposes absolute hygiene, sterilisation and immunisation (Esposito 2011) against any danger of contagion. Indeed, the living being *is* contagion, or else it would not be a living being at all: '[m]ake a rhizome. But you don't know what you can make a rhizome with, you don't know which subterranean stem is effectively going to make a rhizome, or enter a becoming, people your desert. So experiment' (Deleuze and Guattari 1987: 251). To abandon the 'I' means to leave behind – or better, simply to distance oneself from, since without an 'I' there is no 'back' but simply an anonymous movement – the stifling and deathly enclosure of subjectivity, and open oneself up to the experimentation of the living.

What I am describing is an irrational and romantic leap in the void. A gesture of utter renunciation of ethics and politics. This is the truth, and we should frankly acknowledge it: there is no ethics without a subject. Indeed, even so-called 'deep ecology' (Næss 1973) – which at first sight does not present itself quite as an ethics – actually cannot escape from the trap of subjectivism. According to Næss this radical approach would be grounded on the 'rejection of the man-in-environment image in favour of the relational, total-field image. Organisms as knots in the biospherical net or field of intrinsic relations. ... The total-field model dissolves not only the man-in-environment concept, but every compact thing-in-milieu concept' (1973: 95). However, the presence of a subjectivist approach emerges clearly in Næss's discussion of the difference between 'complexity' and 'complication': 'a multiplicity of more or less lawful, interacting factors may operate together to form a unity, a system' (1973: 97). What else is the environment as unitary form, as *Gestalt*, if not yet another appearance of the subject? It is clear how Næss is still think-ing in these terms when he discusses the position of humans within his vision of a 'deep ecology': 'applied to humans, the complexity-not-complication principle favours ... integrated actions in which the whole person is active, not mere reactions' (1973: 97). But what is more humanistic than the action/reaction, active/passive couples? After all, Næss himself makes it explicit how his 'deep ecology' is an ethics, and therefore both presupposes and entails the presence of a subject: 'it should be fully appreciated that the significant tenets of the Deep Ecology movement are clearly and forcefully normative' (1973: 99). Animality, on the other hand, is not normative – for a cat cares nothing about religion, or a worm about economy. Animality is dangerous.

It is therefore necessary to take Derrida's 'heterogeneous' multiplicity seriously, because to talk about living beings is not enough. Indeed, even the concept of 'living being' implicitly contains a violent act of power, of exclusion – like Heidegger's dropping the stone in the pond, because inert, non-living and 'world-less': a simple *thing*. Indeed, if 'heterogeneous multiplicity' is open to exchanges between living beings, and between living beings and things (since living beings are things among things), it follows that it is also open to exchanges with what – perhaps due to our impatience or lack of imagination – we call non-living, like stones. As Francis Ponge (1899–1988), the French prose poet of the world of things, writes (turning Heidegger's ideas on their head):

> To die and live again, plants, animals, gases and liquids move more or less rapidly. The great wheel of stone seems to us practically, and even theoretically, immobile; we can only imagine a portion of its slowly disintegrating phase.
>
> So that contrary to popular opinion, which makes stone in man's eyes a symbol of durability and impassiveness, one might say that stone, which does not regenerate, is in fact the only thing in nature that constantly dies. (Ponge 1974 :73)

Derrida's 'heterogeneous multiplicity' is composed of 'organizations of relations between living and dead, relations of organization or lack of organization among realms that are more and more difficult to dissociate by means of the figures of the organic and inorganic, of life and/or death' (2008: 31). Thus, another crucial element of Heidegger's scheme is put into question: the distinction between human death and animal ceasing-to-be. What does it mean to die when the processes that define death assume different values according to the temporal frame of reference we adopt? When does a dog die? When its heart stops beating or when the last atom of its body has been assimilated by another body, a mineral, or a cloud? And when does a human body die? When it becomes unable to say 'I', or when the heart stops beating, or perhaps when every metabolic process at the cellular level (that 'residual life', as thanatology defines it, which can last several hours, or even days after death) finally halts? The distinction between death and ceasing-to-be seemed so neat and precise, and yet we discover that it is all but clear-cut: indeed, perhaps it is not a distinction at all, but rather a prescription, or a hope.

106

'These relations', Derrida continues, 'are at once intertwined and abyssal, and they can never be totally objectified. They do not leave room for any simple exteriority of one term with respect to another. It follows that one will never have the right to take animals to be the species of a kind that would be named The Animal, or animal in general' (2008: 31). This vision undermines the naïve yet persistent account of evolution that puts the human at the top, and presents other species as more or less imperfect and tentative forms of the human. As if a chimp was to be considered only to the extent that it (allegedly) prefigures the human, and not because it is an autonomous and utterly singular form of life. The image of an animality to come – the one we are attempting to think here – is precisely this 'heterogeneous multiplicity' of living beings, mobile, contaminated and never crystallised into any kind of 'I' or subjectivity. Because '[t]here is a reality of becoming-animal ... [i]t is a question of composing a body with the animal, a body without organs defined by zones of intensity or proximity' (Deleuze and Guattari 1987: 273, 274). We can find an example of such an *animal* multiplicity – that aspires to no unity, that seeks no *Gestalt*, no harmony, and is capable of shifting from shape to shape, from animal to plant, and indeed from life to death – in the extraordinary tale of Philemon and Baucis, told by Ovid in his *Metamorphoses*:

> Meanwhile in the foothills of Phrygia
> There are two trees, a lime tree and an oak
> That grow within the ruins of a wall.
> . . .
> Long, long ago, Jove in his mortal dress
> Came to this country with his lively son –
> The one who stemmed from Atlas, a brisk boy
> Who'd dropped his wings but held a magic wand
> They knocked for shelter at a thousand homes
> And learned a thousand gates were locked against them.
> At last a cottage roofed with straw and grass
> Swung its doors wide. Within these shabby walls
> Old Baucis and wife Philemon survived,
> Equal in age, both pious and reserved.
> When they were very young and gay and married,
> They chose the little cottage as their home,
> And there they lived till they'd grown old; the couple
> Made light of being poor by making certain
> The little that they owned was truly theirs:
> The two were servants and their own sweet masters. (Ovid 1958: 226–7)

Philemon and Baucis live a humble life, but they have everything they need, for their home and their mutual companionship is their whole existence. A life without desires – if such a life is at all possible for human beings – because they have what they need and do not need what they lack: to this extent, theirs is a full life. Their generosity, too, has no hidden agenda. They offer what they have simply because they can: water to the thirsty, food to the hungry. A generous gesture that pays no heed to transcendence: it rather means that, free from desires, they also do not need to stockpile a private reserve. So, theirs is a kind of non-ethical generosity – one would want to say an *animal* generosity:

> So when the heavenly visitors arrived
> And bowed to enter the low-ceilinged door,
> Old Baucis rose to offer them a seat,
> Dusted a bench, and soothed a rug across It,
> While Philemon stirred up a dying fire,
> . . .
> Then food was served, first came Minerva's fruit,
> The ripe brown olive and September cherries
> Spiced with a measure of sweet wine, new lettuce,
> Creamed cottage cheese, pink radishes, and eggs
> Baked to a turn, and all were handed round
> On plates of country-fashioned earthenware –
> And of the same make came a large bowl, then
> Small wooden cups, all lined with amber wax,
> The service for the soup poured at the hearth,
> Then came the table wine and the next course.
> Set to one side, nuts, figs, and dates, sweet-smelling
> Apples in a flat basket, grapes just off the vine,
> The centerpiece a white comb of clear honey.
> But happier than the simple meal itself,
> A halo of high spirits charmed the table. (Ovid 1958: 227–8)

The old couple's hospitality is generous and rich, noble and not at all ostentatious. The gods are very impressed and grateful, and when they punish the country for its lack of hospitality – by sending a flood – they save the old couple's hut, and turn it into a temple of which Philemon and Baucis will become priests. They will only ask one thing of Jupiter: the paradoxical desire of having no desires, to keep living the same life, and to be able to die together, as they lived. The god happily grants this wish, because the flux that kept them together during this life will again unite them in the next. That is because, for the gods, every individuation is nothing but a moment in a continuous movement:

When at last
In frail old age they stood at ease before
The temple's doors and spoke of years gone by,
Baucis saw Philemon shake leaves around her,
And she herself saw Baucis do the same.
Around their faces branches seemed to tremble,
And as bark climbed their lips as if to close them,
They cried, 'Farewell, good-bye, dear wife, dear husband.'
In Thrace the natives show their visitors
Two trees so close together that their branches
Seem to grow upward from a single trunk. (Ovid 1958: 229)

Note

1. It is interesting to note that such a possibility has been always operative in non-Western cultures, as in the case of the Amerindian ones described by Eduardo Viveiros de Castro in *Cosmological Perspectivism in Amazonia and Elsewhere* (2019). Such cultures represent a completely different way of living beings, anthropomorphic but not anthropocentric, based on a non-dualistic ontology composed by a multiplicity of gazes, human and nonhuman.

5

Becoming-human

The 'Rat Unit' and the Maze

The animal, the *animot*, is the generic living being that *lacks* something
– typically, language. To avoid misunderstandings and accusations,
especially from some animalists, let me clarify this: the fact that
nonhuman animals do not have a (human) language does not entail
that other forms of communication are uncommon among them. The
point is not that a mouse, for example, cannot speak English – for
then we should ask ourselves why a human being cannot use a bat's
echolocation system. No, the problem is not what the animal – *any*
animal – lacks, but rather what its 'degree of power' is (Deleuze and
Guattari 1987: 256). It is necessary to leave behind the comparative
logic that always favours the human animal, and consider every
individual body in itself, and not in relation to another. The identity
machine establishes that something is an *x* by virtue of being a *non-y*;
however, this means subordinating affirmation to negation. On the
contrary, animality means that an affirmation does not oppose anything, nor does it differentiate itself from anything: it is pure affirmation, because 'difference is affirmation' (Deleuze 2001a: 55). The
objective is that of seeing animality in itself, and not in relation to
humanity. That a trout has no language is no more meaningful than
the fact that a human mammal has no feathers.

Let us return, then, to the voiceless animal. According to the
anthropocentric standpoint, this amounts to a lack. So, if the animal
cannot talk, we are still unsatisfied: for even the quiet animal will not
be left alone by us. That silence perturbs the loquacious living being:
does it mean that animals have nothing to say to us, or are ignoring
us? And so, we try to teach them to speak our language – as has
been repeatedly attempted from the 1960s onwards (Wallman 1992;
Lyn 2012). The goal of these experiments has never been clear: to
demonstrate that animals can talk like humans, or that they cannot?
Either way, clearly the object of interest was never *their* language
(Despret 2002). The sad history of these experiments is particularly

instructive, for it teaches us more than what was ostensibly discovered by performing them, which was very little indeed; for example, the fact that a chimp (or a dog, or a parrot) can learn to productively and reflectively use a few hundred symbols (although exact figures are debated). But we have always known this; the problem is that the animal has no language, and not because it is unable to communicate (nobody who has ever known an animal has doubted this), but because the very definition of animal is *a living being with no language*. To say that the animal cannot talk is akin to saying that a bachelor is an unmarried man. The obtuse inability to go beyond the ANIMAL makes it impossible to see *this* cat and *this* monkey. What is most striking, when considering these research projects, is the way in which they are constructed, where the same scheme is reproduced in thousands of only superficially different experiments: a human being asking the animal to perform an action it has no interest in performing (Waller 2012).

The animals' position – chimps, orangutans, dolphins, parrots, gorillas and so on – is as subordinates who must obey orders (it is no coincidence that they are locked in cages), and their first problem is trying to understand what the human in a white lab coat demands of them. The animal asks nothing at all. If desperate enough, in the end it understands that it is supposed to perform some actions that the human standing outside of the cage considers very important. If not sufficiently desperate, on the other hand, the animal refuses to do anything, stubbornly resisting. In these experiments we see at work language's primary and primordial performance, a language made 'to be obeyed, and to compel obedience' (Deleuze and Guattari 1987: 7). The cage, like the infamous 'Skinner box' (Skinner 1951), does the 'thinking' for those who conduct the experiment. Such an apparatus amounts to a hierarchical procedure through which someone with the power to ask questions orders someone else to behave in a way that the scientist deems most 'correct' – a behaviour that, for the caged animal, is completely meaningless. The 'Skinner box' is a distillate of the absolute power of language over bodies and life: '[w]ords are not tools, but we give children language, pens, and notebooks as we give workers shovels and pickaxes. . . . Language is not life; it gives life orders. Life does not speak; it listens and waits. Every order-word, even a father's to his son, carries a little death sentence – a Judgment, as Kafka put it' (Deleuze and Guattari 1987: 7). The animal demands nothing because only a subjectivity can ask for or order something. The animal – not a subjectivity but an impersonal singularity – *reacts*, like a released spring. Indeed, according to Heidegger animals simply exhibit a 'behaviour' (the response, whether learnt or innate, to a stimulus), and not a 'comportment' (which entails a rule that is voluntarily followed or transgressed): the 'possibility of "responding"' (Derrida 2008: 111) is thus foreclosed to the animal. In other words, we do not expect to be surprised by the animal, any more than we would expect the unexpected from a wall, or a washing machine. The point that needs stressing is not the mere fact that the animal does not respond (as if this was a discovery); rather 'the animal does not respond' is a *definition* of what the animal is.

The typical structure of these experiments requires a hungry animal (for otherwise it would not waste its time with humans), a sign to be learnt, and a reward (a grape, for example). The experimenter presents a sign to the animal, together with the object it is supposed to refer to; when the animal correctly repeats the action (after a long series of extremely boring and pedestrian presentations of the sign) it receives the reward. It is already clear how the whole experiment is designed for the animal to be unable to ask for anything, other than to beg for something to eat, or a gesture of affection. Not because it cannot ask for anything else, but because the experimental apparatus excludes the possibility of posing questions.[1] The (alleged) discovery that animals use the language we teach them only to ask for food (Terrace et al. 1979) is not a discovery at all, for it simply reiterates what we already *believe* we know about animals, and which therefore does not surprise us. But we are not surprised only because we have forced the animal into a situation that excludes any possibility of surprise. If we stop asking whether or not the animal has a language akin to ours, and pay attention to what the animal is actually saying, we suddenly *see it*, as in the case of Washoe the chimp. Washoe – who got her name from the Nevada county where she was raised by a couple of psychologists who endeavoured to teach her sign language (Gardner and Gardner 1969) – learnt to use hundreds of different signs. In the vast majority of cases, Washoe used the language she was taught to ask for either food or affection, as we would expect from an intelligent animal who has learnt that her human captors will feed her only if asked through the gestures she has learnt with great effort. And yet, occasionally Washoe also managed to request something else. 'Please', she would sign by holding her right hand to her chest, next to her heart, and moving it in a circular motion. 'What do you want?', the experimenter enquires. 'Outside', Washoe would reply by taking her right hand out of the clenched fingers of her left hand.[2] On another occasion, Washoe asked 'Come' by point-ing both her thumbs towards herself. 'What do you want?', she was again asked. 'Open', she replied, by showing the palms of her hands slowly moving away from each other, like the two halves of a large portal (Linden 1974: 41). It is not hard to understand what Washoe's desire was, even if we do not know if she considered 'Open' to be a word or a phrase, a sign or a meaningless gesture, part of a language or not. Washoe wanted to *get out*. All of a sudden, we see what decades of experiments failed to discern: an ape that does not want to be trapped in a cage or in an experimental setting; a human that talks and plays with language; and a life that wants to escape – because the animal is '*[a] line of escape, and not freedom*' (Deleuze and Guattari 1986: 35).

What is at stake, between ape and human, is not the animal's mind. The cruel linguistic game that Washoe is forced to play is designed to answer a different question: what are the effects of words on animals? As Lacan puts it: '[s]ince the limit . . . is constituted by the fact that there are beings who speak, people wonder what the knowledge of those who do not speak could be. They wonder about it. They don't know why they wonder about it. But they wonder about it all the same. So they build a little maze (*labyrinthe*) for rats' (1998: 139). What is a rat, for the human experimenter? And why a maze? 'They do not take the rat as a being, but rather as a body, which means that they view it as a unit, a rat-unit . . . [T]hey identify its being with its body' (1998: 140). In the maze, the rat stops being a living singularity, and becomes an abstraction, a generic 'rat-unit' (an *animot*). This is the same machinery that turns a living being into an animal, just like the anthropologic machine produces a uniform series of interchangeable 'I's. The rat-unit coincides with the body that it is: it is not separated into two parts, as in the case of the human being, an 'I' who *has* a body (Miller 2001: 75). We throw the rat in the maze precisely because we cannot stand its being simply the animal it is, and nothing more. The maze is a punishment for its animal condition, it has the purpose of transforming the rat's 'environment' into a 'world', and indeed it produces distance, doubt and uncertainty:

The maze leads not only to nourishment but to a button or flap that the supposed subject of this being must figure out how to use to obtain nour-ishment. Or it has to recognize a feature, a lit or colored feature, to which the being is capable of reacting. What is important is that the question of knowledge is transformed here into that of learning. (Lacan 1998: 140)

The spontaneous knowledge of the rat, the one it employs to survive, is bodily and perceptual: it is an immediate knowledge, in direct contact with experience. But, in the maze, this knowledge is useless and indeed dangerous, for it is now necessary to learn that food can be (maybe) reached if a button is pressed, if a certain direction is chosen, or if a certain colour is recognised. Now and forever the screen of signs, of equivocation and of deception, lies between the rat and its food, because this is what the maze and the network of language are.

For the same reason, only the talking living being could design such an experiment:

> Now, the experimenter is the one who knows something in this business, and it is with what he knows that he invents this montage consisting of the maze, buttons, and flaps. If he were not someone whose relation to knowledge is grounded in a relation to llanguage [*lalangue*], in the inhabiting of llanguage or the cohabitation with llanguage, there would be no montage. (Lacan 1998: 141)

What Lacan calls 'llanguage' is precisely the merging of body and language that characterises human biology; llanguage is not a determinate language, but the possibility of any language, an inseparable tangle of signs which are connected to other signs, and so on. Llanguage 'evinces knowledge that, for the most part, escapes the speaking being', and 'articulates things by way of knowledge (*de savoir*) that go much further than what the speaking being sustains (*supporte*) by way of enunciated knowledge' (Lacan 1998: 139). To place the rat in a maze means to observe first hand the birth of a rat-unit, of an animal, just like the human is born out of language. Because – and this is the moral of Lacan's analysis – the rat is in the maze like the *infans* is in language.

The most disturbing aspect of this cruel game (still disguised as a science) is that it is completely lost on the rat, just like 'llanguage' is lost on the human who speaks a determinate language, and is convinced of knowing what he or she is saying when referring to it:

> The only thing the rat-unit learns in this case is to give a sign, a sign of its presence as unit. The flap is recognized only by a sign and pressing its paw on this sign is a sign. It is always by making a sign that the unit accedes to that on the basis of which one concludes that there is learning. But

this relation to signs is external. Nothing confirms that the rat grasps the mechanism to which pressing the button leads. (Lacan 1998: 141)

Suddenly, a light shines in the maze. The rat cowers in fear and hits a lever that opens a door, from which a peanut rolls out. The light – as well as the lever – might be a sign, perhaps; but the mechanism that governs this cruel game remains mysterious. What is certain is that the rat scuttles around in fear, and its every action is now doubled: it is what it is – the movement of a paw, for example – but it is also the meaning that such action might have with respect to another sign. Hesitation, uncertainty and sadness have now been introduced into the maze along with signs. Because once inside, the simple vitality that (in the 'outside' uselessly signed by Washoe) merges gaze and object, paw and action, animal and world is forever lost. Time begins in the maze and, along with it, regret.

If we turn to the 'two positions of knowledge' regarding the animal of which Derrida speaks – one group considering animals as 'something seen and not seeing' (more or less everyone, including so-called animal lovers) and a much smaller group composed by those 'poets or prophets . . . who admit to taking upon themselves the address that an animal addresses to them' (Derrida 2008: 13, 14) – we can certainly consider Kafka as a member of the latter group. His 1917 short story 'A Report to an Academy', is particularly relevant: this is the tale of an ape called Red Peter who, taken very young from Ivory Coast and brought to the civilised world (the world of an Academy), learns how to talk and becomes a world-renowned attraction (exactly Washoe's story). The narration is in the first person – it is the ape who speaks – but Red Peter's becoming-human crosses its path with Kafka's becoming-animal. 'I came down for a drink at evening among a troop of apes. They shot at us; I was the only one that was hit; I was hit in two places' (Kafka 1952: 170). The first encounter with humanity is traumatic, it leaves a scar – a *trace* – that will never be erased. Becoming-human is nothing but living through the aftermath of that primordial trauma: '[i]t is because there is the unconscious – namely, llanguage, insofar as it is on the basis of the cohabitation with llanguage that a being known as speaking being is defined' (Lacan 1998: 142). The trace/scar is a sign, and a sign refers to something else (to a meaning) which requires another sign to be comprehended, and so on: this is the maze of language into which Red Peter is thrown. His sadness is that of a living being who, like the 'rat-unit', is transformed into a two-sided being, split between subject/person and 'bare life', thought and action, past and future: 'it is in that respect that the subject turns out to be – and this is only true for speaking beings – a being (*un étant*) whose being is always elsewhere. . . . The subject is never more than fleeting (*ponctuel*) and vanishing, for it is a subject only by a signifier and to another signifier' (Lacan 1998: 142). The Ivory Coast is forever lost, because even returning to it would not mean being reunited with a warm and welcoming natural 'environment', but merely coming back to a 'world', one among many, incomprehensible and hostile.

The trip towards the rich Western world is gruelling, and the monkey quickly understands – just like the 'rat-unit' and Washoe did – that in order to survive it will be necessary to renounce the past, and to forget the Ivory Coast. It is a painful transition: the 'environment' is discovered just when it is being abandoned, because as soon as its presence is felt there it also vanishes, since for an 'environment' to exist it is necessary for those within it to be unaware of it. And so, a newly discovered past immediately turns into regret and desperation: 'I could never have achieved what I have done had I been stubbornly set on clinging to my origins, to the remembrances of my youth. In fact, to give up being stubborn was the supreme commandment I laid upon myself; free ape as I was, I submitted myself to that yoke' (Kafka 1952: 168). Thus, Red Peter claims his (heretofore unacknowledged) freedom only to immediately renounce it, since it is discovered when the ape is forced to forfeit it, and to live the existence others will impose upon it according to unknown rules, in an alien world. This is the paradox of the anthropologic machine, which fabricates an autonomous 'I' only to then impose how to live and what to think:

> After these two shots I came to myself – and this is where my own memories gradually begin – between decks in the Hagenbeck steamer, inside a cage. . . . The whole construction was too low for me to stand up in and too narrow to sit down in. So I had to squat with my knees bent and trembling all the time. . . . Such a method of confining wild beasts is supposed to have its advantages during the first days of captivity, and out of my own experiences I cannot deny that from the human point of view this is really the case.
>
> But that did not occur to me then. For the first time in my life I could see no way out; at least no direct way out; directly in front of me was the locker, board fitted close to board. (Kafka 1952: 171)

The cage in which Red Peter is trapped cannot but be too narrow, simply by virtue of being a cage. This is the first and the most important of the ape's realisations: it has become a caged living being. In truth – before being an instrument of containment – the cage is a conceptual apparatus, the first and most fundamental biopolitical tool: the omnipresent attempt to grasp and 'immunise' life. From this point of view the cage does not discriminate between animals (in zoos) and humans (in prison): the pictures of the children of Central American 'illegal' immigrants locked in cages by the US police serve as a paradigmatic example of how the cage 'works' equally with all forms of life (and, in this sense, a houseplant's pot is a cage too). Red Peter had never before experienced this kind of sensation, and not simply because he was free to roam the Ivory Coast's forest, but rather because that was an 'environment', i.e., an *open* space. When Peter realises himself to be living in an 'environment' he also becomes aware of the fact that it is nothing but *a* possible environment so that, paradoxically, he understands himself to be living in a 'world', i.e., to be locked in a cage. In his cage below deck Red Peter, who until then had no name, becomes aware of his own life (*Homo sapiens* is both this discovery and the regret of knowing it). So far, he had simply lived: '[b]ut over and above it all only the one feeling: no way out'. Only an 'I' can realise its own mortality, and only an 'I' can experience the feeling of having no way out (that death cannot be eluded): 'Until then I had had so many ways out of everything, and now I had none. I was pinned down. Had I been nailed down, my right to free movement would not have been lessened' (Kafka 1952: 172). Red Peter is no longer an ape , but neither is he a man: he is an intelligent animal – like the 'rat-unit'. If this is the nature of the game, it is best to learn it quick:

> I had no way out but I had to devise one, for without it I could not live. All the time facing that locker – I should certainly have perished. Yet as far as Hagenbeck [Peter's captor] was concerned, the place for apes was in front of a locker – well then, I had to stop being an ape. A fine, clear train of thought, which I must have constructed somehow with my belly, since apes think with their bellies. (Kafka 1952: 172)

This is a radical solution: to stop being an ape. Becoming-human means to stop being an animal: 'freedom was not what I wanted. Only a way out' (Kafka 1952: 173). To find this way out means abandoning the quest for a way out. Red Peter applies all of his intelligence to the purpose of becoming human, or quasi-human, because only then will he be accepted into their world, and thus survive (just like Washoe had to learn the human's game). He immediately understands what is expected of him: to speak. Nothing unsettles the *sapientes* more than the animal's silence – or what they perceive as such. With a tremendous effort he eventually manages to enter into language:

> because I could not help it, because my senses were reeling, called a brief and unmistakable 'Hallo!' breaking into human speech, and with this outburst broke into the human community, and felt its echo: 'Listen, he's talking!' like a caress over the whole of my sweat-drenched body. I repeat: there was no attraction for me in imitating human beings; I imitated them because I needed a way out, and for no other reason. (Kafka 1952: 178)

The ape from the Ivory Coast is now gone, and the anthropologic machine reveals its cruel and violent face: '[a]nd so I learned things, gentlemen. Ah, one learns when one has to; one learns when one needs a way out; one learns at all costs. One stands over oneself with a whip; one flays oneself at the slightest opposition' (Kafka 1952: 179). This is indeed what happens when an animal becomes an *animot*, a 'rat-unit', or more precisely an 'animal model' – the euphemism used to define animals that take part in experiments. If the animal is 'a creative line of escape that says nothing other than what it is' (Deleuze and Guattari 1986: 36), *Homo sapiens* is, on the contrary, the living being who, in order to become 'human', needs to obstruct all lines of escape. It follows that a more apt definition of the human would be *Homo biopoliticus*, the living being who fears and controls life: law, religion, economy, language, psychology, ethics – these are all forms of the primordial fear of life. A life that, in itself, is neither wild nor violent, neither good nor sweet.

The Forest Without Trees

Heidegger, as usual, does not mince words: 'in a fundamental sense the animal does not have perception' (1995: 259). But, for example, what can elude the hawk's eye, an animal with a proverbially keen sight? Human becoming pivots on the question of language, as Red Peter frankly acknowledges. And becoming human means learning *to see in a human way*, i.e., linguistically. Heidegger's example is that of a foraging bee, flying towards a flower. It does so because it is looking for nectar, the sweet substance that is secreted by flowers precisely in order to attract insects, and used by bees to produce honey. And so bees bring pollen from flower to flower, thus becoming the unwitting agents of the reproduction of flowers. But what does the bee properly *see* when it looks at a flower? It sees a certain shape, for example,

118

to which it is naturally more sensitive than others which do not attract its attention as much (von Frisch 1953). But Heidegger does not question whether or not they see something, but rather if they see the flower *as* a 'flower', as a distinct botanical entity, separate from the grass and the trees, the sky and the clouds. Can a bee see the flower as an *individuated object*? Why is Heidegger so concerned with this question? Because a separate and distinct object can exist only if there is a *subject* that observes it. And a subject knows itself to be one precisely by setting itself apart from the objects of everyday dealings. If put in these terms, we know how the story ends: an animal cannot be a subject, and therefore it cannot handle objects nor – consequently – can it perceive anything (it cannot enter into a sensible relation with an object). Heidegger's aim is to establish whether or not an animal can perceive something *qua* something, i.e., as an isolated object – which ultimately means that it can be assumed as the referent of a *name*. The bee, an animal, cannot have any relationship with the '*qua*': when it sucks the flower's nectar, we should talk of a 'behaviour rather than comportment on the part of the bee toward the honey which is present or no longer present' (1995: 241). A 'comportment' is a norm-bound human *action*: it can be evaluated as either right or wrong, it has a purpose, and it is part of an explicit project. That of the bee, on the other hand, is mere 'behaviour', an action 'terminated through an inhibition (drive and disinhibition)' (1995: 243). The bee leaves the hive in search of food, for itself and for the hive. This action is triggered by an internal, instinctual process over which the bee has no control whatsoever. The sight of a flower triggers another behaviour (i.e., it disinhibits it), and so the bee proceeds to harvest the nectar. In this sequence of actions, the bee is dragged step by step by the stimuli it receives, and so this instinct 'is merely another form of captivation' (1995: 243) since the bee acts automatically, without being aware of what it is doing.

Throughout this process the flower never plays the role of something 'which is present or no longer present': the flower is part of the bee's behaviour because it bears the natural meaning of 'source of nourishment'. When the bee's hunger is satiated, its interest in flowers is over, since these only exist as means to reach nectar. In this sense the bee, for Heidegger, does not properly perceive the flower, because the flower means nothing to it – the only thing that exists is the flower as an intermediate passage leading to the nectar, the biological end of its behaviour. This is the link between 'captivation' on the one hand, and lack of objectivity on the other: the bee is *always* captivated, and therefore unable to perceive something *qua* something: '[t]o say that captivation is the essence of animality means: The animal as such does not stand within a manifestness of beings. Neither its so-called environment nor the animal itself are manifest as beings (1995: 248). The bee's captivation entails the impossibility of perceiving itself as a subject or the flower as an object. Thus, the bee is structurally indifferent to the '*qua*'; it is not just unable to perceive it, for its very biological constitution makes it impossible to access it. Thus for Heidegger the animal is 'poor in world', precisely because its 'environment' – the acuity of its senses notwithstanding – would be, paradoxically, less rich than ours, lacking objects and including only irresistible behavioural sequences: '[t]he striking indifference of . . . animals toward anything that does not directly address their instincts, toward whatever does not fit into their species-specific environment, can be attributed to the monotony and "lack of ability" of their senses *and* movements' (Gehlen 1988: 143).

However, this description of the nonhuman animal world could be completely reversed: it is not the bee who fails to perceive the flower *qua* flower, but rather the linguistic animal who looks at the 'flower' without seeing the nature to which the flower – as well as him- or herself, as a being who assigns names – belongs. The bee is nature itself, taking the form of a flying insect. The talking being, on the other hand, is an isolated entity – the subject/person – unable to discern the infinite links that bind together those that, to the human mind, appear as distinct entities. Indeed, when the need to establish once and for all who is a subject and who an object – who is active and who is passive – is overcome, nature reveals itself as an infinite field of operations of 'recognition' and 'communication'. Returning to the example of the bee flying in search of flowers, we see that not every plant-form is, for it, a flower; however, when one is recognised as such the bee plunges into it, looking for its precious nectar. If we look at the same event from the flower's point of view, we can say that it tries to be recognised by the bee, so that the bee will coat itself in pollen, thus pollinating the next flower it will visit. The flower thus 'communicates' to the bee, by means of its form and scent, its 'suitability' for reproduction. In both cases there is no break in the reciprocal relation established between bee and flower. In the end, the bee is a flower with wings and sting, a flying flower. In the biological world there is no individual *qua* individual; there are only fluxes of becoming. The becoming-flower of the bee and the becoming-bee of the flower:

We are impressed by the concept of the individual because we live long lives and we see many things change around us, while 'individuals' remain constant. In reality, nothing is as ephemeral as a biological individual. Its very anatomy changes several times during its lifespan, and it hosts within itself a number of other individuals, and is itself hosted by others. Continually devoured, it devours. Finally, it dies, but that is a transitory phenomenon, just like its 'individual life' was. What has taken place was simply a furious and urgent aggregating and desegregating of molecules in a relatively limited space. (Pierantoni 1977: 219)

How is it possible, then, to transition from the bee's lack of perception to the human gaze, grasping the flower as something subsistent? How to transition from the bee and the flower to Heidegger? It is necessary to make explicit what Red Peter reminded us of: 'one learns at all costs. One stands over oneself with a whip; one flays oneself at the slightest opposition.' How can one learn to see the world in this strange and unnatural way? And, most importantly, what is lost when one learns to see the flower *qua* flower? From a psychological standpoint, the history of the *'qua'* is that of how a primate of the species *Homo sapiens* learnt how to control (here again the whip appears) its own attention. Because to see a flower *qua* flower I need to learn to see – i.e., to selectively pay attention to – a flower even when, if I am a bee for example, I am not hungry or when it holds no nectar. Vygotsky and Luria reconstruct this process in their 'Tool and Symbol in Child Development'. The two great Soviet psychologists' description of the perceptual abilities of the child is very similar to Heidegger's discussion of the bee. At the beginning the child's gaze is irresistibly attracted by the perceptual scene, forcing upon her not just *what to see*, but also *what to do* in that context. The child, that is, appears to be a 'slave of the field of vision' (Vygotsky and Luria 1994: 127):[3] to see an apple, for example, means to immediately try to grasp it, just like the sight of a flower dictates to the bee which 'behaviour' to adopt. According to this description, the child does not strictly speaking perceive a distinct object – say, an apple – against which she would position herself as an equally distinct subject; the child rather partakes in a unitary flux of 'perception-movement' (Vygotsky and Luria 1994: 127), a becoming-apple that does not permit the distinction between active and passive, doer and object, thinker and (object) thought. It is clear that, in the process of the child's becoming-apple, Heidegger's apple *qua* apple completely vanishes.

A machinery capable of interrupting the flux of the child's becoming-apple is needed to move towards the specifically human form of perception, allowing the separation and crystallisation of the two positions of subject and object: on the one hand an 'I' and on the other the apple *qua* apple. Language is this machinery, which 'introduces an analytical factor into perception, and thus supplants the natural structure of apperception by a complex and psychologically indirect one' (Vygotsky and Luria 1994: 126). Through the introduction of language, the child, on the one hand, begins to think of *herself* as an 'I' while, on the other, she begins to *see* the apple through the meaning of the *word* 'apple': since the 'apple' is different from the 'pear', they are separate objects, one there, one here – just like 'I' is different from 'you'. Language – and in particular its interiorised form that becomes 'verbal thought' – allows the child to introduce distinctions where hitherto there was nothing but an undifferentiated stream, flowing from the eye to the arm to the apple, and vice versa:

> this primary natural relation between perception and movement, their inclusion in a common psycho-physical system, disintegrates in the process of cultural development, and is replaced by relations of a quite different structure, beginning from the moment when words or some other sign is introduced between the initial and concluding stages of the reactive process, and the entire operation assumes an indirect character. (Vygotsky and Luria 1994: 128–9)

In 'natural perception' – as opposed to 'cultural' or 'artificial' perception, mediated by language – the attention is completely guided by the event within which the child is trapped; in 'artificial' perception the situation is completely reversed:

> The essential point in the development of this process, however, is that the child, unlike the animal, proves to be capable of transferring its attention actively and independently, reconstructing its perception and thus freeing itself, to a tremendous extent, from submission to the structure of the given field. Linking the use of tools with speech at a certain stage of development . . . the child in this way transfers the activity of its attention to a new plane. With the help of the indicative function of words, noted above, the child begins to master its attention, creating new structural centres of the perceived situation. By this means . . . the child evaluates not the degree of clarity of one or the other part of the perceived field, but its 'centre of gravity' (*Schwerpunkt*), the importance of its separate elements, singling out ever new 'figures' from its background, and thus limitlessly widening the possibilities for mastering its activities. (Vygotsky and Luria 1994: 132)

What is at stake in this dramatic process – one that literally and violently transforms a living being into a subject/person, an 'I' – is the establishment of a hierarchy of commanded and commander: the constitution of an 'active' and 'independent' actor, capable of breaking out of the slavery of the perceptual field and 'mastering its attention', i.e., its eyes and hands. This process of the mastery of attention splits the human animal in two: the subject/mind on the one hand (the active instance), the executor on the other (the passive instance, the 'bare life'). Prior to the separation between human and animal, then, there is that between mind and body. The first fracture will not be recomposed before the second, for the two proceed (or fall) together.

Yet, if we go back to a time preceding this fracture, what do we find? *How* does the child becoming-apple, or the bee becoming-flower, see? There is a passage in Heidegger's text dedicated to the theme of animality where the philosopher of Being seems to sense the depth of the loss occurring in the transition to the '*qua*' mode of perception. He wonders what the bee perceives, since it does not perceive the flower:

> if behaviour is not a relation to beings, does this mean that it is a relation to nothing? Not at all. Yet if it is not a relation to nothing, it must always be a relation to something, which surely must itself *be* and actually *is*. Certainly, but the question is whether behaviour is not precisely a kind of relation to . . . in which *that to which* the behaviour relates in the manner of not attending to it is *open in a certain way* for the animal. (1995: 253)

He then proceeds to explain that 'open' should not be interpreted as '*manifest as a being*', and this should not be surprising, for only the human can have access to beings *qua* beings. It refers, rather, to an ecstatic condition, obtuse but radically freeing, and for this very reason foreclosed to the human. It is as if Heidegger could sense that the animal's 'captivation' is not just a lack, an index of its being 'poor in world', but that, on the contrary, it can also be understood as a vital fullness that is utterly foreclosed to the 'world-forming' human. That is to say, it is not so much a matter of considering the animal as a living being that lacks something the human possesses, but rather inverting the point of view: the animal lacks nothing, it is the human who is marked by a surplus, something in excess. The animal is not to be compared to a (not yet) human being; rather, the human is a not- (anymore, or not yet) animal. Agamben hints at this possible reversal of perspective by returning to the example of the tick, once again tormenting the philosophers' dreams: the signs in its environment force the tick into 'an intense and passionate relationship the likes of which we might never find in the relations that bind man to his apparently much richer world. The tick *is* this relationship; she lives only in it and for it' (Agamben 2004: 47).

Vygotsky does not want the human to be a 'slave' of perception. This requires going from the animal 'natural' attention to the 'artificial' attention proper to language – and ultimately unnatural. In order to consider not just what is gained but also what is lost in this transition, let us consider autistic zoologist Temple Grandin's *Animals in Translation*, a book presenting theses that we can, paradoxically, consider to be very near to those of Heidegger concerning the '*qua*', as exposed in his *The Fundamental Concepts of Metaphysics*. The difference is that Temple Grandin wrote a book from the point of view of animality, therefore foregrounding what Heidegger neglects and despises: the possibility of a way of living untouched by language, i.e., not oppressed by the structure of the '*qua*'. What does it mean, then, to *see* something without the mediation of language? Heidegger and Vygotsky have explained the meaning of seeing through language – to see the flower *qua* flower (for example). But to see *a* flower means to see it as a representation of a class of entities, the class of all flowers. Essentially, it means seeing the exemplary nature of the flower, displayed right in front of our eyes; but what makes a flower exemplary – what allows it to stand *for all flowers* – is the same thing that makes it impossible to see how *this flower*, right *here* and right *now*, actually is. To see a flower '*qua*' flower makes it far more difficult to pay attention to the details of the flower we assign a name to (besides, the process of nomination interferes with the memory of the experience we name; see Schooler and Engstler-Schooler 1990). The animal's sensory world is lush with details which, to a human eye, go entirely unnoticed; not because the animal's sight is keener than that of a *Homo sapiens*, but because the latter is confused by the generalising interference of language: '[w]hen an animal or an autistic person is seeing the real world instead of his idea of the world, that means he's seeing detail. This is the single most important thing to know about the way animals perceive the world: animals see details people don't see' (Grandin and Johnson 2005: 31). Animals can see these details because their attention is entirely captivated by the perceptual field, and there is no separate and distinct mind – no 'I' is in charge – which would command their attention: the visible appears in its full pressing evidence 'as a swirling mass of tiny details' (2005: 67). In order to really pay attention to a detail it is (paradoxically) necessary not to be distracted by attention: '*[h]umans are built to see what they're expecting to see*, and it's hard to expect to see something you've never seen. New things just don't register' (2005: 51). If a living being capable of feeling something as an integral aesthetic experience – i.e., a purely sensorial experience, without the involvement of additional cognitive processes – exists, that is only the nonhuman animal:

> A lot of what animals see normal people see, too, but normal people don't know they're seeing it. Instead, a normal person's brain uses the detailed raw data of the world to form a generalized concept or schema, and that's what reaches consciousness. Fifty shades of brown turn into just one unified color: brown. That's why normal people see only what they expect to see – because they can't *consciously experience* the raw data, only the schema their brains create out of the raw data.
>
> *Normal people see and hear schemas, not raw sensory data.*
>
> (Grandin and Johnson 2005: 65)

The animal can be completely immersed in the sensible, because its eyes see without the interference of (explicit and, mostly, implicit) thoughts that the machinery of the '*qua*' constantly engenders: '[a]nimals definitely act like they see everything, because you can't get anything past a cow' (2005: 51). We cannot even imagine the power of such a gaze, because to be a member of the species *Homo sapiens* means to have traversed the anthropologic machine, having thus become a linguistic animal; and it is language that stops us from seeing what a cow can see. The human animal, the animal who can perceive beings as subsistent, reaches the cognitive achievement of seeing the forest (seeing a linguistic entity, the abstraction FOREST) while animals 'might not see the forest at all. Just trees, trees, and more trees. Animals are like that' (2005: 218). Heidegger's position must then be reversed: the 'captivation' of animals is not a condition of disadvantage, but actually a sort of 'enchantment' (Wheeler 2018: 337), because the animal – free from the burden of subjectivity – can abandon itself to the marvels of the world. Strictly speaking, the animal does not abandon itself, as if there was *someone* 'deciding' to relinquish its subjectivity: animality (human and nonhuman, living and non-living) is nothing but this abandon, without any residue or destination. Animality is this marvelling, this 'base feeling-tone of all life', this dwelling in the world's marvel.

Caged

The 'captivation' which, according to Heidegger, characterises animals is an 'absorption', a condition that 'never involves an attending to beings, not even to itself as such' (1995: 259). The animal is not a subjectivity, an 'I' observing the world as something separate from itself. Animality means to coincide with a flux, to be placed within the continuum of events, and to be wholly seized by a single detail: 'being hyper-specific means you see the differences between things a lot better than you see the similarities' (Grandin and Johnson 2005: 218). To experience a detail – which is the meaning of being 'hyper-specific', something unimaginable for the linguistic animal, the concept- and abstraction-monger – means perceiving everything as if it was seen for the *first time* (an unthinkable world of tokens without types). That is why animals dislike novelties: because a novelty is extraordinarily new and always in need of evaluation. Is it a danger? Is it harmless? Is it good, or indifferent? What happens when such a mind is put to work? When, for example, it is asked to solve a problem that, in its native environment, would never be encountered? In this case what is relevant is not so much the difficulty for the animal of finding the problem's solution (Huber and Gajdon 2006). Rather, the challenge is for it to understand what is being asked: to perceive the world as a problem in need of a solution. The animal really wants to say: the world is as it is, there is no problem at all. On the other hand – and Heidegger is here absolutely correct – the human is 'world-forming', and keeps on changing the world. From this point of view, the Anthropocene began with the apparition of *Homo sapiens*.

When an animal is placed in an experimental setting and asked to solve a problem, what is really expected of it is to become a subject, subtracting itself from the vital 'cycle' it belongs to as a living being: to think before acting. The experiment is an attempt to transform the animal into a human being. Indeed, even when the animal manages to solve the problem it is presented with, it does so differently than a human would. It tries to resolve it, that is, as if the problem was always presented anew – even if it has encountered it many times before. It does not rely on past experience, but on what it sees when the problem is presented. Not because of the lack of good memory, or of intelligence, but because the situation's details are never exactly as they were the previous time. The animal's life takes place entirely in its present moment, it is a life under the sign of immanence.

Let us consider Wolfgang Köhler's famous psychological experiments with chimps, a scientific project the biopolitical value of which has not been sufficiently highlighted yet. In one of these experiments, the task was that of getting to a fruit dangling from the ceiling, out of reach of the chimps' hands. Some wooden crates were also placed in their cage. The problem is clear enough: the chimps are hungry, there is some food, but it cannot be easily reached. It occurs to one of the most enterprising chimps, called Chica, to climb on top of a crate in order to get closer to the fruit and finally grasp it. Problem solved. What really happened though was that *this* problem was solved, not this *type* of problem. Because the animal does not think according to categories; the animals sees the trees, not the forest. Indeed, when the same problem was presented again, the chimp struggled with it as if it was the first time: 'it is interesting to observe how an animal, who has already found the correct solution to a task in one situation, cannot for some reason, use it in another' (Vygotsky and Luria 1993: 53). The problem was not the same as the previous time, it was not the repetition of a general scheme. There is no such scheme, and so 'Chica tries her best to seize the banana suspended from the ceiling, but does not attempt to make use of the box standing in the middle of the room, even though on several occasions she has already used this very box as a stairway' (1993: 54). What is it that the chimp *cannot see*? When it solved the problem, the crate was already directly below the hanging fruit, so that the solution was evident, directly visible. What the chimp cannot see is the *structure* of the problem (a structure designed by a linguistic being thinking according to schemes and stereotypes). The chimp sees the tree, but not the forest:

> The ape exhausts herself by jumping up and trying to tear away the fruit. All the while she sees the box, even sits down on it more than once to have a rest, but does not make the slightest effort to drag it toward the goal. All this time another animal, Tercera, is lying on the box. When the latter incidentally gets up, Chica immediately seizes the box, drags it toward the target, and gets hold of it. (1993: 54)

What was different now as compared to previous, failed, attempts? The crate had now changed its 'meaning', because it entered into a new perceptual configuration as compared to when Tercera was lying on it: for as long as Tercera was lounging there, the crate was, for Chica, nothing but a resting place. Once Tercera gets off it, the crate becomes available for another kind of use. The truth is that Chica, like Agamben's Franciscan monks, *uses* the world without either appropriating it or forcing it into predetermined categories: '[u]nder these circumstances, the ape in no way links the box with the target; the box seems to be included in a different structure and therefore cannot be incorporated as a tool in the main experimental situation'

(1993: 54). Chica's difficulties depend on the fact that her thought (and to be an animal means precisely that thought is *never* owned) is not organised according to the general schema 'problem/instrument/goal'. In order to follow this pattern of thought, it is necessary to possess a self-image *qua* the 'I' of a subsistent object – the dangling banana, in this case – as well as the notion of a third element, the 'instrument' serving as an intermediary between the first two. Only the linguistic animal thinks in this way, the animal who was taught to see the forest before the trees. Conversely, this pattern of thought is completely alien to a chimp. But the human animal cannot even imagine a different way of thinking than his or her own. And so, the animal, as an eternal allegory of something else, is described as lazy, or indolent:

> The same animal behaves quite extraordinarily, when one tries to teach him something in which he is not interested. Once, he was required, in the evening after all the animals had been fed, to collect the fruit skins which were lying about, and put them in a basket. He quickly grasped what was required of him, and did it – but only for two days. On the third day he had to be told every moment to go on; on the fourth, he had to be ordered from one banana skin to the next, and on the fifth and following days his limbs had to be moved for every movement, seizing, picking up, walking, holding the skins over the basket, letting them drop, and so on, because they stopped dead at whatever place they had come to, or to which they had been led. The animal behaved like a run-down clock, or like certain types of mentally-deficient persons, in whom similar things occur. It was impossible ever to restore the matter-of-fact ease with which the task had at first been accomplished. (Köhler 1927: 297)

The animal is neither lazy nor indolent, because laziness and industriousness can only apply to talking and working animals. What is odd in this passage is Köhler's peculiar lack of imagination: why would a chimp make the effort to learn 'something in which he is not interested'? What is truly noteworthy is the psychologist's incapacity to adopt the animal's point of view, from which the task imposed by the scientist appears as completely nonsensical. Köhler incarnates a clear example of anthropomorphic myopia: the human standpoint – that of the scientist – is the only possible point of view. He writes that: '[n]ever could I achieve educational effects lasting beyond the time of my actual presence by frequently repeating prohibitions and by punishment' (1927: 297). What value can a prohibition have for an animal who lives every instant of its life as if it was the first – and the last? Köhler's book reveals more about its author than it offers

128

insights into the apes' behaviour it purports to describe. Rather than describing their mentality, it actually offers us a glimpse into the psychologist's unreflective standpoint. One day, he discovers that a chimp – called Nueva – 'had a special fancy for knots' (1927: 312). Köhler immediately thinks to exploit this to teach her some 'manual craftmanship', aimed at the production of textiles: '[w]hen I prepared for her a wooden frame with strips of leaf fastened to one side of it for plaiting, she turned aside and devoted herself to her usual knots; the slightest pressure towards anything stable and "productive" extinguished her joy and interest at once, and she let the frame fall in sullen displeasure' (1927: 312). Köhler's lack of imagination here turns into bad faith. Nueva is a caged animal, hungry and forced to spend her time solving meaningless problems; how can anyone expect her to take 'pleasure' in performing 'manual craftmanship'? Here is the human's ideal animality: a slave thankful to have been turned into one. The novelist John Maxwell Coetzee managed to see what Köhler couldn't, and described the world as seen through the eyes of Sultan, the most laborious of Köhler's chimps. This is what the animal sees and thinks from behind bars:

> Sultan is alone in his pen. He is hungry: the food that used to arrive regularly has unaccountably ceased coming.
>
> 'The man who used to feed him and has now stopped feeding him stretches a wire over the pen three meters above ground level, and hangs a bunch of bananas from it. Into the pen he drags three wooden crates. Then he disappears, closing the gate behind him, though he is still somewhere in the vicinity, since one can smell him.
>
> 'Sultan knows: Now one is supposed to think. That is what the bananas up there are about. The bananas are there to make one think, to spur one to the limits of one's thinking. But what must one think? One thinks: Why is he starving me? One thinks: What have I done? Why has he stopped liking me? One thinks: Why does he not want these crates any more? But none of these is the right thought. . . . (Coetzee 1999: 28)

Notes

1. Indeed, if we modify the learning scenario – to one where the animal is not limited to obeying orders – even a parrot suddenly becomes able to pose questions (Pepperberg 1999). What remains unthought in animal experimentation is the hierarchical position of the experimenter who, hiding beyond his or her role as a 'scientist', is not aware of his or her power, even if motivated by a genuine love for animals, the same animals he or she wants to show as capable of empathy and consciousness. As

Cary Wolfe argues, referring in general to the field of animal studies (but these observations could also be applied to comparative psychology): 'this suggests two important things about animal studies: first, that it studies both a material entity (nonhuman beings) and a discourse of species difference that need not be limited to its application to nonhumans alone and, second, that taking animal studies seriously thus has nothing to do, strictly speaking, with whether or not you like animals' (2009: 567). In truth, research like that of Pepperberg on Alex the parrot, of Terrace (1987) on Nim the chimp, or Savage-Rumbaugh's on Kanzi (Savage-Rumbaugh and Lewin 1994), has revealed far more about the human researchers than the animals they so carefully and stubbornly studied. First of all, these are animals who received a name, an important and all-too-often neglected point. The assignment of a proper name is a fundamental humanising procedure; that 'Alex' can speak then becomes implicit in the experimental procedure itself. Once named, 'Alex' couldn't but speak, as anyone who shares a house with a cat – a cat that 'talks' to us – knows. But behind all these experiments lies a heretofore unarticulated question: why do we want to demonstrate that a nonhuman animal can talk? Why is language so important? Ultimately, what do these experiments really demonstrate (Lestel 1995)? Can Alex and Kanzi talk like a child? Clearly not, and not for lack of intelligence but because, for both animals, language is a difficult machinery to which they need to painfully adapt in order to receive food and attention. If they do talk at all it is only to please the experimenters, who clearly hope to be able to boast that their animal 'sons and daughters' are good and smart enough to have learnt language. As Tomasello (2017) observes, reconstructing decades of experiments on nonhuman animals (involving dolphins, chimps, parrots, orangutans and gorillas), if, on the one hand, it is undeniable how these animals possess many (but not all) of the cognitive prerequisites to handle language, on the other hand it is just as evident how they have no interest in using it. They do it only because humans want them to, at least as little as they can manage. Animals are not interested in language – sooner or later we will have to come to terms with this fact.

2. It is extremely interesting that one of the few confirmed, and non-controversial, uses of human signs by animals is precisely the gesture that, in ASL, means 'outside'. The chimp Nim Chimpsky (named in ironic homage to Noam Chomsky) used this sign almost every time he came into contact with humans (Hess 2008), whether they used sign language or not. Perhaps nonhuman animals lack our syntactic abilities, but they are very forthcoming about their desire not to be confined in a cage, even if in a laboratory. Animality is outside, it is the *outside*.

3. As already mentioned in Chapter 3, note 2, some doubts have recently been cast on the textual fidelity of the writings published under Vygotsky's

name, including those written with Alexander Luria (see Yasnitsky and Van der Veer 2016). However, the ideas included in 'Tool and Symbol in Child Development' – one of the clearest and most explicit papers among those attributed to the great Soviet psychologist – can be found in other texts of more certain attribution, as can be also inferred from the recent publication of some handwritten notes of Vygotsky's (Zavershneva and van der Veer 2018).

6

The Artistic Beast

Nulla può essere unico e intero
che non sia stato lacerato?
    [Can anything be unique and whole that hasn't been lacerated?]
                                                    (Pasolini 2001: 849)

The Animage *and the Artist*

The animal is the *animot*. The animal is always told, imagined and represented. Although some artefacts that – to a modern observer – might appear like artistic phenomena precede the emergence of *Homo sapiens*, the fact is that the accomplished humanity of the human essentially coincides with the appearance of visual representations of animal life (Tattersall 1998; Guthrie 2005). The human has become itself by painting the animal. Indeed, in art, 'we recognize two key elements: (1) an extraction from direct instrumental communication; and (2) a duplicitous logic of representation: there is what it is or presents, and there is what it conveys only in some figurative form' (Deacon 2006: 22). Without wholly adopting a Kantian standpoint we can say that art presupposes a somehow 'disinterested' gaze, that is to say that a visual representation of a buffalo (for example) has no explicit and clear biological purpose. The image, that is, is not directly linked to survival, unlike a fur pelt or an axe, products with a clear biological purpose. At the same time, as stressed by Terrence Deacon, the artistic gaze implies a doubling, between that which is shown and what this 'means'. But this doubling, in turn, presupposes an even deeper and more radical separation between the representer and the represented, the subject and the object. The anonymous painter who, in a Pleistocene era cave, traced the contours of an animal's shape on the wall was also declaring him- or herself to be different from that animal. He or she was marking a difference by stating: I am not that buffalo. In this sense, a visual representation of an object – and art in general (both representational and non-representational) – attests to the cognitive distance separating the human from the rest of the natural world. I paint; therefore I am not an animal. According to Deacon, this cognitive peculiarity of human art forms is linked to art's role as a symbolic activity: indeed, 'art seems to have a sort of cognitive complementarity to language' (2006: 23). The very same anthropologic machinery can produce a living being who both says 'I' about itself and who is able to produce visual representations of the world (thus 'declaring' its non-congruence with what is represented). In both cases, that machinery produces a subject, separate from the world.

It is especially interesting that one of the earliest – if not the very first – records of this separation was precisely the pictorial represen-tation of nonhuman animals. Thus, human art was born as a distanc-ing from the world in general, and from animality in particular. Appearances notwithstanding, to paint an animal means something completely different than what is believed by the most naïve forms of animalism: it does not express a closeness to the animal, but on the contrary conveys the unbridgeable distance that separates *Homo sapiens* from the living world. As we will see, this means that an 'animal art' (in the human sense of the term) doesn't and cannot exist (Cimatti 2017). Not because animals would lack the 'technical' skills needed to produce artistic objects, but because the nonhuman animal never presents itself as *someone* separate from the world. The animal is always already in the world, and therefore has no interest in *representing* it. This has at least two important consequences: human art, even that which appears to be 'animal friendly', is always underpinned by an unspoken humanistic background. Animal art (an expression whose ambiguity, between art about animals and nonhuman art, is worth preserving (see Baker 2000; Broglio 2011; Aloi 2012a, 2012c; Caffo and Sonzogni 2015)), if it exists at all (and we will soon see that it does not), would be completely different from human art. To deal with animal art, therefore, means trying to imagine a human art that would take animality seriously. Not an art that would merely tap into its inner animality – both as a model (to mimetically reproduce) or more straightforwardly as a material (like the tiger shark in Damien Hirst's 'The Physical Impossibility of Death in the Mind of Someone Living') – but an art that would *become* animal art. The philosophical theme of bestial art, then, is neither that of the representation of the animal nor that of how 'artis-tic' (by human standards) animal art really is. What is at stake in this bestial art is the production of a space of indeterminacy, indifferent to both the identity of the artist and the content of the art itself. As

Giovanni Aloi puts it, discussing a multichannel video installation by British artist Marcus Coates:

> *Dawn Chorus* uses the animal as tool to undo and challenge the human condition . . . through the processes involved in the becoming animal, and the use of the animal as a vehicle, a multitude of departures may effectively present the opportunity, if nothing else, to explore further our human condition, more so than animality, from different and less predictable perspectives. But what about the animal? (Aloi 2011: 9)

Although Agamben, in his *Creation and Anarchy: The Work of Art and the Religion of Capitalism*, does not directly examine animal art, he does describe the – in his opinion utterly necessary – transition from artwork-oriented art (human art) to the becoming-art of the human animal. The centrality of the *artwork* in contemporary aesthetic discourse does nothing but reinforce its dualistic and humanistic character. As long as we keep referring to an artwork, we are talking about someone – the subject-artist – who either produced or created the object. On the contrary, art will have a future only if we rid ourselves of this dualism and concentrate on the space of indeterminacy that opens between artist and artwork. This space, if it exists, is beyond the subject/object distinction. This is a bestial space. For Agamben, the first step is deconstructing what he calls the 'artistic machine', wholly analogous to the 'anthropologic machine' that produces the (linguistic) unity of the human:

> The hypothesis that I would suggest at this point is that *ergon* and *energeia*, work and creative operation, are complementary yet incommunicable notions, which form, with the artist as their middle term, what I propose to call the 'artistic machine' of modernity. And it is not possible, even if it is always attempted, either to separate them or to make them coincide or, even less, to play one off against the other. We are dealing, then, with something like a Borromean knot, which binds together the work, the artist, and the operation; and as in every Borromean knot, it is not possible to release one of the three elements that compose it without irrevocably breaking the entire knot. (Agamben 2019: 8–9)

Artist, artistic operation and work of art. These are the elements of the metaphysical machinery to be deconstructed. Because it is a machinery that continuously engenders separation and dualisms: of subject and object, of image and model, of human and animal. From this point of view, the whole of animal-oriented art does nothing but restate, its intentions notwithstanding, the very same dualism which it aimed to radically undermine. Indeed, in order to overcome the human/animal dualism, it is not enough to put animals into art, or to seek at all costs 'artistic' value in animal productions. On the contrary, the animal is always again trapped in the *animot*, or in what we could call the *animage*, i.e., the (visual) representation of the animal. Concerning oneself with animals does not suffice to relinquish one's anthropocentrism. This is an important point, often neglected by animalist thought. The 'anthropologic machine' – just like the 'artistic' one – cannot be willed out of existence. These are machineries that 'operate' well beyond our intentions or feelings. Even the most animal-friendly human never ceases to be a member of the species *Homo sapiens*. This is an anthropological, rather than ethical, issue. For this reason (as we will see again in the last chapter) the question of animality pertains, more than to *Homo sapiens*, to the human/no-longer-human (or perhaps finally fully human) that is the posthuman.

For Agamben, then, it is necessary to untangle that Borromean knot that binds together, in a suffocating embrace, the artist, the artwork and the operation. Agamben employs an extremely interesting example – the Borromean knot – the same concept used by Lacan to discuss the indissoluble link between the Symbolic, the Imaginary and the Real. For Lacan, the intersection of these three 'registers' defines human life, made of the Symbolic (language and cultural structures), the Imaginary (what humans think and imagine about themselves and the world) and the Real (reality as filtered by both the symbolic and the imaginary). Employing once again von Uexküll's terms, the Borromean knot that binds together the Symbolic, the Real and the Imaginary is our '*Umwelt*'. For Lacan, a philosophically more refined thinker than von Uexküll, *Homo sapiens* coincides, without residue, with its '*Umwelt*'. In his Seminar XXIII, dedicated to Joyce, Lacan essentially poses the same question asked by Agamben: can the Borromean knot be untied? That is to say: can we come to terms with the anthropologic machinery? Is it possible, for a living being who becomes human only at the price of being absorbed and moulded by this machinery, to achieve a position of independence? Once again, this is not an ethical question, because the problem raised by Lacan does not pertain to the freedom of the human subject with respect to the (biopolitical) machineries that engender it. Freedom is an attribute of the subject, but the subject exists only as a by-product of the Symbolic-Imaginary-Real Borromean knot. In this sense, Lacan enjoins the human to free itself from its own freedom. This is why I have said that Agamben's question, like Lacan's, pertains to the posthuman (placed beyond the subject and its freedom) rather than the human (i.e., the ethical field of the subject and its freedom). Although neither Lacan nor Agamben explicitly talks of posthumanism, this – and only this – is their field of interest. For Lacan, the problem is not just that of untying the Borromean knot – since that knot is the human itself – but rather of finding a wholly singular way to inhabit that knot.

The point is to transform – and Heidegger is once again useful to think this transformation – the 'environment' into a 'world' as well as, conversely, to see one's 'world' as an 'environment'. Art is that 'know-how' located in the indeterminate space floating between 'world' and 'environment'. The point is that there is nothing artistic about this 'art', as if there was an artist, creator of artworks (Baker 2013): art, here, is a life without subjects and without artworks. In order to describe this condition Lacan created the term 'sinthome'. A 'sinthome' is a way – by definition unique and ineffable (and for this reason intrinsically artistic) – to cope with the forces that have shaped each human being (the Symbolic, the Real and the Imaginary). Lacan's formulation is paradoxical and contradictory, but could not have been otherwise: '[o]ne is only responsible within the limits of one's *savoir-faire*. What is *savoir-faire*? It is art, artifice, that which endues a remarkable quality to the art of which one is capable, because there is no Other of the Other to perform the Last Judgement' (2016: 47). The 'savoir-faire' – that is, the 'sinthome' – is the non-ethical (for it is an artifice) capacity to act on the 'anthropologic machine'. If being a *sapiens* means being a living being spoken by language, the 'sinthome' as 'art' is the capacity of silencing that language; it means having no need to say anything. This is not a matter of assuming an active position with respect to a previous, and passive, stance: passivity and activity are forms of the subject, and without a subject this venerable dualism disappears. The 'sinthome' as an 'artifice' is the only option available to the human, since 'there is no Other of the Other': there is no transcendence, no ethics or politics – only a life that can be lived.

As we have seen, Agamben too starts from the same injunction: that of finding a way to cope with the Borromean knot, composed by the interlinked functioning of the 'anthropologic' and the 'artistic' machines. The exemplary figure here is clearly Duchamp, who – for this very reason – 'was not working as an artist' but as one who would 'blow up' and 'deactivate the work-artist-operation machine' (Agamben 2019: 12). In Duchamp's ready-mades, 'nothing here comes to presence: not the work, because we are dealing with some industrially produced object of use, nor the artistic operation, because in no way is there *poiēsis* or production, and least of all the artist, because the one who signs the urinal with an ironic false name does not act as artist' (2019: 12). What of the 'artistic machine'? Duchamp's gesture collapses it, and what is left is a urinal, a laughter, the life of a man who turned the lack of artworks into an artwork. Duchamp's 'sinthome' is this artwork without work. In this sense Duchamp is not an artist, and not even a human anymore, precisely because he has completely renounced those constructions (subject, artwork, identity) to which humans are so tenaciously attached. Duchamp is his life, and nothing more. *His* life in a very radical sense: in fact, Duchamp does not 'own' his own life; quite the contrary, such a life does not belong to anyone:

> An artist or poet is not someone who has the potential or faculty to create, which one fine day, through an act of will or by obeying a divine injunction (the will is, in Western culture, the apparatus that permits us to attribute actions and techniques in possession to a subject), he or she decides, like the God of the theologians, to put to work, who knows how or why. (Agamben 2019: 13)

The artist is to the subject as the subject is to law and ethics. Without a subject there is no law; without an artist there is no art. What of art then? And what of those we insist on calling 'artists'? They 'are rather living beings who, in the use and only in the use of their members and of the world that surrounds them, gain experience of themselves and constitute themselves as forms of life' (Agamben 2019: 13).

But what are these 'forms of life' if not – singular and thus unutterable – human ways of living, not as subjects but rather as bodies? In these forms of life, the distinction between the subject – owner of objects – and the objects it produces and owns is collapsed. This is still a human life, because it is the life of a being who self-constituted itself by distinguishing the 'world' from its natural 'environment'; but this is also a being who manages to live a life free from transcendence (since 'there is no Other of the Other'). And what else is this if not a finally *animal* human life?

> Art is only the way in which the anonymous ones we call artists, by maintaining themselves constantly in relation with a practice, seek to constitute their life as a form of life: the life of the painter, of the carpenter, of the architect, of the contrabassist, in which, as in every form-of-life, what is in question is nothing less than their happiness. (Agamben 2019: 13)

The Irreparable

The question of the animal corresponds to the entanglement of the crisis of humanism, the Anthropocene (Barbaj 2015), and happiness and immanence. Animal art is an art that presents itself as an escape route from the 'artistic machine' and therefore from the artist-operation-artwork metaphysical nexus. Such an art does not merely represent animality, or use it to demote the human from its privileged position. Rather, it is animal art in both a subjective sense – i.e., produced by animals – and in an objective sense. This is the art that, using Agamben's words, questions 'happiness' – not that of the artist but of the 'form of life'. Agamben employs the concept of 'form of life' in order to thematise human animality. It is a human life – i.e., the life of a living being who has been processed by the 'anthropologic machine' – and yet it is also a life free from the constraints of the subject/person machinery. An impersonal, artistic life; precisely because art is not the artwork, but the life of life. The aim is '[r]eaching this impersonal zone of indifference, in which every proper name, every copyright, and every claim to originality fade away' (Agamben 2019: 15): a life of immanence, as complete adherence to the world, without a subject, without an object, without private property, laws, names or money. An artistic life then, not in the sense that it would represent or depict the world, but rather a life wherein the human being relinquishes the need to do something to and of the world (and so, *pace* Heidegger, a human life without 'world-forming' beings): 'being a poet means being at the mercy of one's own impotential', which means putting an end to 'the blind and immediate thrust of potential toward the act' in order to prevent 'potential from being resolved and fully exhausted in the act' (Agamben 2019: 19). It is not a matter of doing, but of being; not a matter of self-affirmation with respect to the world but a coincidence with the world: not saying 'I' but rather turning one's voice into a kind of natural song, like the buzzing of bees around the hive. The crucial point of this fully human and fully animal condition is that it 'implies, first and foremost, the deactivation and the abandonment of the apparatus subject/object' (Agamben 2019: 24). This is why the question of animal art is central, because art is the condition where *something* is present – the artistic event – the *author* of which is irrelevant. In art, the world takes the centre stage, in the sense that art is the human way to let the world emerge. For this reason, art is intrinsically human, because only a dualist living being can attempt to overcome that very dualism. Art is the becoming-animal of the human.

In *The Coming Community*, Agamben defines this situation as that of 'the irreparable': when the world and things 'are consigned without remedy to their being-thus, that they are precisely and only their *thus*' (2007: 39). Here the nexus between art and animality is made explicit: things are thus and so, the world is made in such a way that things are here and such. This is, for example, the way of being of a spider, who never wonders why the world is just so: this is the world, and there are no others. On the other hand, the human is that living being who always projects a different (and possible) 'world' beyond the present one, since *Homo sapiens* is the animal of the subject/object dualism. And yet, the human is also the living being who can *deliver* things to their being thus and so. Art, the irreparable, is then the destitution of the human subject, who leaves the world as it is. It is an emptying, from the inside, of human dualism. The 'irreparable' world is the world as lived by the spider. Art is the human way to experience the world as a spider would see it, 'without refuge and nonetheless safe – safe in its being irreparable' (Agamben 2007: 100).

If there is a contemporary artist who is able to display the 'irreparable', it is Romeo Castellucci, the theatre screen player of the Socìetas Raffaello Sanzio (Guidi et al. 2001; Castellucci et al. 2008; Di Matteo 2015), someone who makes of the work on animality one of his most distinctive marks. The beast is the animal that has no relation with language, that was never contaminated by it. The beast is the real of the world. When a beast comes onto the stage, it is not entering the scene like an actor. The beast does not play, does not represent, does not allude to anything. From the spectator's point of view, the beast is a pure tautology: the beast is the beast, yet only from the spectator's standpoint, i.e., from that of the *animal fictivus*. In Romeo Castellucci's theatre, the beast is not a metaphor for something else: for example instinct, animality or savage nature. If that was the case, the beast would still be a fictional one, a symbol. On the contrary, the beast – like the bull in *Moses and Aaron* (from the unfinished opera by Arnold Schoenberg, represented at the Paris Opéra in 2015) – is *a bull*, and nothing more. This is why the Socìetas' theatre is iconoclastic, because it refuses any image, any symbolism and any word.

The point – and herein lies the idea of an iconoclastic theatre – is that the beast is what it is precisely because it *neither* wants *nor* knows itself to be one. Only the non-beast can see a beast. The beast, in virtue of its position before language, is also placed before the consciousness (as well as the unconsciousness) of knowing (as well as of not knowing). To be a beast means nothing more than to be *this* beast – to be the irreparability of bestial being. Being a beast is to be before meaning and intelligence, but also before meaninglessness and stupidity (Kubiak 2012; Chaudhuri 2017). This is why the beast breaks, once and for all, the representational machinery, because the beast – literally – has no meaning. Indeed, according to Romeo Castellucci: 'the work with animals never aims at a particular goal, result. They do not play any specific role, neither are they decoration. They are pure presence, introducing a contradiction, because they are the point in which the very representation-fiction collapses. After all, animals do not pretend' (Semenowicz 2016: 177). The beast breaks the representational and hermeneutic spell, and simply offers the world as world, since it 'operates beyond the linguistic sphere' (Castellucci 2000: 24). But where is the beast located? Before or beyond language? Beyond language as far as the beast – and its simple being bestial – is concerned; and beyond language for the spectator – the talking animal – who, in the beast, sees not just the absolute lack of meaning of his or her own existence, but also the pointless becoming of representation and therefore of language. Indeed, the beast on stage is the becoming-thing of language, and therefore of the actor – the voice of language on the scene (Cimatti 2018). The beast is, then, the beyond of language. In fact, talking about his *Oresteia*, Castellucci observes that:

> This *Oresteia* wants to fall into an infantile movement of *catabasis*, a mysterian movement where the real world alludes to theatre, where language must necessarily be reborn through its own death, traversing things, animals, beings, and place, divesting itself of its codified royalty Language rests on the same level as the elements. It becomes elementary, something unnameable, because names withdraw themselves. (Guidi et al. 2001: 156–7)

What is at stake for the beast, then, is language. Romeo Castellucci's theatre is a continual attempt to come to terms – *within* language – *with* language (as well as *within* theatre *with* theatre). The point is that language is a force that overpowers the speaker. As we have seen in the previous chapters, the paradigmatic example of this over-powering is the dualism between subject/person and body. From the moment a living being first says 'I' it affirms its own lordship over the body which, from that moment onwards, will be *its* body. The person, indeed, is nothing but the owner of the body ('bare life'). One says, naively, that the body speaks; but it speaks like the ventriloquist's puppet does, for its voice is really the voice of the master. Nobody has yet ever heard the non-linguistic voice of the body. This would be an absolute voice, non-semantic, non-representative and – precisely – non-linguistic. Such a voice, even if it could be heard, would not be understood: it would be a purely bestial voice. Romeo Castellucci's theatre seeks this voice, because the human body only hears – and, crucially, *can* only hear – meaningful voices. The voice of the body is like the sound of things, the wind through tree branches, the squeal of breaking tyres, the rhythmic rumble of a combustion engine. The voice of the body is, like the beast itself, a *thing* of the world (Bennett 2010). In this sense the beast announces the becoming-matter and becoming-thing of the actor. Castellucci, then, seeks the corruption of language within language, i.e., its interminable fading away:

> My starting point is that art is not pure. Nobody will ever convince me that art sets the human free. Art's soteriology seems to me nothing more than a marketplace rumour. For me, art assumes – needs to assume – its corrupting condition. Art is corrupt, but this is not simply a negative term; all of art's beauty consists in its corruption, in its awareness of corruption. The 'real' word, the poetic word, has no meaning in theatre. It has no meaning because language, the word, is always without me: there is no more adherence to the body. Speaking is not a pleasant experience, and it never was. Words always express a separation, a coldness. While speaking, I am not myself. It is not my place: it is unknown to me. While I speak, I am not there; and I am therefore assuming language in its fullness, its over-abundance, and proceeding into rhetoric. Rhetoric consciously takes upon itself its own corruption and shamelessly exploits the means of the word, of the reformulation of a language. . . . But what I wanted was to oppose, on the one hand, rhetorical language – far from our experience – and on the other the concreteness and the truth of a body. (Guidi et al. 2001: 276–7)

The beast is to the theatre as language (rhetoric, in Castellucci's words) is to the body, because 'while speaking I am not myself', i.e., I am not the animal irreparability of the body. The aim is to bring this body to the forefront, but not simply to – once again – let it speak. On the contrary, the goal is to expose it as a body-thing, as matter, as an 'elementary' entity. The body as we know it is nothing but the other of the person, the body as the remainder of the word, mind's possession, non-person, 'bare life'. The body of the beast, on the other hand – a body that was never split – is a thoroughly exemplary body, a pure and mute body that has nothing to say, and has no use for meaning. The beast, then, is the thing, the speaking body that, finally and for the first time, becomes thing and matter. We can thus explain Romeo Castellucci's hostility towards the actor/performer. The actor, like the beast, must become a thing, an appendix of the stage. The actor needs to literally become a 'machinic assemblage' as Deleuze and Guattari put it in *A Thousand Plateaus*. In fact, according to Castellucci, the actor is nothing but a stage element:

> The actor is no longer he or she who acts, but is rather acted upon by the stage. The actor knows how to return to and merge with the stage, suspended thanks to the incredible use of his or her voice and by means of the homeopathic effect of the assumption of an extraneous element: language. The actor is the point of maximal crisis of language. (Guidi et al. 2001: 81)

The actor, like the beast, is the becoming-thing of the theatre, of representation, and ultimately of language: 'a good theatrical piece can be condensed into an image, that of an organism, of an animal' (Guidi et al. 2001: 270). Thus we can grasp the sense – which is an absolute non-sense – of the presence of beasts in Castellucci's theatre.

It is not an allegory, the usual and harmless allusion to the natural, to an alleged bodily innocence. The beast is a *thing*. A thing that can be reached starting from theatre. The beast is a representation that stops representing, thus showing its naked material reality. The beast is the real of the theatre, a real that can *show* itself only by inverting the rhetorical artificiality of theatre into its opposite. The real, like the beast, is not before representation. On the contrary, the real of the theatre can only be announced through the artificial machine of the representation. That is because theatre, since its inception, is representation and therefore dualism, gaze and spectacle, mind and body, sense and meaning. Theatre, for Castellucci, is the art of reversing the theatrical machinery upon itself. In the end (but also at the beginning) of this path, there is the beast. It can now be understood how the theatrical beast is the exact opposite of the irruption of the natural on the scene. The beast is the most extraordinary and elaborate technical artifice there can be to reverse the artificial procedure of theatre. For this reason, it is possible to speak of the 'animal's super-technique', because the animal does not know (for the beast is precisely this radical lack of consciousness) any 'fear of making mistakes' (Guidi et al. 2001: 270).

For Romeo Castellucci the beast becomes the prototype of the actor.[1] Not because the actor should be a docile instrument at the mercy of the director's theatrical inventions. The point is rather that the actor must become, like the beast, a thing – to be like the stage, or the mechanical devices used in theatre. Through Castellucci's theatre there unfolds a single movement: bestial, machinic and material. At the same time, this operation of maximal artificiality turns into its opposite, the maximal bodily adherence to the stage. But the actor is such only insofar as they renounce their actorial and expressive ambitions:

> I don't need technology, because the paradoxical beauty of my alienation sets me free, finally, through the most powerful affirmation of the body. Sacrifice has nothing to do with it. It is a matter of indifference. The cold indifference of any real beauty. A super-technique cannot be acquired; it is there since our very first step. Super-technique is, therefore, a *call*. This is no mysticism: it is rather a turn towards the cavity of an exact matrix. As a destiny. The body – animal, thing, actor – that is called finds its adherence with the stage far before all the technique's efforts, because it is exposed *in* it. (Guidi et al. 2001: 87)

This is what matters when the beast makes its appearance: bodies and things – actors or animals. The bestial theatre is the theatre of bodies 'as that which eludes any attempt at representation' (Di Matteo 2015: 11). It is a theatre of bodies in this radical sense of the body, and not merely a theatre of the lived body of phenomenology (a lived and meaningful body, but still too humanist), nor of the natural body (there is no Nature without Artifice), nor of the carnal body – since 'flesh' remains too vitalist, too romantic a name. No, the body of the bestial theatre is the *thing*-body, a body of absolute immanence. Theatre, for Castellucci, is art artificially producing – through representation, and therefore by means of the dualism of the sign – its own erasure. The beast as a radical indistinction between mind and matter, meaning and referent, form and content. The beast is located beyond the actor, the person, the gesture and the voice. It is beyond the body itself. The beast is the *real*, the only real accessible to the human being, the real of representation. Castellucci's theatre – like that of Carmelo Bene, according to Deleuze – is a subtractive theatre that aims to reach the thing, the bestial matter:

> it isn't an anti-theatre, a theatre-in-the-theatre, or a theatre that negates theatre. . . . It is an altogether more precise operation: we begin with subtracting, detracting all that constitutes an element of power, in language

and in gestures, in the representation and in the represented. This cannot even be called a negative operation, since it begets and puts into motion a large number of positive processes. Structure is removed, because it is the synchronic mark, the set of all invariant relations. The constants are removed too, along with stable or stabilizing elements, for they belong to the major use. The text is amputated, because the text is like the dominion of language over the word, and it still attests an invariance or a homogeneity. Dialogue is suppressed, because dialogue transmits to the word the elements of power, and allows its circulation. . . . Enunciation is removed as well, along with action. . . . What is left? Everything is left, but in a new light, with new sounds, new gestures. (Deleuze, in Bene and Deleuze 2012: 97–8)

Everything is removed in order to reach the essential, which was obscured from sight by all the rest – the real. This is why, in the end, 'everything is left', because the real *is everything*. The beast, *qua* real of the representation, takes theatre beyond itself, i.e., pushes language beyond sense. And for this reason, it also takes it beyond the voice – a voice that can find its place, in theatre, only as long as it loses every sacrality, every carnal subjectivity, every actorial complacency. The voice of the beast is not beautiful, nor mesmerising. The voice is either bestial or the usual innocuous, expressive – and therefore meaningful – sound. The beast is the becoming-thing of theatre. The beast is the irreparable.

Without Work

Let us return to the gesture that sparked modern art (an explosion that keeps exploding), Duchamp's urinal. This operation could 'work' because what can be 'seen' in that object is not just its function, but also the possibility of having no function at all. Duchamp, that is, plays on the hesitation that occurs when we realise that an 'environment' is also a 'world', and that a 'world' is always in the process of decaying into an 'environment'. However, it is now worth asking ourselves: what would a cat see, if facing that very ready-made object? It is here, rather than in the more or less convincing attempts to show that even nonhuman animals are *somehow* capable of having artistic experiences (Dissanayake 2015; Renoult 2016), that the problem of bestial art resides. Whether or not human artistic activity has its biological origin in that of animals should not be an issue. On the one hand, it is in some way obviously the case, but on the other it is far from clear in which sense these activities tell us something meaningful about human art. Real or imagined similarities between human and nonhuman art (pretending we do not know that human art *in general* does not exist) notwithstanding, the – stunningly puzzling – fact remains that nonhuman animals do not produce art in the same way that humans do:

> Why don't cats paint? . . . Indeed, why don't any other species engage in quite this form of behavior or even seem to appreciate its products? And why is it so nearly universal in some form in humans if it is so culture-dependent and culture-bound? And, of course, why do these activities produce the special kinds of experiences that they do, which can be both powerful and seriously sought after? (Deacon 2006: 24)

The truth is not only that cats do not paint, but also that they seem to have a very different way of observing what we consider paintings (i.e., images). Let us go back to the urinal. What happens when someone observes it outside of a contemporary art museum, as for example in the men's toilet in a cinema? Will this person see the *same* object that can be admired in the museum, or something different? And if, as seems to be the case, he or she sees something different – at least in the sense of seeing it *otherwise* – what is properly *seen*? What lurks in this question is a well-known philo-sophical issue: when something is seen, is the visual act unitary (so that, for example, we see a 'urinal' or the 'ready-made') or is it – at least in principle – divided into two moments: a purely receptive and epistemically 'neutral' (sensation) stimulation of the eye by the light bouncing off the object, and a (perceptual) moment consisting in some kind of 'interpretation' broadly conceived (albeit implicit and unconscious) of what was given in the first moment? What is at stake here? In the first case, seeing would be a 'simple' act, requiring neither conceptual knowledge nor the possession of language: this is what Dretske (1969: 79) simply calls 'seeing', i.e., a 'non-epistemic seeing', a way of seeing that perhaps we share with cats. But in the second case, seeing would always be a 'seeing as'. This is the kind of seeing that takes place when something defined is seen (*this* or *that*), even when we are not able to explicitly state *what* we are seeing. Indeed, even in this case an 'object' (for example) is seen, and this already implies a 'seeing as' – we are seeing something *as an object*. In this case then, 'seeing as' is a seeing linked to the way in which the words of our language describe the world – even if we are not aware of it. 'Seeing as' means seeing on the grounds of a certain 'descrip-tion' of what we are seeing: 'seeing as' is mediated and indirect (Marr

1982; Rock 1997). In this sense, 'seeing as' is strictly connected to language and linguistically articulated concepts. In the first case, conversely, the perceptual process is independent from language, which intervenes – if at all – only at a later stage. In this case there is first a 'seeing' (Michaels and Carello 1981) and then, later, a 'seeing as'. So, perception and the language/conceptual system would be separate.

What does this have to do with the problem of art, and animal art in particular? What is especially relevant here is the case of the perception of images, i.e., of (iconic) *signs* that 'send to' something else. Let us consider, for example, a still life by Cézanne. How can we see a certain visual object as an 'image' that 'represents' a carafe next to some apples and oranges on a white tablecloth? In order to see something as an 'image', a 'seeing as' is always necessary. But this entails that someone lacking language and a conceptual system would be unable to see an image *as an image*, i.e., as a visual representation of something. So, our question becomes: do nonhuman animals see images (or better, what we consider to be images (see Weisman and Spetch 2010)) *as* images? The case of nonhuman animals is interesting because we can be reasonably certain that in their cognitive world language (in the human sense of language) plays, at best, a marginal role. Therefore, if 'seeing as' can also be found in nonhuman animals, it follows that there is no necessary link between art and language. Indeed, much of what we call art is composed by images, so the question of 'seeing as' in nonhuman animals can be used to confirm – or disprove – the art-language link.

In a famous experiment (see Watanabe et al. 1995) it was demonstrated how pigeons are able – after a period of training – to tell Claude Monet's works apart from those of Pablo Picasso. The pigeons were given a reward when, asked to choose between the reproductions of Monet's or Picasso's paintings, they chose the 'right' one, i.e., the one assigned to the group they were part of (one group was rewarded with food when 'choosing' Monet; the other when 'choosing' Picasso). What does this experiment really demonstrate? That a nonhuman animal is able to construct classes of percepts: one including those pictures that, *according to the experimenters*, are reproductions of Monet's paintings, while another including reproductions of Picasso's. It certainly does not demonstrate that pigeons have considered what they saw to be images. What they probably saw – from their point of view – are complex configurations of visual stimuli, that they rapidly learnt to classify, i.e., to tell apart. But the problem was not that of establishing whether or not nonhuman animals are able to categorise perceptual stimuli, but rather that of figuring out if they are able to see a certain visual pattern *as* an image. From this point of view, Arthur Danto fails to appreciate the problem: 'pictures as such are not like propositions, nor can we speak of a pictorial language, as Wittgenstein endeavored to do in his *Tractatus*, since animals demonstrably have pictorial competence while animal propositional – or sentential – competence remains undemonstrated' (Danto 1992: 20). It is a mistake to assign a 'pictorial competence' to pigeons, since what they actually see are not pictorial representations, but visual stimuli, no different from any other visual stimulus: it is actually 'a serious error to assume that pigeons see pictures as representations of places and objects in the world' (Weisman and Spetch 2010: 118).

The crucial point is that a visual image *represents* – according to a particular system of transformations and correspondences, so in a way that is neither immediate nor 'natural' – what it reproduces. The image is an (iconic) *sign* for what it represents: 'to understand pictures as pictures, it is necessary to mentally represent the concrete object itself (i.e., the picture) and its abstract relation to what it stands for' (Parron et al. 2008: 351). That a human being, raised in a linguistic and symbolic environment, is able to see the image of a three-dimensional event in a two-dimensional visual surface is not surprising. But that is so precisely because *Homo sapiens* has always had commerce with language, i.e., with a representational system. What happens in the case of an animal with no symbolic experience? In the experiment conducted by Parron and her colleagues, a group of fifty-five baboons – who had never had any contact with pictures, videos or paintings – were presented with a choice: whether to grasp a real banana slice or a picture of a banana slice. The result is clear: in many cases 'baboons did not process the pictures as representations, but rather mistook the real piece of banana and their depiction' (Parron et al. 2008: 355); indeed, what often happened was that 'a large number of baboons ate the banana pictures', confirming that, for the animal, the image is *not* at all an image, but *the thing itself*. To further insist on the non-natural character of images, it should be noted how something similar happens with young human beings. In an experiment conducted with nine-month-old children, it was observed how these infants try to suckle on pictures that depict a baby bottle (DeLoache 2004: 68), just as if they were the real thing. This goes to prove that those images are actually not yet seen *as* images, i.e., as signs (see Fagot 2000; Fagot et al. 2010). In general, this kind of experimental research does not prove the existence, in nonhuman animals, of the ability to 'see as' an image something that, to an adult of the human species, clearly appears to be an image. In the case of the chimp, the most studied animal in this respect:

> the ability of chimpanzees to recognize pictures is not genetically pro-grammed, but should be acquired as a skill after birth. This is related to the findings that chimpanzees did not draw any representational images . . . It may not be reasonable to expect chimpanzees to recognize repre-sentational images because they do not draw representational images themselves. (Tanaka 2007: 178)

Yet another way to verify the linguistic competence of nonhu-man animals is through images produced by the animals themselves (Morris 1962). Morris observes that – at least in the case of the chimp called 'Congo', the main subject of his study – 'paintings' produced by this animal were the result of a series of radial gestures, having as an approximate centre the body of the 'painter', which marked the contours of a kind of 'owned' space. Essentially, according to Morris, these would not be images at all, but rather the repetition of the gestures performed by a chimp preparing its nest on a tree where it has decided to spend the night. This hypothesis is as good as any, but what seems to characterise these kinds of objects is that they never seem to have a representational role (see Smith 1973; Boysen et al. 1987; Saito et al. 2014). These are gestures, not representations. Without denying the performative value of images, the point is that an image is an *image* only insofar as it is a *sign* for something else.

Finally, another method for exploring the capacity of nonhuman animals to see something as an image is that of their much-debated ability to 'recognise' themselves in a mirror (see Taylor Parker et al. 1994; Guenther 2017). At the source of this debate, still raging today, there is Gallup's infamous experiment, which we have already encountered in the Introduction. In a recent version of the same experiment, an elephant observes in a mirror a white cross above its right eye (Plotnik et al. 2009). The reflected image is a sign, something that stands for something else. It therefore presupposes the existence – logical before factual – of an 'original' (what is reproduced by the image) and a 'copy' (the reproduction of the original). Now, this dualism is problematic in the case of nonhuman animals. In order to see in the 'image' something else besides what the image ostensibly shows, keen eyes do not suffice. The fact that the elephant touches the cross it sees in the mirror with the tip of its trunk does not at all imply that he sees it as a *reproduction* of an 'original', located else-where (in this case, on 'its' body). There is no reason to suppose that the elephant – or the chimp in Gallup's original experiment – thinks of itself as an object (or, even less so, as a subject) separate from the rest of the world, nor is there any reason to think that it sees, in the reflected image, an image *of something*. An image is not an image in itself, but only if it is observed *as an image*. The elephant has learnt that there is a way to reach an otherwise invisible part of its 'own' body by means of the mirror. That is all. Moreover, to see a mirror as a 'mirror' – i.e., a device that reflects that which stands before it – it is necessary to *already* possess the concept of 'image'. The mirror alone, therefore, does not explain what an image could be. On the contrary, one must already know what an image is in order to see a mirror *as* a 'mirror'. Clearly, here we are not questioning the elephant's intelligence (animals, in their own way, are all equally intelligent (Macphail 1987)), but rather the way of seeing the world of an animal that has no idea of the distinction between copy and original, i.e., of the dualism between sign and reference. Language is such a dualism, between word and reference, between proposition and world.

What does this long (and somewhat depressing) series of empirical analyses really show? Many different things. First of all – but this is something we have encountered many times before – it shows that if philosophy is obsessed with animals, the same is true (and probably more so) in the case of science. In the course of all these experiments it never occurred to anyone to ask what the animal might *feel* about this complex experimental apparatus (Marchesini 2016). The animal is a challenge, for the philosopher as much as for the ethologist: 'at the limit of our perception we encounter the friction and opacity of other ways of being that remain inaccessible to us' (Broglio 2011: 23). Actually, what these experiments show is not so much the fact that animals don't see images as images, but rather that their way of seeing the world is utterly *different* from ours. Ours is a world that speaks (the 'seeing as'); theirs is a world that has nothing to say, and that they love precisely because of its silence. For humans seeing is a mode of saying, and vice versa: '[t]he only plausible hypothesis seems to be this: perception and language condition each other, one presup-poses the other, and they constitute a *strict correlation*' (Garroni 2005: 41). On the contrary, animals see the world without the need to utter it. Their seeing is not a kind of saying. And this – it should be clear by now – is not a lack or a deficiency. On the contrary, it is the animal's greatest resource. That is because animals, unlike humans, are not frightened by the silence of the world. Consequently, while human art *says* and *produces* something, animal art neither says nor produces anything. The nonhuman animal is *without craft*.

The animal is an artist, but not because it produces an artistic 'object'. Let us take the famous case of the satin bowerbird (*Ptilonorhynchus violaceus*), which builds complex and garish bowers, composed of all sorts of objects, from whatever it finds – fruits, berries, mushrooms, pieces of aluminium foil, or plastic fragments, which are sometimes coloured with natural pigments by means of a special 'brush' kept in its beak (see Collias and Collias 1984) – in order to attract the females during mating season. Does this bird create an *artwork*? In truth, this 'object' has no value in itself. On the contrary, it is functional within the 'love life' of the artist-animal; the bower it builds is not an object it owns, but its way of using the world, an entirely temporary use at that. The movement of life does not terminate in the (art)work; rather, the satin bower-bird's bower is its becoming-art, becoming-love, becoming-colour. For this reason, then, the artist-animal is the ultimate (or the first) figure of the human, because the animal-artist, finally, manages to use the world without appropriating it, to be an absolutely singular thing without being someone, and to live the world's immanence. According to Agamben, this is the life lived according to the inhuman – indeed, animal – Franciscan rule:

> The specific eschatological character of the Franciscan message is not expressed in a new doctrine, but in a form of life through which the very life of Christ is made newly present in the world to bring to completion, not the historical meaning of the 'person' in the economy of salvation, so much as his life as such. The Franciscan form of life is, in this sense, the end of all lives (*finis omnium vitarum*), the final modus, after which the manifold historical dispensation of *modi vivendi* is no longer possible. The 'highest poverty,' with its use of things, is the form-of-life that begins when all the West's forms of life have reached their historical consummation. (Agamben 2013: 143)

Note

1. As the poet and *Teatro Valdoca*'s screenwriter Mariangela Gualtieri writes: 'I believe that the actor should have as large a soul as that of an animal. A silent void in the middle, like the animal. I believe that no virtuoso will ever touch a heart if not moving from the splendour, or the

mud, of this animal soul. And technique can be fatal for such a soul. Just as the lack of technique can be' (2018: n.p.). Human animality is always subhuman and superhuman, both before and after the human. The role of 'technique' is fundamental: it takes effort to 'become-animal'. In this sense acting is a possible field of experimentation of human animality.

7

Becoming-animal

The animal is a transformation disguised as an object or being.

(Valèry 2010: 160)

The Indian and the Horse

We never seem to manage to consider animals, including and perhaps most of all those we hold captive in scientific laboratories (Hess 2008), as simple and real living beings. We look at them, but we cannot truly see them for what they are (animality is invisible, by definition; *Homo sapiens* is human precisely because it cannot see the animal).

In front of us, for example, there is a dog: consider the case of Princess Marie Bonaparte – Freud's psychoanalyst friend – and her famous Topsy, an exemplar of the Chow-Chow breed. Her beloved Topsy is actually nothing but a substitute, replacing her son and daughter who have left the family house. But Topsy is also a 'talisman', since it bars 'the entrance of [her] room to a worse ill, and even to death' (Bonaparte 1994: 79). Topsy, that is, is a symbol – it is other than itself, beyond itself. A living being that cannot just be the life it is, is nothing but a substitute bound to disappoint – such as when Topsy, after a period of sickness, prefers to run with Bonaparte's youngest daughter, or even with the maid. Freud's reply, however, is surprising, because he does not merely restate the allegorical character of the animal, but takes it a step further: 'Actually', he writes, 'the reasons why one might love an animal with such a singular intensity . . . are sympathy without ambivalence, the simplification of life, the beauty of a self-completed existence' (Freud, unpublished; my translation). So far, however, the human's point of view is still privileged, and the dog plays a secondary and exemplary role. But there is more, Freud adds, for there is a 'feeling of intimate kinship, of indubitable affinity'. Now, the dog is not merely a sign, it is once again a living being of flesh and blood, with its own intrinsic worth, and with whom it is possible to establish a somewhat egalitarian relationship: 'often, while petting Jofi [Freud's dog] I caught myself humming a melody that I, an absolutely non-musical man, had to recognize as the aria of friendship from *Don Juan*' (Freud, unpublished). Freud – the man who, as we have seen in the case of the Wolfman, never speaks of animals as animals – finds himself humming (music does not explain anything, music is not a language or form of reasoning): it is Freud's own body which takes pleasure in spending time with Jofi, not his analytical mind always seeking a reason for any event, including his affection for a dog. Psychoanalysis notwithstanding, the body of Jofi is still a body, and we all have to come to terms with such a body, Freud included. He reiterates this in another letter – this too addressed to a woman, Lou Salomè – wherein he confesses how much he misses another dog Lün, Jofi's sister, which recently died: 'I miss her now', Freud writes 'almost as much as my cigar' (Freud and Salomè 1972: 188) – which he was forbidden to smoke after having been diagnosed with mouth cancer. The parallel might seem outrageous: a dog like a cigar. And yet here Freud – the atheist materialist – is talking about the body, and nothing is more important than the body: something that no one comprehends better than a cancer patient. Here, life itself is at stake – its meaning is not in question any more. A dog, then, is a body, and that of the great Freud himself is nothing but a body as well – and a cigar is a sort of body too. All of a sudden, Heidegger's careful (and gatekeeping) tripartition – 'worldless' stone, 'poor in world' animal and 'world-forming' human – seems to collapse under its own ponderous weight. A cigar, a dog, a man. Granted, the Freud who composed the famous epigram 'where the Id was, there the Ego shall be' (*Wo Es war, soll Ich warden*) has no truck with the desire to erase all borders, to confound the human with the animal, the I and the Id. And yet, in his discussion of his dogs, a view onto a completely different way of considering the body – something that perhaps Freud never explored – seems to be revealed.

This is because the problem of animality is the problem of the body and of how to set it free from the anthropologic machine's control, because '*the* difference' between human and animal 'has no meaning' (Despret and Porcher 2007: 29). Here, rather, we are interested in the complex and murky means through which a body becomes something different from that which it is, when essences and identities renounce their narcissistic pride. Once again, it is Kafka who can guide us on this path, just as he previously showed us the violence of becoming-human. Indeed, becoming-animal is a wholly different affair than becoming-human. While the latter is a process that engenders a subject – and therefore an 'I' and a body, separate from each other – becoming-animal is a movement that proceeds beyond subjectivisation, beyond language (because the 'I' and language proceed in lockstep), and so beyond 'bare life'. Becoming-animal should not be understood as a process of animalisation, akin to a 'going back' to an animal condition. There is really no animal condition to return to, for the animality of becoming-animal is in the future rather than the past, it is to be built rather than recovered. Kafka's short story 'The Wish to be a Red Indian' is as short as it is incisive:

> If one were only an Indian, instantly alert, and on a racing horse, leaning against the wind, kept on quivering jerkily over the quivering ground, until one shed one's spurs, for there needed no spurs, threw away the reins, for there needed no reins, and hardly saw that the land before one was smoothly shorn heath when horse's neck and head would be already gone. (Kafka 1979: 242)

The Indian is not *on* the horse, it is not an 'I' commanding and guiding the beast's body – the horse recklessly galloping on the prairie. The horse's 'neck and head would be already gone' because there is no longer a horse and an Indian; there is a running horse-Indian, a becoming-horse that knows no subject and no object, no rider and ridden, no guide and guided. This short story is not an allegory for freedom, or for the encounter between human and animal. Rather, it plays on the fact of their indistinction: the Indian-horse riding until 'one shed one's spurs', where asking who this 'one' might be utterly misses the point. Becoming-animal is precisely beyond any question around the self, its limits, and what sets it apart from the non-self. Becoming-animal means nothing more than the dissolution of this question. Not because the answer would be uninteresting, but because there is no longer anyone who can pose it. Becoming-animal, in this sense, is not an ethical act, and even less so a political one (for both ethics and politics need a subject). Rather it is the relinquishment of the venerable juridical-religious figure of the person: 'becoming animal does not consist in playing an animal or imitating an animal, it is clear that the human being does not "really" become an animal any more than the animal "really" becomes something else. Becoming produces nothing other than itself. (Deleuze and Guattari 1987: 238). Becoming-animal is the simple fullness of becoming, i.e., the overcoming of identities that always again territorialise themselves. That is because, in becoming-animal, '[w]hat is real is the becoming itself, the block of becoming, not the supposedly fixed terms through which that which becomes passes' (Deleuze and Guattari 1987: 238).

D. H. Lawrence's novella *St. Mawr* (1925) tells the interwoven story of a couple – she American, him Australian – taking place in the immediate aftermath of the First World War. Theirs is a successful existence: he is a promising painter, she is a wealthy young woman still looking for her calling. The man is very attracted by social life, while the woman – Lou – struggles to find it equally alluring even while having no particular objection towards it, or at least until she gifts a horse to her husband. St. Mawr is a beautiful stallion with a difficult temper that has caused more than one accident to its previous owners. The horse's presence radically changes Lou's perspective, and the woman gradually develops a clearer insight into her own existence. St. Mawr is really not a bad animal, he simply refuses to accept the life that is forced upon him. This is how Lou realises that another life is possible. And she realises it precisely because St. Mawr stubbornly and obtusely refuses to be simply what humans expect him to be: a good horse making his owners look good. 'Isn't it extraordinary', a friend says to Lou, talking about the horse who has just unsaddled her husband, 'that you never get a *really*, perfectly satisfactory animal! There's always something wrong. And in men too. Isn't it curious? There's always something – something wrong – or something missing. Why is it?' (Lawrence 2006: 146). Lou sees something about herself in the horse's obtuse and headstrong tenacity, speaking of her own dissatisfaction and unease. It should be noted that, in this tale, St. Mawr is not an allegory – it is a horse with a temper, just that and nothing more. It is not the symbol of a natural and wild life, because Lou immediately realises that this would not be a plausible path for her. The point is not to return to a primordial existence (which never was) but rather to find a way to be the body one is – the body of the speaking animal – while being also an *animal* body. The animality of becoming-animal is not behind us, but in front of our eyes. What her friend deems to be 'wrong' in St. Mawr, just as 'in men', is precisely what Lou seeks to reach and to protect. The horse's 'great animal sadness' (2006: 103) really represents his hope, and it will become – as the story unfolds – Lou's as well.

The first step is taken when Lou realises that the stallion is not a horse, i.e., an exemplar of the species *Equus caballus*: 'Just think of St. Mawr!' Lou says to her mother, 'I've thought so much about him. We call him an animal, but we never know what it means. He seems a far greater mystery to me, than a clever man. He's a horse. Why can't one say in the same way, of a man: *He's a man?* There seems no mystery in being a man. But there is a terrible mystery in St. Mawr' (2006: 79–80). The 'mystery' is *this* horse with his peculiar temper – at the same time both obedient and violent – and his reddish coat, so sensitive and quivering. We lack the words to describe this individuality (and the eyes to see it), but on the other hand we know very well what 'man' is. And so, an individual man, *this* flesh and bone man right here, disappears – just like *this* horse disappears, eclipsed by the 'horse' – and all that is left is a generic and indistinct 'world-forming' creature. St. Mawr does not accept this, and he rebels against it in his own way: kicking, shaking his head and refusing the company of those docile horses which, instead, quietly stand in their small stables, munching hay. St. Mawr awakens Lou to this utterly unthinkable possibility, flying in the face of our usual preoccupation of getting 'a perfectly satisfactory animal'. The stallion, quite simply, has no intention of being 'satisfactory', i.e., he does not want to be a 'horse'. This is what fascinates Lou: St. Mawr's radical individuality. Not the 'call of the wild' nor an alleged primordial natural condition for which she has no use. She very clearly explains it to her mother who, at first, does not understand the daughter's agitation:

> 'And don't misunderstand me mother. I don't want to be an animal like a horse or a cat or a lioness, though they all fascinate me, the way they get their life *straight*, not from a lot of old tanks, as we do. I don't admire the cave man, and that sort of thing. But think mother, if we could get our lives straight from the source, as the animals do, and still be ourselves.' (Lawrence 2006: 81)

What Lou feels to be lacking from her life is the fullness of animal life, i.e., their getting 'their life straight'. This fullness entails an existence that stays anchored to things, unencumbered with a transcendence that would distance and distract: '[w]hy isn't men's thinking quick like fire mother? Why is it so slow, so dead, so deadly dull?' (2006: 81). Lou does not want to renounce her humanity in order to turn into a 'horse or a cat or a lioness'. The adjective *sapiens* cannot be freely removed from *Homo sapiens*. It is not a matter of divesting one's role as *Homo sapiens*, but rather of trying to live in a way that approaches that of animals. Lou's mother, still puzzled, asks: 'What do you want Lou? You *do* want the cave man, who'll knock you on the head with a club' (2006: 81). Lou's reply is clear, for it is obvious that she desires something completely different:

'Don't be silly mother. That's much more your subconscious line, you admirer of Mind – I don't consider the cave man is a real human being. He's a brute, a degenerate. A pure animal man would be as lovely as a deer or a leopard, burning like a flame fed straight from underneath. And he'd be part of the unseen, like a mouse is, even. And he'd never cease to wonder, he'd breathe silence and unseen wonder, as the partridges do, running in the stubble. He'd be all the animals in turn, instead of one, fixed, automatic thing, which he is now, grinding on the nerves – Ah no, mother, I want the wonder back again, or I shall die.' (2006: 82)

Now, the condition of 'wonder' consists in one's being exposed to sensible experience in an absolutely radical manner. This is the theme of the 'details' explored by Temple Grandin. In order to *see* a detail, one should be able to see this tree right here and right now, without being distracted by the sight of the 'forest'; in this sense, a detail is no longer a 'detail', just because there is no longer a 'whole' to which the details would belong. It is no coincidence that even for Lawrence the theme of wonder interweaves with that of language: the language of a 'real human being' who is still to appear (the becoming-animal of the human), will be '[a] world dark and still, where language never ruffled the growing leaves and seared their edges like a bad wind' (2006: 124). Here, even a leaf is something to be observed for what it is – its colour, texture, smell and shape, where every detail attracts our attention. In such a world, a leaf is no longer a LEAF.

What is at stake in becoming-animal, then, is the experimentation of a humanity that would not be trapped in the cage of the subject – that of the 'I' and the 'you', of the 'I' over here and everything else over there (the world as object). This reminds us of Kafka's desire to become Indian-horse: not a horse serving the human nor a human turned into a horse. It is a longing for the overcoming of the limits of our individuality, for becoming flux and prairie and experiencing a new form of life. This is nothing but the desire felt by those who are burdened by the weight of their own individuality, as well as that of others. It is not surprising, then, that one of the most effective descriptions of this desire can be found in Temple Grandin's work:

Horseback riding was joyous for me. I can remember being on a horse sometimes and we'd gallop in the pasture and that was such a big thrill. . . . I remember what it looked like, the trees whizzing by; I remember that really well to this day. Riding becomes instinctual after a while; a good rider and his horse are a team. It's not a one-way relationship, either; it's not just the human relating to the horse and telling him what to do. (Grandin and Johnson 2005: 6)

Becoming-horse and becoming-prairie – without any fear of losing one's 'I' – to completely coincide with the flux of the riding, getting one's life 'straight' as Lou longed for: this is the animality of the human, a project for the future rather than a past to be restored:

> Finally one day I decided to just lie down flat on my back and see what happened. They all came up to me and sniffed and licked and sniffed and licked. . . . When a cow comes up to explore you, it's always the same. They'll stretch out their heads toward you and sniff you; that's always first. Then the tongue will reach out and just barely touch you, and as they get less afraid they'll start licking you. They'll lick your hair and chew on it, and they like to lick and chew your boots, too. I usually don't let them lick me on my face because cattle have extremely rough tongues and I could get a scratched cornea, although I sometimes just close my eyes and let them go ahead. I don't mind if the tongue goes down my neck. That's okay. And I let them lick my hands. I think they probably like the taste of the salt on your skin. Sometimes I'll kiss them on the nose. (Grandin and Johnson 2005: 45–6)

'Becoming-wolf'

One day – decades after his analysis sessions with Freud – Sergej Costantinovič Pankejeff, the Russian nobleman better known as the Wolfman, was asked what he thought about Freud's interpretation of his famous dream:

> In my story, what was explained by dreams? Nothing, as far as I can see. Freud traces everything back to the primal scene which he derives from the dream. But the scene does not occur in the dream. When he interprets the white wolves as nightshirts or something like that, for example, linen sheets or clothes, that's somehow farfetched, I think. That scene in the dream where the windows open and so on and the wolves are sitting there, and his interpretation, I don't know, those things are miles apart. It's terribly farfetched. (Obholzer 1982: 35)

Naturally, the Wolfman's opinions about psychoanalysis – and about Freud's interpretation of his dreams – are as good as anyone's; if the dream cannot be separated from its interpretation, the one offered by the dreamer is no more valid than Freud's. The contentious point is not whether or not Freud offered the correct interpretation of that particular dream (Ginzburg 1982; Davis 1992). Rather, what should be pondered is the kind of analytic automatism by means of which animals are immediately classified as something else. Sergej dreams of a wolf – or wolves – but he is *really* dreaming of his father: the wolves are white, like night-gowns, and have long tails, indicating a preoccupation with his penis. Still, they were wolves:

> Freud obviously knows nothing about the fascination exerted by wolves and the meaning of their silent call, the call to become-wolf. Wolves watch, intently watch, the dreaming child; it is so much more reassuring to tell oneself that the dream produced a reversal and that it is really the child who sees dogs or parents in the act of making love. Freud only knows the Oedipalized wolf or dog, the castrated-castrating daddy-wolf, the dog in the kennel, the analyst's bow-wow. (Deleuze and Guattari 1987: 28–9)

This is just like Topsy's case, the allegorical dog we encountered earlier. Of course, Sergej Pankejeff really did become the Wolfman – that is how he answered the phone when someone called his house: '*Wolfsmann*'. Yet one cannot help but wonder if he became the Wolfman through psychoanalysis, or if he remained so in spite of it.

The question of the wolves, then, is important. As is the fact that there were more than one: their number is crucial. That is because the wolf is a gregarious animal – there is no wolf, as there is a Mr John Smith, but there's always a *pack* of wolves. In this sense, the question of animality is that of imagining a post-subjective humanity, and the wolf (wolves) is a way to imagine this humanity to come:

> You can't be one wolf, you're always eight or nine, six or seven. Not six or seven wolves all by yourself all at once, but one wolf among others, with five or six others. In becoming-wolf, the important thing is the position of the mass, and above all the position of the subject itself in relation to the pack or wolf-multiplicity: how the subject joins or does not join the pack, how far away it stays, how it does or does not hold to the multiplicity. (Deleuze and Guattari 1987: 29)

The subject – Mr John Smith – is identified by the tag on his door, i.e., the enormous territorialising apparatus made of barriers and borders that separate him from all other John Smiths in the world – doors, locks, alarms, private properties, passwords, security boxes, privacy measures, 'mine' and 'yours', and so on. 'Becoming-wolf' places itself well beyond this scenario. One of the principal effects of having traversed the 'anthropologic machine' is that of believing there is only one way to be an individual: the one manifested – to others as well as to oneself – through the pronoun 'I'. It is as if only two alternatives were possible: either to be an 'I', or to be nothing; either a subject/person or an object. 'Such a perspective . . . assigns an ontological primacy to the constituted individual' (Simondon 2013:

23). The wolf is really a singularity, a body with its own metabolism and psychology. And yet these characteristics are not sufficient to create a flesh and blood wolf, a living one: what is still missing is what Simondon calls 'group individuation', a third (and necessary) level of individuation along with the 'vital' and the 'psychic' one. Simondon writes that

> It is incorrect to speak of the influence of a group on the individual; indeed the group is not constituted of individuals, bound together by means of certain links, but of grouped individuals, i.e., *group individuals* [*individus de groupe*]. Individuals are group individuals just as groups are groups of individuals. The group cannot be said to exercise an influence on the individuals, because this action is contemporaneous to – and not independent of – the life of individuals. Neither does the group consist of an inter-individual reality, but rather of a complement of individuation on a large scale, which binds together a large number of individuals. (2013: 290)

The 'group individual' is neither a wolf together with other wolves – as if the pack was just the sum total of the relations between the various wolves – nor a group as an entity with its own life, swallowing and obliterating the single wolves: neither an isolated individual, nor a totalising group. On the contrary, it is a way of being *this* wolf that still cannot be separated from the fact of its inclusion in the unitary movement of the pack of wolves. The 'group individual' cannot be thought if we remain shackled to the 'I'/subjectivity entity, because such an individual can be constructed only by stressing its difference from the group: the 'I' can exist only as opposed to a 'not-I'. We are looking at 'becoming-wolf' to find an unprecedented and anonymous subjectivity. Anonymous because 'I' is actually the word of the Other (who taught us to talk, who offered us the language we use to talk and think), so that linguistic subjectivity affirms itself only to the extent that it self-submits to the language of the Other. For this reason, on the contrary, the 'group individual' is anonymous because it does not need language in order to individuate itself, since it does not *define* itself an 'I'. But it is anonymous for another reason too, since only if the 'I' is absent can one truly be an individual: once absorbed by language, *this* animal immediately becomes the 'animal', but in this way its inexpressible singularity is lost, precisely because it is not a radical singularity. The 'group individual' is a non-linguistic individual, but not one closed onto itself, isolated and self-sufficient. It is a way to remain oneself when among others without being forced to renounce – as happens when we say 'I' – that utterly individual core that makes us what we are. Indeed, for Simondon, the 'group individual' is richer than an individuality that stops at 'vital' and 'psychic' individuation: 'Being is not simply what it is *qua* manifest, for that manifestation consists . . . of a single phase; while that phase actualizes itself, other latent and real phases – just as actual – exist as energetically present potentials, and being consists in them as much as it does in the phase through which it achieves entelechy' (2013: 308). 'Becoming-wolf' is not so much a renunciation of subjectivity as it is the acquisition of new and diverse forms of non-subjective individuation, the opening of a 'polyphasic being' which clearly 'cannot be considered within the schema of common kinds and specific differences' (Simondon 2013: 308): a traditional classificatory schema based on the so-called proper name – yet never really proper, precisely because it is always the name of an Other (we are always named by an Other):

> The proper name can be nothing more than an extreme case of the common noun, containing its already domesticated multiplicity within itself and linking it to a being or object posited as unique. This jeopardizes, on the side of words and things both, the relation of the proper name as an intensity to the multiplicity it instantaneously apprehends. (Deleuze and Guattari 1987: 27–8)

'Becoming-animal' is a way to think of non-subjectivised individuality, single bodies that are not an 'I' but 'group individuals' (the challenge of animality lies within this oxymoron). But at the same time these bodies are extraordinarily more powerful than those trapped in the cage of subjective identity, and derive this power precisely from their not being stifled by the fear of losing their 'I'. New and previously unthought vital possibilities are thus disclosed, combinations that break the boundaries of the body, forming fluxes where distinguishing between who is active and who is passive, who is a subject and who is an object, who is human and who isn't, no longer has any meaning. 'Becoming-animal' is thus a twin process of 'deterritorialisation' (the process of opening up frontiers, thus blurring the lines between territories) and 'territorialisation' (the process through which new territories, new aggregates and new fluxes are born):

> The orchid deterritorializes by forming an image, a tracing of a wasp; but the wasp reterritorializes on that image. The wasp is nevertheless deterritorialized, becoming a piece in the orchid's reproductive apparatus. But

it reterritorializes the orchid by transporting its pollen. Wasp and orchid, as heterogeneous elements, form a rhizome. (Deleuze and Guattari 1987: 10)

The orchid goes out of itself (i.e., it opens its territory) by assuming a form that will be completed by the wasp, thus forming a common territory; the same goes for the wasp, as it becomes part of the reproductive circuit of the orchid. The difficult point to bring into focus is that this new space is not the result of some kind of 'juridical' pact between two distinct individualities. Rather, it is the constitution of a 'group individual', of a becoming-animal-vegetal, within which evaluating the wasp's contribution as compared to that of the orchid's – as if they were two different territories – has no meaning. The becoming-wasp of the orchid, just like the becoming-orchid of the wasp, dismantles the territorial mechanism:

> Each of these becomings brings about the deterritorialization of one term and the reterritorialization of the other; the two becomings interlink and form relays in a circulation of intensities pushing the deterritorialization ever further. There is neither imitation nor resemblance, only an exploding of two heterogeneous series on the line of flight composed by a common rhizome that can no longer be attributed to or subjugated by anything signifying. (Deleuze and Guattari 1987: 10)

There is no pre-constituted order, no plan and no direction. The rhizome extends itself, and is 'not amenable to any structural or generative model. It is a stranger to any idea of genetic axis or deep structure' (Deleuze and Guattari 1987: 12). Only the subject needs a defensive order, which must remain faithful to a genetic scheme, and not transgress the borders of tradition; becoming-animal is the dangerous space of contingency and opportunity: '[i]t is composed not of units but of dimensions, or rather directions in motion'. Most of all, this is a becoming that 'is reducible neither to the One nor the multiple' (1987: 21). Where does the wasp end, and the orchid begin? Where is the border, without which we would not know what to think or say?

> There is a block of becoming that snaps up the wasp and the orchid, but from which no wasp-orchid can ever descend. There is a block of becoming that takes hold of the cat and baboon, the alliance between which is effected by a C virus. There is a block of becoming between young roots and certain microorganisms, the alliance between which is effected by the materials synthesized in the leaves (rhizosphere). (Deleuze and Guattari 1987: 238)

The wolves return, along with the challenge they pose to the little Sergej, and to the analyst who quickly brings them back into the enclosure of subjectivity: 'every animal is fundamentally a band, a pack' (Deleuze and Guattari 1987: 239). That is why there were so many wolves in that tree. Because just as the animal does not exist, neither does the wolf; what is seen is a pack of roaming wolves – in the woods, coming now closer, now farther – observing us, calling us and keeping us at a distance (as in Malaparte's tale, recounted in Chapter 3). Animals are always a 'multiplicity' that undermines the 'I' and its borders: the animal is the 'effectuation of a power of the pack that throws the self into upheaval and makes it reel' (1987: 240). Becoming-animal has no use for the comfortable binary thinking of the subject – either the 'I' or a 'not-I' – for becoming fully unfolds within those two alternatives, in the infinity of combinations and encounters that open up when border lines are crossed: 'I am legion' (1987: 239),[1] responds the animal, and perhaps even the Wolfman would have wanted to reply thus. The 'multiplicity' of the wolves is what truly frightens. Not because the wolf is dangerous (the wolf is dangerous as an animal, before being dangerous as a predator), but because the wolves are many, a 'multiplicity' that calls for an 'alliance' between unequal, different enemies:

> This form of evolution between heterogeneous terms is 'involution,' on the condition that involution is in no way confused with regression. Becoming is involutionary, involution is creative. To regress is to move in the direction of something less differentiated. But to involve is to form a block that runs its own line 'between' the terms in play and beneath assignable relations. (1987: 238–9)

This 'creative involution' – that is not an evolution, a progress, or an improvement (operations that refer to a subject and to a project) – is the outcome of animality: '[u]nnatural participations or nuptials are the true Nature spanning the kingdoms of nature. . . . These combinations are neither genetic nor structural; they are interkingdoms, unnatural participations. That is the only way Nature operates – against itself' (Deleuze and Guattari 1987: 242).

Sergej's wolves announce a movement of discharge of a subjectivity locked within the 'I'. Indeed, those wolves are a pack (a 'group individual' – neither group nor individual), they observe us, they wait in a tree, they are patient and tenacious animals. 'Becoming-animal' is a last resort of the subject – neither dialectical nor evolutionary – to get out of itself: '[b]ecoming produces nothing other than itself. . . .

What is real is the becoming itself, the block of becoming, not the supposedly fixed terms through which that which becomes passes' (Deleuze and Guattari 1987: 238). A philosophy of animality, then, is a philosophy of the *between*, a 'between' that is not a place of passage from one place to another, but rather a transit coming from nowhere and going nowhere. Animality means inhabiting this transiting that is a transit no more. A becoming nothing, stubbornly becoming itself. That is why this is no evolution, because there is no goal to reach. The goal is not a goal, but becoming itself. In becoming-animal all the dualisms that entrap thought – and the ethico-juridical antino-mies that keep making it impossible for us to be in the world like a leaf or a wolf – are collapsed. The *use* of the world is nothing but the becoming-animal of the human. This is why when Agamben talks of the 'use of bodies' this formula needs to be understood as having a double meaning: in general, bodies (human and animal, living and non-living) *use* the world; the world is nothing but how bodies use it. There is no body, here, opposed to a world over there. The body is the use of the world – a non-proprietary, non-juridical and non-subjective use of the world: '[h]uman being and world are, in use, in a relationship of absolute and reciprocal immanence; in the using of something, it is the very being of the one using that is first of all at stake' (Agamben 2016: 30). A 'human' who can use the world thus is no longer a member of the species *Homo sapiens*. 'Becoming-animal' means knowing how to use the world.

The Creature and Immanence

The most difficult point to grasp about 'becoming-animal' is that it really becomes nothing at all, since it is a 'block of becoming' that requires no completion, no absolute knowledge and no happy ending where everything would be finally accounted for. It is a complete adherence to the world, it is *being* the world of which one partakes. But what is becoming-animal's mode of being if not that of an 'I'? Is there something left of the subject? On this topic, Deleuze and Guattari speak of 'haecceity', i.e., 'subjectless individuations' (1987: 266). A haecceity is something, yet without being a self-conscious subject: '[n]othing subjectifies, but haecceities form according to compositions of nonsubjectified powers or affects' (1987: 266). Haecceity is a certain degree of power, a particular intensity, a spe-cific timbre. It is something, and thus, finally there is nothing but 'a becoming of everybody/everything' (1987: 280). Like a murmuration

164

of birds assembling into a shifting pattern in the sky – a becoming-flock where all birds resemble each other – each of them preserving their particular colour, their specific sound, and their absolute and unmistakable haecceity. Now, this life is 'pure immanence' (Deleuze 2001b: 27). Gone are the obstacles created by the 'I' and by the divisions that accompany it when one thinks (and presents oneself) as a subject – therefore demanding an object to lord it over (for without the object, the subject is lost (Cimatti 2018)), a before and an after, a here and a yonder. A haecceity lives its life, and nothing more. The reassuring distinction between an 'environment' and a 'world' can now no longer be applied: it is a life, no less and no more. Let us return to the flock of birds in the sky – i.e., the birds' bodies use of the sky – a combination of bodies to form a body, but a body without any purposeful organisation, whose movement has no goal, whose beauty has no observer (surely unseen by the birds themselves), yet all the more beautiful for this very reason. Immanence means nothing else: there is no beyond, not even that of beauty. All there is in the becoming-flock of birds is there on display, with no one to behold it: 'not immanence to life' – where a difference between life and immanence still holds, allowing the intrusion of transcendence – 'but the immanent that is in nothing is itself a life. A life is the immanence of immanence, absolute immanence: it is complete power, complete bliss' (Deleuze 2001b: 27). It is complete for otherwise it would be a power lacking something, therefore no longer being an 'immanence of immanence'. For the same reason it is – in Spinozian spirit – 'bliss' because immanence desires nothing: it is not marked by lack, by regret or by nostalgia.

The question of immanence, i.e., of animality, can begin to be posed only once the nature of a body is no longer defined by language. Indeed, to be the talking animal means to project one's experience beyond the present moment lived by the body. It means using an expressive gesture – a word, for example – to indicate something that is not present at the moment of enunciation. Transcendence enters into *Homo sapiens'* life through language (Agamben 2006). Immanence is fullness. For example, for immanence holes do not exist, since from the world's point of view a hole 'is just as much a particle as what passes through it. Physicists say that holes are not the absence of particles but particles traveling faster than the speed of light. Flying anuses, speeding vaginas, there is no castration' (Deleuze and Guattari 1987: 32). The very idea of *castration* – the human, according to Freud (1961), becomes truly human only after accepting castration – is inconceivable without language: castration is an absence (indeed, a hole) which sends back to an absent presence the designated object that is missing when the enunciative act takes place. Castration, as a symbolic act, can exist only for those who think the world through language. Indeed, only a linguistic mind can consider a presence – like a certain bodily configuration (a vagina) – as something lacking from something else: only the talking animal, the animal educated in the use of symbols, sending and transcendence, can see in something that which is not directly perceivable:

> It's very clear that the object of privation is only ever a symbolic object – this is completely clear. That which is of the order of privation, that which is not in its place or, to be exact, that which is not in its place from the point of view of the real, this means absolutely nothing. All that is real is always and necessarily in its place, even when we disturb it. The real has the foremost property of wearing its place on the soles of its shoes – you can disturb the real as much as you like but, regardless, our bodies will still be in their place after they explode, their place of pieces. The absence of something in the real is something purely symbolic; that is, as long as we define by means of the law that it should be there, an object is missing at its place. (Lacan 2018: n.p.)

Immanence, on the other hand, lacks nothing: '[a]bsolute immanence is in itself: it is not in something, *to* something; it does not depend on an object or belong to a subject' (Deleuze 2001b: 26). Once the bodies have escaped from the cage of language, new and absolutely extraordinary possibilities for non-subjective individuation open up and haecceity is no longer forced to coincide with a material body, and even less with an 'I':

> a summer, an hour, a date have a perfect individuality lacking nothing, even though this individuality is different from that of a thing or a subject. They are haecceities in the sense that they consist entirely of relations of movement and rest between molecules or particles, capacities to affect and be affected. (Deleuze and Guattari 1987: 261)

In one fell swoop, Heidegger's perplexing tripartition between stone, animal and human (what of plants, and the millions of non-animal living beings?) is overcome. A haecceity is

> *a body ... defined only by a longitude and a latitude*: in other words the sum total of the material elements belonging to it under given relations of movement and rest, speed and slowness (longitude); the sum total of the intensive affects it is capable of at a given power or degree of potential

(latitude). Nothing but affects and local movements, differential speeds.
(Deleuze and Guattari 1987: 260)

In immanence the cognitive trap of the *name* – that crops out and sets
apart by tracing confines, hierarchies and levels – disappears. The
world is filled with unprecedented presences, crossing the sanitised
boundaries of substance, of the proper and the improper, of mine
and yours: a world that is now literally bursting with new, impossible
and contaminated lives. Becoming-animal coincides with this movement, this deflagration, this extraordinary richness. The challenge
of animality, then, is not that of retrieving the lost animal in us –
something both impossible (because the *human* condition cannot be
dismissed at will) and useless (because we never truly stopped being
animals) – rather, the goal is that of making possible this radical
operation of decentring with respect to linguistic subjectivity. As
Deleuze and Guattari put it:

> You have the individuality of a day, a season, a year, a life (regardless of
> its duration) – a climate, a wind, a fog, a swarm, a pack (regardless of its
> regularity). Or at least you can have it, you can reach it. A cloud of locusts
> carried in by the wind at five in the evening; a vampire who goes out at
> night, a werewolf at full moon. It should not be thought that a haecceity
> consists simply of a decor or backdrop that situates subjects, or of append-
> ages that hold things and people to the ground. It is the entire assemblage
> in its individuated aggregate that is a haecceity; it is this assemblage that is
> defined by a longitude and a latitude, by speeds and affects, independently
> of forms and subjects, which belong to another plane. It is the wolf itself,
> and the horse, and the child, that cease to be subjects to become events, in
> assemblages that are inseparable from an hour, a season, an atmosphere,
> an air, a life. The street enters into composition with the horse, just as the
> dying rat enters into composition with the air, and the beast and the full
> moon enter into composition with each other. (1987: 262)

The world of immanence is a brand-new world, a world entirely
here and one that desires nothing more than being here – with no
beyond, no before, but only the *right here*. This 'here', however, now
assumes a different value, because it does not define itself in opposition to the times of yore, nor to what is still to come. Quite simply,
immanence does not project itself – immanence is quite still, like the
wolves observing Sergej, or Derrida's cat. Stepping into this world
means discovering a richness the existence of which we did not even
suspect. This is animality's call: to try stepping into this world. Of
course, doing so is a challenge, because there is a very high admission

price: we need to leave our 'I' at the door. But this is what animality is. The world, then, will burst with life: '[c]limate, wind, season, hour are not of another nature than the things, animals, or people that populate them, follow them, sleep and awaken within them. This should be read without a pause: the animal-stalks-at-five-o'clock (Deleuze and Guattari 1987: 263).

This field of absolute immanence is the 'open', as Rainer Maria Rilke calls it: '[a]ll other creatures', i.e., the animals, 'look into the Open with their whole eyes' (1975: 55). They see it 'with their whole eyes', i.e., directly, because there is no screen between creature and world. They see it in all of its richness of detail, as we know, as they see it for what there is to see. 'Creatures' partake in the world, they simply *are* their use of the world. Only 'creatures' can see the world, and '[w]e know what's out there only from the animal's face' (Rilke 1975: 55) (perhaps this is why the caged chimp Nim Chimpsky kept signalling 'outside' with his hands). This simple and radical vision is precluded to the human – linguistic – animal (*Homo sapiens* is this preclusion), because it is hindered by language, and therefore by the subject/person. Thus, Rilke reverses Heidegger's position (although he wrote his *Duino Elegies* before Heidegger's *Fundamental Concepts of Metaphysics* lecture course): the animal is not 'poor in world'; on the contrary, the real of the world, in its entire power and splendour, can only be perceived and lived by the nonhuman animal. The human, and not the animal, misses the fullness of the world. For the latter, unburdened by the preservation of the 'I', is not bound to a subjectivity cast into time and into boredom – it is, ultimately, '[f]ree from death' (Rilke 1975: 55). Not because animals do not die, but rather because only the 'I' can cease to exist, all of a sudden. A haecceity, on the other hand, passes into another 'block of becoming', as the 'dying rat enters into composition with the air': when it comes to the creature, 'his being is infinite, incomprehensible, and blind to his condition, pure, like his outward gaze. And where we see the future, he sees all, himself in all, and whole forever' (1975: 57). On the contrary, 'we only see it [death]; the free animal always has its destruction behind and god ahead, and when it moves, it moves toward eternity like running springs' (1975: 55). Here 'god' is not to be understood as a form of transcendence, but rather as the achieved fullness of immanence, a never-ending becoming, 'like running springs'. The 'open' is 'that pure space ahead of us, in which flowers endlessly open. It is always World and never Nowhere without No: that pure, unguarded space we breathe, always know, and never crave' (1975: 55). The 'No' is the mark of the human world, the most important of linguistic operators, since it establishes that which *is not*. The 'No' is the deployed power of language. Transcendence begins with the 'No', just like immanence begins there where the 'No' ends. The 'open', on the other hand, is never a 'Nowhere' – a presence hinting towards an absence – nor is it the dialectical negation of this 'Nowhere'. It is rather anterior to this distinction – which it has no use for – and it is an 'unguarded space we breathe' even if nobody knows anything about it, for it is an infinite knowledge, without bearer and immanent. To imagine human animality means imagining a way to see the 'open' in order to abandon our condition of suspended living beings, lacerated by language:

> And we: spectators, always, everywhere,
> looking at everything and never from!
> It floods us. We arrange it. It decays.
> We arrange it again, and we decay.
> Who's turned us around like this,
> so that whatever we do, we always have
> the look of someone going away? Just as a man on the last hill
> showing him his whole valley
> one last time, turns, and stops, and lingers –
> so we live, and are forever leaving. (1975: 59)

Note

1. 'He asked him, "What is your name?" He replied, "Legion is my name. There are many of us" (Mark 5:9).

8

Beyond the Apparatus

'In sum, the ideal would be to get rid of the symbolic.'
(Lacan, *L'insu que sait de l'un béuve*, unpublished)

The Saint

In order to *see* the open, following both Rilke and Deleuze and Guattari, it is necessary to see the world for what it really is: an immanent fullness. Such a world is full, without gaps, without 'castration' – it is free from the de-realising power of language. For Lacan, 'castration' is the distinctive trait of the symbolic, and it indicates that, at the centre of the human, lies a fundamental lack, a *void*. On the contrary, Nietzsche's Zarathustra is the no-longer-human human (the human's becoming-animal) who is able to both see the world as it is (so bypassing the deforming screen of language/castration) and – and most importantly – able to fully adhere to the world. Indeed, it is: 'the kind of man [who] . . . conceives reality *as it is*: it is strong enough for that – it is not alienated from it, not at one remove from it, it is reality *itself*' (Nietzsche 2007: 92). These are the stakes of animality: reality itself.

The problem is that we cannot find the animality of the human in other animals, because *Homo sapiens* exists only insofar as it separates itself from all other animals – a gesture that is repeated each time a word is spoken. There is no *Homo sapiens* without *animalitas*, and vice versa. Any human who attempts to regain contact with animality will not cease to be an individual of the species *Homo sapiens*. The condition of the 'I' cannot be abandoned through sheer force of will, or good intentions. The problem of the relationship between human beings and animals is here not an ethical, but a biological one. The first kind of problem can be solved – perhaps – with education, empathy and some form of renunciation. The latter cannot, because one's biological condition is beyond the power of the will. A good 'I', one who loves animals and only eats fruit and vegetables,[1] does not for this reason stop being a subjectivity. And if it is a subjectivity (an 'I') it will never stop affirming its difference from the animal – whether it wants to or not. This is why human animality is to be sought in the *human*, and not in animals. The problem is that the apparatus – the anthropologic machine – through which we become human excludes any pact with animals, with the exception (in the best of cases) of us trapping them in a zoo, or a natural reservation.

> The fact that the human being can have the 'I' in his representations raises him infinitely above all other living beings on earth. Because of this he is a *person*, and by virtue of the unity of consciousness through all changes that happen to him, one and the same person – i.e., through rank and dignity an entirely different being from *things*, such as irrational animals, with which one can do as one likes. (Kant 2006: 109)

Kant here is very explicit, presenting the fundamental question with brutal clarity: human subjectivity – the 'person' – is the incarnation of a being that is completely different from all other living beings. Of course: *Homo sapiens* is an animal, many minds and animal languages exist, empathy and ecological imperatives exist – all of this is true and indubitable. But the fact remains that a 'person' is an utterly unique kind of living being, and that the *condition of possibility* for its existence is the continuous restating of its difference from all other animals. No ethics can erase this biological fact (and here biology blurs into metaphysics). Kant does nothing but clearly present what is more hypocritically displayed by a cling-film-wrapped piece of chicken breast in a supermarket (packaged in such a way to make us forget we are being offered the piece of a corpse): animals are things 'with which one can do as one likes'. It should be clear that this is not an empirical observation, but rather a *definition* of what an animal is. Even if we were to reverse this definition, holding that the animal is a sapient being with reason and interests, we would still put ourselves in the position of deciding about the life or death of other living beings.

Would it really be impossible to *respect* animals – as held by animalist thought? The point is that the condition of subjectivity confers on the human a power that no ethics can contain. Egoism is not a human defect, eventually eradicable through an enlightened education – rather, it is its principal biological trait:

> From the day that the human being begins to speak by means of 'I', he brings his beloved self to light wherever he is permitted to, and egoism progresses unchecked. If he does not do so openly (for then the egoism of others opposes him), nevertheless he does so covertly and with seeming

self-abnegation and pretended modesty, in order all the more reliably to give himself a superior worth in the judgment of others. (Kant 2006: 16)

The sad destiny of animals in the human 'world' – their condition as 'things' – does not depend on an evil disposition that a better human being will one day rectify: it depends on the fact that this 'I' *is an* 'I'. The ecological disaster we are heading towards is not caused by human malice, but by the fact that every 'I' – in an ever-growing way, as more means become available to it – tries to affirm itself at everyone else's expense. Fire does not destroy because it is evil, but because it burns. Sure, fire can be confined in an oven, and thus controlled. But the fact that we seek protection from its flames means that it will keep consuming wood, coal or whatever else with which we feed its destructive nature.

The link that holds between language, the 'I' and the destruction of animals is shown in exemplary manner by Flaubert in his *La Légende de Saint Julien l'Hospitalier*. This is the tale of a young prince, which begins with his discovery of the pleasure of killing a living being:

> One day, during Mass, he noticed as he raised his head a little white mouse coming out of a hole in the wall. It scampered on to the first altar step, and after turning two or three times to right and left, ran back in the same direction. The following Sunday he was disturbed at the idea that he might see it again. It did come back; and every Sunday he would wait for it and find it irritating, until he began to hate it and resolved to get rid of it. So, shutting the door, he sprinkled cake crumbs over the steps, and posted himself in front of the hole, with a stick in his hand. After a very long while a pink nose appeared, followed by the whole mouse. He struck it a light blow, and stood astounded in front of the little body, which no longer moved. A drop of blood stained the flagstones. (Flaubert 1999: 45)

Julian sees a white mouse, pays attention to it; that uncontrolled and uncontrollable life bothers him. He is in church, and perhaps he is preoccupied that a mouse might defile that sacred place, or maybe he simply discovers the intoxicating power implicit in his being an 'I'. Indeed, the mouse is neither a danger nor food – it is just a 'mouse', something there that Julian can decide to make disappear. His whim is more than sufficient to condemn the mouse to death. Now, a 'mouse' is nothing but *a* mouse, or 'mouse number one'; to kill it once is not enough, because a second will come after the first, and then a third, and so on:

> All kinds of little birds used to peck up seeds in the garden. He had the idea of putting peas into a hollow reed. When he heard twittering in a

tree, he would come up softly, then raise his tube and puff out his cheeks, and the little creatures would rain down on his shoulders so thick and fast that he could not help laughing with pleasure at his mischief. (Flaubert 1999: 46)

Julian is not compelled to hunt by need, hunger or fear: his desire has no straightforwardly biological explanation. Julian kills. First a mouse, then some birds, and then '[h]e killed bears with a knife, bulls with an axe, wild boar with a spear' (1999: 48), without stopping. What is most striking in his behaviour is the numerical element: every number is followed by another, and another, and so on, so that each of his prey is always next to last because there is no last prey, no larger number of all. But numbers are linguistic entities. Indeed, Julian is held hostage by language: 'the subject is led to behave in an essentially signifying way, indefinitely repeating something which is, strictly speaking, mortal' (Lacan 2018: 9). It is 'mortal' both for animals and for Julian himself, since he is trapped in a machinery that overpowers him, that drags him along and literally 'thinks' on his behalf. Because Julian is not evil: he is the talking animal, and therefore the counting animal, fascinated by the inexplicable fact that 1 is followed by 2, and then 3 follows 2, and so on, towards infinity (arithmetic is the hidden and unsettling face of language (Danesi 2016)). So, it happens that '[o]ne winter morning he set out before dawn, well equipped, with a crossbow over his shoulder and a supply of arrows at his saddlebow' (Flaubert 1999: 49): he departs because he is compelled to 'infinitely' repeat what the machinery orders him to do. The secret of the human lies in that *infinity*. According to Chomsky, human language is essentially a machinery – allowing 'recursion, providing the capacity to generate an infinite range of expressions from a finite set of elements' (Hauser et al. 2002) – that constantly 'engenders' new statements, starting from a pre-existent set. What needs underlining, and yet is constantly elided, is that this machinery is *not* at the speaker's service, precisely *because it works*. Julian is dragged by this recursive machinery – not because he is sick or evil, but because he is human.

And so, the massacre begins: '[a] wood-grouse, stiff with cold, was sleeping at the end of a branch, its head tucked under its wing. With a backward slash of his sword Julian severed its two feet and went on his way without picking it up' (Flaubert 1999: 49); then, on a mountain peak, he sees two wild goats, 'crouching and barefoot he finally reached the first goat and plunged a dagger under its ribs.

The second leaped terrified into the void.' Next it is the birds' turn: '[c]ranes, flying very low, passed over his head from time to time. Julian knocked them down with his whip and did not miss one' (1999: 49). But the slaughter has just begun:

> A roebuck bounded out of a thicket, a fallow deer appeared at an intersection, a badger came out of its sett, a peacock on the grass spread out its tail; and when he had killed them all, more roebuck appeared, more fallow deer, more badgers, more peacocks, and blackbirds, jays, polecats, foxes, hedgehogs, lynx, creatures in endless profusion, more numerous with every step. (1999: 50)

Why don't animals flee? They cannot, for there is nowhere safe from human beings, because Julian will catch them either way. As soon as the 'I' exists animals become those '*things*', as Kant told us, 'with which one can do as one likes'. The epilogue to Flaubert's story takes place in 'a valley shaped like an amphitheatre' where stags were 'huddling close together' (1999: 50):

> For a few minutes the prospect of such carnage made him choke with pleasure. Then he dismounted from his horse, rolled up his sleeves and began shooting. As the first arrow whistled by, all the stags turned their heads with one accord. Gaps appeared in their ranks; plaintive cries rose up and the herd shook with a great shudder. The rim of the valley was too high to pass over. They sprang about in the enclosed space, trying to escape. Julian aimed, fired; and the arrows slashed down like rain in a thunderstorm. The stags fought together in their frenzy, reared up, mounted each other; their bodies, with their antlers tangled together, formed a great pile, which kept collapsing as it moved. At last they died, lying on the sand, frothing at the mouth, their entrails hanging out, their heaving bellies gradually subsiding. Then all was still. . . . Julian leaned against a tree. He gazed wide-eyed at the enormity of the massacre, without understanding how he could have done it. (1999: 50–1)

What happened exactly during this massacre? Julian has killed all the stags that were trapped in the valley. But his actions are wholly analogous to those of Adam, when he assigned names to every animal. Flaubert explicitly mentions this:

> Sometimes in a dream he would see himself like our forefather Adam in the midst of Paradise, among all the animals: stretching out his arm, he would put them to death; or else, they would file past, two by two, in order of size, from elephants and lions down to stoats and ducks, as on the day when they went into Noah's ark. From the shadow of a cave he would hurl at them javelins that never missed; others would appear;

there was no end to it; and he would wake up with his eyes rolling wildly. (1999: 56)

Adam stood before the animal and gave it a name (those creatures are 'animals' precisely because they have been given a name). By doing so he made it unhappy and mortal, because he transformed it into an individual entity: something that begins and that sooner or later will end. Only individuated entities can die, for everything else was never born and will never die – it simply passes from one form to another. This is why Adam's act is nothing but the prefiguration of Julian's slaughter. Indeed, Julian is not looking at a particular stag; he is aiming at a STAG, and then another, and then another. Blinded by language and number, he is chasing an abstraction.

The challenge is that of interrupting this mechanism – this is the theme of the rest of Flaubert's tale – or better yet, to escape from it. In fact, this machinery cannot be stopped via a voluntary act – as if Julian, in a moment of clarity, could suddenly realise all the evil that he has so far perpetrated. This is impossible because it has always been clear that there is no justification for the bloodlust. But most importantly because if killing animals is bad, Julian is not guilty of it, for he has inherited his desire from Adam's primordial act. Indeed, Julian *is* that evil. This is why the issue of animality is not an ethical problem (Diamond 2008). The turning point of Flaubert's tale can be found in the curse cast by the last surviving stag, just before collapsing, killed by an arrow to the head: '"Cursed! Cursed! Cursed! One day, savage heart, you will murder your father and your mother!" He bent his knees, slowly closed his eyes, and died' (Flaubert 1999: 92). Julian, terrified, flees from his native castle, enrols as a mercenary in a faraway land, performs heroic deeds, and marries an emperor's daughter. His life is now happy, seemingly changed. And yet he feels the curse looming upon him, not so much on account of what he has done, but because of what he is. Moreover, it should not be forgotten that Julian, in order to understand the meaning of his actions, had to *listen* to a curse cast upon him. Language dooms, and language saves. This is why animality is beyond language, not before it. Indeed, his caution notwithstanding, Julian ends up killing his elderly parents who had spent years travelling, looking for him (like Oedipus, he is stained with a pre-existing guilt, for which he is not responsible). This time, his escape is radical. Having spent a long time desperately wandering the lands, he settles to become a ferryman on a river, carrying people from one bank to the other, asking for no compensation. He does it simply because there is nothing else for him to do, but also because a ferryman makes a living from a constant transition, having no fixed identity to defend – the ferryman is the becoming-river of the human. One night, a leper appears, asking to be ferried to the other side of the river. It is a stormy night, and Julian offers him shelter in his hut, giving him food and water. '"My bones are like ice! Come beside me!"' says the leper, '[a]nd Julian moved aside the canvas and lay down on the dead leaves next to him, side by side' (1999: 69). But that does not suffice:

> The Leper turned his head. 'Take off your clothes, so that I can have the warmth of your body!' Julian undressed; then, naked as the day he was born, settled back on the bed; and he felt against his thigh the Leper's skin, colder than a snake and rough as a file. He tried to hearten him, and the other answered with gasps: 'Oh! I am going to die! . . . Come closer, warm me! Not just with your hands! No! No, with your whole body! Julian lay full length on top of him, mouth to mouth, chest to chest. (1999: 69)

We have reached the tale's denouement. Julian – the descendant of Adam, who named animals in order to then slaughter them, realising the prophecy contained in that name – is now face to face with the same death he had so generously and obtusely spread across the 'world'. In order to return to this death, and to finally deliver himself from it, he had to traverse that of his parents and get rid of this cursed inheritance. The price Julian has to pay to unburden himself of the massacres he has committed is extremely high. But there was no other way: by killing his own parents he has killed himself, the one who brought death with his arrows, like Adam did with his words. Now, perhaps, a new Julian can appear:

> Then the Leper embraced him; and his eyes suddenly shone as bright as stars; his hair streamed out like the rays of the sun; the breath from his nostrils was as sweet as roses; a cloud of incense rose from the hearth, the waters sang. Meanwhile delights in abundance, a superhuman joy came flooding into the soul of Julian, who lay in a swoon; and the one whose arms still clasped him tight grew larger, larger, until his head and his feet touched the walls of the hut. The roof flew off, the firmament unfolded. (1999: 69–70)

The Real of the Body

The paradox of the I is what both allows it to become an 'I' and forbids its full realisation. The body that proclaims to, at last, be an 'I' cannot say the truth about itself. In order to utter this truth it would be necessary to use someone else's words, the language of the Other: but the *I* that desires to announce itself is *this body* – right here and right now – and nothing more. However, no language has the expressive resources needed to indicate this absolute individuality: 'I' is just a word in a language that, like any other word, anyone can use. There are as many 'I's as there are bodies who utter this word. The very same moment I say 'I' to indicate that which is most singular in me, I am also admitting my inability to grasp this core, precisely because there are no words to say this absolute individuality of mine – and mine alone. The anthropologic machine does not know this body, just as it ignores the diversity of life; it can only know the generic ANIMAL, and can only indicate this interchangeable 'I'. What interests us here is the unspeakable truth of the *body*, a truth that linguistic meaning cannot articulate. The body, not as a 'bare life' (for this is nothing but the converse of the subject/person), but as a pure *non-sense*:

> We lose our rooting at 'the body.' Here, 'non-sense' doesn't mean something absurd, or upside-down, or somehow contorted. (We won't be touching on the body in the work of Lewis Carroll.) It means, instead: no sense, or a sense whose approach through any figure of 'sense' is absolutely ruled out.
>
> Sense making sense where sense meets its limit. A mute, closed, autistic sense – yet without *autós*, without 'itself'. Autism without an *autós* for the body, making the body infinitely less than a 'subject,' but also infinitely other, *thrown*, not 'subjected,' but just as hard, intense, inevitable, and singular as a subject. (Nancy 2008: 13)

Now this absolutely unknown body (precisely because the only body we can know is that of 'bare life', the product of the anthropologic machine) lies where sense 'fails', because it is a kind of sublimation of sense, appearing only when language loosens its grasp, leaving the body free to be itself. A body that is not a subject (because a subject exists only by means of an 'I') but not any less 'singular' – indeed the opposite is true. This body would not even be an *autòs*, since only an I has borders to defend, only an 'I' can be egotistical. A body to be imagined, traversing language (the same difficult path that Julian had to take in order to relinquish Adam's legacy) in order to at last get rid of it: '[p]erhaps *body* is the word without employment par excellence', Nancy argues, because language ignores this body; and so 'in any language, it's the word in excess' (2008: 21). Such a body endures, 'like a piece of bone, a pebble, a stone, a granule, falls right where we need it' (2008: 20). Language cannot digest the body. Here we hear an echo of Lacan's discussion of the *objet petit a* which stands, like a gap or a residue, against the Other, the Symbolic and language. This *petit a* – and the issue of animality hinges entirely on the use one can make of it – is a residual product of (big) A; indeed, it is 'an effect of discourse that produces a reject' (Lacan 2007: 43). Language 'eats' the human animal thus producing, on the one hand, the subject/person and, on the other, a 'bare life'. However, this operation leaves behind a residue: the unspeakable singularity of the body, the *object petit a*. Nancy talks of this body that can only exist as a reject of the Symbolic. But this means that human animality can only be that of the little *a*, coming after language. Once again, the human was never an animal, but at the same time it is nothing but an animal.

But how can we, finally, simply be a body? According to language, as we know, the body is the substrate of the mind/subject, and therefore invisible. Otherwise, it is taken as a sign for something else, as happens with so-called body language: that is to say, the body is never considered in and for itself. A certain kind of psychoanalysis – utterly blind to the body save when taking it as an allegory of some hidden meaning to be interpreted and revealed – is here exemplary:

> It's . . . surprising . . . that a certain psychoanalytic discourse would seem to insist, while denying its object, on making the body 'signify', rather than flushing out signification as something that always screens off the spacings of bodies. . . . Hence, it would seem, hysteria is instituted as exemplary: a body saturated with signification. And hence no more body . . . (Nancy 2008: 22–3)

The hysteric body speaks through its symptoms, but nonetheless it *speaks*. But if it speaks, it is no longer a *body*. Instead, what interests us here is a body that has nothing to say, a body that is simply what it is – both its power and its weakness. Julian realises the simplicity of the body – after having slaughtered hundreds of them, without ever seeing them – only when he holds the leper close to him, in a lethal and abjectly erotic embrace. It is as if words finally admitted their limit, for they cannot go beyond that point – and hence the leper, the wounds, the disgust, the pleasure and death. The body can appear only when language collapses: '[i]f it's a sign, then it's not sense: therefore, it has to have a *soul* or *spirit*, which will be the "body of sense"' (Nancy 2008: 69). Where the body is, there finally is no more spirit, no soul and no transcendence. A new fissure opens up through which the body appears as if for the first time, as if it had never been, or as if we had never truly observed it – as Julian never truly observed the stags he killed by the hundreds, and again, and again, without end.

The body, then, appears as the stumbling block of meaning, when the word spins idle and falls silent. Now, there are two ways to consider this body, finally revealed: we could look at it from the standpoint of sense – that of language and of the 'I' – thus seeing it as the *negation* of sense (a mute body, incapable of talking); or else, from another point of view, we could see it as a new existential possibility (like that of Julian beyond himself) and therefore like a body that no longer needs language. In order to imagine this body-beyond-the-body we can refer to Lawrence's extraordinary last novel, *The Man Who Died*, written during the final and tormented part of his life. Lawrence tells the story of Christ who, after his crucifixion, rises from death as the body of a man among men, and not as the Son of God. No longer the Son of God, he is but simply the body – wounded and in pain – of a man who died and inexplicably came back to life. This is a life that, at first, he does not want, because all existence meant to him was pain and treason. Life has now recalled him, even though in the end – when suffering on the cross – all that he longed for was death. Yet he is alive once again and, despite himself, he discovers that he can finally be the body he is: '[H]ow good', he said, 'to have fulfilled my mission, and to be beyond it. Now I can be alone, and leave all things to themselves, and the fig-tree may be barren if it will, and the rich may be rich. My way is my own alone' (Lawrence 1994: 33). This is what passing through death and language is like: the fig-tree is just a fig-tree, with no injunction to produce fruits – it is all the same, the figs can be found somewhere else. At last, the world is just the world, sense-less yet not meaningless. For Lawrence's Christ, like for Nietzsche's Zarathustra, the reality of the world is simply 'the way it is'. In such a world the body is no longer 'bare life', because through the Passion the body/subject (the 'Son' of God) has died. The body can still talk, but its relationship with language has changed. It talks, but the word does not distance it from the immanence of its own existence. It is a living body, and nothing more. Indeed, Christ has finally set himself free from language, i.e., the machinery of transcendence:

The Word is but the midge that bites at evening. Man is tormented with words like midges, and they follow him right into the tomb. But beyond the tomb they cannot go. Now I have passed the place where words can bite no more and the air is clear, and there is nothing to say, I am alone with my own skin, which is the walls of all my domain. So he healed of his wounds, and enjoyed his immortality of being alive without fret. For in the tomb he had slipped that noose which we call care. In the tomb he had left his striving self, which cares and asserts itself. Now his uncaring self healed and became whole within his skin, and he smiled to himself with pure aloneness, which is one sort of immortality. (Lawrence 1994: 33)

Let us go back to Julian then, and try to follow this human, and yet no longer human, path. Julian kills animals, this is his truth. Indeed, he also kills many human beings during his time as a mercenary, but the animals he encounters are his favourite target. He kills them, one after another. As we have already seen, he is agitated by something like a deadly numerical compulsion (Wiese 2003). But if it is true that only those who are individuated by means of a name can die, then this numerical compulsion is a synonym of death. Julian is under the spell of a drive that forces him, almost despite himself, to kill every life form he encounters. He ultimately kills his own parents – not too surprising considering that they were responsible for transmitting to him this murderous compulsion. Up to this point Julian has lived in the condition of he who 'finds his home at a point located in the Other that lies beyond' (Lacan 2014: 47). Here we have it: Julian has never lived in his own home, because to be human means that your home always belongs to someone Other. Finally, this is what is at stake in the question of animality: will Julian ever be able to live in his own home? An important misunderstanding needs to be avoided: it is not a matter of freeing Julian from the social conditioning that would inhibit the 'spontaneous' development of his 'I'. On the contrary, Julian needs to be freed from his own 'I'. The problem is not Julian's impossible self-realisation, the point is rather to liberate him from the conditioning that the 'I' imposes on the body he is. The 'I' is a linguistic construct; the challenge facing human animality is that of delineating a *somehow* still-human life, unbound by the need for identity and the egoism of the 'I'. Only an 'I' can feel the need for self-realisation; but since 'the man's desire is the desire of the Other' (Lacan 2014: 22), what the 'I' believes to be *its* desire is nothing but the desire of the Other, 'this Other that steals away in the indeterminate echo of significations, this Other in which the subject no longer sees himself except as fate, but fate that has no end, fate that gets lost in the ocean of histories' (2014: 46). We cannot touch the Other, for it is the sum total of the conditionings, the traditions and the 'histories' that we must assimilate in order to become human. It is no coincidence that Vygotsky defined this process of humanisation as a veritable 'revolution', where 'the external operation became internal' (in Rieber and Carton 1997: 117). The complete realisation of the 'I''s desire, the dream of any liberated subjectivity, indeed coincides with the highest degree of subjugation. The challenge is not that of freeing the 'I' but rather to be freed *from* it.

Indeed, there is a crucial difference between *human* animality and the body under the 'I's dominion ('bare life'): the fundamental characteristic of subjectivity, according to Lacan, is a 'lack', precisely because the 'I' cannot find, within itself, that which defines it as an 'I'. That can only be found outside of itself, in the Other: '[l]ack is radical, radical in the very constitution of subjectivity . . . as soon as it becomes known, as soon as something comes to knowledge, some-thing is lost' (Lacan 2014: 134). Animality, on the other hand, is full. It is everything it is, lacking nothing, and fully coinciding with itself. We do not ask, of a body, 'What does it lack? What does it need?' Rather, the question becomes: 'What can a body do?' (Deleuze 1990: 81). Julian's body can embrace the leper: it can embrace death, and not just give it. It finally breaks out of the constraints of identity that forced him into the role of hunter or hunted, of person or thing. Now a whole space of possibilities is disclosed, possibilities that were wholly unthinkable as long as one was trapped in the circuit between 'I' and 'You', between agent and patient, subject and object. A body is nothing but this body, in *this* moment, in this place: in order to understand that it is indeed a body, there is no need to ask ourselves if it is an 'I', if it speaks, or if it is rational. A body is what a body can do:

> this here eats grass, that other eats meat. The alimentary regime, you sense that it is about the modes of existence. An inanimate thing too, what can it do, the diamond, what can it do? That is, of what tests is it capable? What does it support? What does it do? A camel can go without drinking for a long time. It is a passion of the camel. We define things by what they can do, it opens up forms of experimentation. It is a whole exploration of things, it doesn't have anything to do with essence. It is necessary to see people as small packets of power. (Deleuze 2007: n.p.)

Julian's becoming-leper dissolves the 'person' that was once called Julian into a pure relational field: Now, in pure immanence, the

Heideggerian tripartition between 'man', 'animal' and 'rock' collapses once and for all. Life can be found even beyond the subject – and perhaps especially there.[2]

In the World

Why is the question of language so important? Every animal, and more generally every living being, somehow communicates – they all know (at least some form of) language. While this is certainly the case, what is also true is that the human being is so permeated by language as to be in fact a *'parlêtre'* (Lacan 2001: 565), i.e., a being made of speech. The speaking animal is entirely shot through with language, for this is not an additional characteristic, but something that defines the kind of animal it is, setting it apart from cats, or lizards. The first and most crucial consequence of the pervasiveness of language is a splitting of the human animal in two: an 'I' and a body that can never come into contact each other. From this split derives the unending 'mind drift' (Ferrari 2005: 67) that is both its natural condition and its eternal curse. Human animality can be found at the end of this linguistic path. An animality trying to reconstitute the fullness of the body. The condition for reaching this fullness is that of transforming language: from a formidable machinery of separation and 'lack' into a locus of re-composition.

The point is that language, by its very nature, is 'two-faced'. There is no *simple* linguistic entity, in the sense that it would simply be what it is: 'a language exists if an idea is attached to a phonic sequence *s+e+a*' (de Saussure 2002: 20). But this means that any linguistic entity distances the speaker from what is *physically* present: there is *this* material object – like the noise 'sea' produced by a human body – but this object has no intrinsic value, for it depends on something else (its meaning) which is not present, in this case the actual *sea*. And indeed, its presence is not at all necessary for that particular phonic chain to be employed. In this sense language is, by its very nature, *transcendent*; that is to say, it gestures towards a different reality than the one the speaker is inhabiting when using it. It is not necessary to believe in God to have an experience of transcendence; to speak – and to expect an answer – is enough: 'as long as we speak, we believe in God. . . . It is the Father who names, who assigns names to things. We receive these names from Him, and believe in them. When we believe in language – when we believe in that which language communicates – we are saying a mass, we are celebrating a mass' (Miller 2004: 40). Every linguistic act presupposes an implicit act of *faith* in language; to speak means to *believe* in language. In fact, as long as one speaks, it is difficult to be truly atheists, because language means faith and belief. Why would 'sea' mean just what I believe it to mean? And how can I be sure that the word I have been taught is indeed the correct one? Faith is what we experience with respect to that which is not present and eludes our control, yet something which, perhaps, might appear tomorrow. We trust our neighbour – just as we trust the law, or the weather forecast – because, as linguistic animals, we are animals of faith. There is no language without faith. But returning to the body means having no need for faith, because the body is *always* here. And if we do not believe in the body that is not because it has betrayed us, but rather because the 'I' cannot truly know it. Because the 'I' is not *in* the body – it rather *has* a body. The experience of immanence presupposes the relinquishment of language, or the use of a no longer 'two-faced' language. This is human animality: immanence.

Psychoanalysis – especially that of Lacanian inspiration – sets itself the goal of fully retrieving this fullness of the body that the 'I' could never know. The 'I' does not only ignore the body, but really *cannot* know it, because an 'I' can exist only where the unity of a body is broken. Psychoanalysis is the attempt (intrinsically unrealisable, since the human animal *is* the '*parlêtre*') to transform the 'I'/ body couple into something unitary. Let us return, for a moment, to Freud's Wolfman. One of his neurotic symptoms was severe constipation; yet Freud recounts how, during the course of his treatment, 'his bowel began to "add its voice" to the work, as if it were an hysterically affected organ, regaining its normal function, which had for so long been impaired, in the course of a few weeks' (Freud 2002: 274). The harmless body, which obeys the rhythm and the rules of the 'I', is the 'speaking' body able to 'add its voice', to listen and to make itself heard. Only a body that is fully conforming to language is allowed, for language is the model of the body. The Wolfman found no other way to know his own body than by subjugating it to the 'I'. But in this way the body loses any autonomy and truth. Indeed, in the end, Sergej Costantinovič Pankejeff literally becomes *the Wolfman*, adopting the name of the clinical case that made him famous: he took the name he was given, that was assigned to him by Freud and by those who subsequently had him as a patient. The only way for Sergej to face his neurosis was to deny it, transforming it into a kind of language that someone – the psychoanalyst – would one day be able to interpret, and thus unveil. And so even his famous dream turns into a kind of puzzle, and his body into a kind of text composed of symptoms (signs) that are to be retraced back to their hidden meaning. There is no body, only the manifestation of something else.

Now, the path we have followed so far is different: the aim is to remain in the body, without distancing it. The goal is not that of explaining the symptom (the wolf as symbolising the father, for example), but rather seeing it as 'something to be used' (Miller 2004: 18), to transform it into a singularising occasion, i.e., the opportunity to be something wholly unique:

> when you know to be afflicted by a symptom, there are two avenues. Either you start looking at dieting programs: taking five capsules per day, going to sleep and waking up at the same time every day, quit smoking, practice sports. . . . Or you do something non-conform. Joyce did not attempt to decipher his symptom. He preferred to . . . cypher it otherwise. (Miller 2004: 80–1)

The fate of the child who was dreaming wolves was that of moving from a name of the Other – Sergej Costantinovič Pankejeff – to another name, *Wolfsmann*, assigned by yet another Other, the Other of psychoanalysis. As if the only possibilities available to him were those offered by Others. For this reason, the goal of psychoanalysis is not that of once again taking the body back to language (psychoanalysis is not hermeneutics). Rather, as Lacanian psychoanalyst Colette Soler writes, 'to analyse is to seek the analphabetic' (2014: 37) within the body of the speaker. This is the paradox offered by animality: to search inside the *'parlêtre'* – the linguistic animal – looking for that wholly individual and transformative core that eludes the grasp of language. The objective then becomes that of discovering the real 'proper name' (Soler 2014: 86), since the one printed on one's passport is nothing but the name given to us by the Other. But what kind of name can be self-assigned? A name nobody can comprehend, because a truly *private* name cannot be employed in *public* communication with others, and it will therefore be utterly incomprehensible (including to those who assign it to themselves). This name will not designate an 'I', because the 'I' is always forced to wear 'the clothes of the Other' (Soler 2014: 111). It will be the proper name of a body that is not an 'I'. This is an absolute and radical singularisation that only *Homo sapiens* can hope to reach; for a language-less animal knows no *I*, nor does it have the problem of being subjugated to – and then liberated from – its rule. On the other hand, only a linguistic animal can attempt to free itself from the 'I' without giving up on its individuality: that is to say, only an 'I' can 'recognize the unimportance of my self-importance' (Tugendhat 2016: 26). The passage from the linguistic body – split into 'I'/subject and flesh/object – to the immanent body, neither fooled nor lured by transcendence, is thematised by Lacan by means of the distinction he draws between 'Freudian symptom' (asking to be given a meaning and an interpretation), and 'sinthome', which is beyond any need of deciphering. The 'sinthome' is an original and creative use of the body and its powers. The 'sinthome' is not the triumph of the 'I', but on the contrary can only appear where both the 'I' and the Other – along with egoism ('I' > others) and altruism ('I' < others) – disappear. The 'sinthome' is beyond language: it is, at last, 'an odd or end of the real' (Lacan 2016: 118):

> To incarnate the symptom is something else, it is the opposite of making significance. When we talk about the grasp of the significant, we do so, ultimately, to say that the detail, the encounter, the singular is transposed, as if by miracle, into the universal of the significant. Here we are dealing with precisely the opposite movement: an incarnation that leads . . . to a structure, the structure of man. (Miller 2004: 23–4)

A 'man', like only an artist can be (for Lacan the model of this process is James Joyce), is someone able to transform the symptom into a new way of experiencing. So, the artist welcomes

> his symptom as something to be used. . . . The symptom is not to be interpreted, but to be reduced . . . there is nothing to heal, but it is presented in order to be used. There is no resonance of resignation here. On the contrary, there is the idea that something is done with the remainder, that the remainder is fertile, that the remainder is a resource. (Miller 2004: 18)

The 'remainder' is precisely that which language cannot make meaningful, what resists and blocks the mechanism of signification; it is necessary to strictly observe that 'remainder' because the unspeakable truth of the body lies therein. The animality of the human is concentrated here:

> a remainder needs to be left behind. . . . A remainder is left to the extent that everyone is without peers, that one's difference resides in the opacity that can never be removed. This remainder is not the impasse of psychoanalysis, but precisely that which constitutes one's value, even as little as one is able to put it into work. It is there, doubtlessly, that one's difference or one's nobility is constituted. (Miller 2004: 137)

To embody oneself – this is the 'sinthome'. To use oneself and to coincide with this use. To traverse the transcendence that language carries with it, in order to finally reach 'a second awakening that would be beyond the awakening that is merely a continuation of sleep in another form' (Miller 2004: 86). An artist is someone who manages to walk this path, going through and beyond the 'I'. In the end, once again, there is only the body – but not as the property of a subjectivity. Rather, a body 'is what is singular to each individual' (Lacan 2016: 147). Becoming-body, becoming-animal, becoming-artist, i.e., someone 'who has earned the privilege of having reached the extreme point of embodying the symptom in himself' (Lacan 2016: 147). The zenith of individuality thus coincides with a sort of eternity, because, if only the living being that has been individuated by a name can die, then the artist with a name that is not a name knows no death. The artist has no 'I' to defend, and thus he or she cannot die. For the same reason, his or her existence – at once infinite and finite – lasts as long as that of an animal, or a stone, or a cloud:

> To be present at the dawn of the world. Such is the link between imperceptibility, indiscernibility, and impersonality – the three virtues. To reduce oneself to an abstract line, a trait, in order to find one's zone of indiscernibility with other traits, and in this way enter the haecceity and impersonality of the creator. One is then like grass: one has made the world, everybody/everything, into a becoming, because one has made a necessarily communicating world, because one has suppressed in oneself everything that prevents us from slipping between things and growing in the midst of things. One has combined 'everything' (*le 'tout'*): the indefinite article, the infinitive-becoming, and the proper name to which one is reduced. Saturate, eliminate, put everything in. (Deleuze and Guattari 1987: 280)

Notes

1. As we have already seen, plant 'behaviour' does exist (Silvertown and Gordon 1989). As already suggested by Aristotle, this means that there exists a plant *sensibility*; but then, why do we concern ourselves with the feelings of a chicken, and not those of a lettuce? We are still there, it is always the HUMAN who decides about the life and death of living beings. We have increasingly accurate knowledge about what is today called 'plant cognition' (Baluska et al. 2018). The possibility of a 'mental life' that would not be based on the workings of a brain and a central nervous system makes all those ethical systems based on the principle of sensibility partial if not downright speciesist. Let us consider Bentham's famous

question: 'the question is not, Can they reason? nor, Can they talk? but, Can they suffer? Why should the law refuse its protection to any sensitive being? . . . The time will come when humanity will extend its mantle over everything which breathes . . .' (1823: 144). Plants have no brains, and yet they feel. If they do, sooner or later it will be necessary to ask when 'humanity will extend its mantle' to protect them, along with other living beings. Does a blade of grass suffer when a goat tears it from the ground? The case of plants is extremely interesting for it foregrounds a 'metaphysical' rather than factual issue. According to our best scientific knowledge, plants 'feel' because they display a 'behaviour' that, *according to us*, is a sign of sensibility and interests. The absence of a brain and a nervous system shifts the problem from a factual to a behavioural level. The unyielding materialist would claim that there is mind only if there is a brain. But we now understand how this criterion is imprecise, if not downright incorrect – there is mind *without* a brain. And what should we say about a sentient 'robot' (Breazeal and Brooks 2005), i.e., an artefact that contains nothing resembling a 'natural' brain, and is indeed made of inorganic materials? The case of plants, then, reveals our still dominating (and unthought) anthropocentrism, according to which sensibility – or better, that which to our eyes looks like sensibility – is the (ethical and scientific) criterion for establishing who is 'alive' and who isn't, who is simply 'simulating' human behaviour and who, on the other hand, really feels. From this point of view, Turing (1950) proposed a much more honest and realistic approach: mind is to act intelligently. But since intelligence is not limited to human organisms, nor to those with a brain, then mind is wherever intelligence is (Brooks 1999). We should then say that cognitive science – if we take its functionalism seriously – is far more advanced than any utilitarian or ecological ethics. A robot, at least in principle, does not think of itself as a 'world-forming' being, nor does it believe itself to be superior to the tick.

2. This point needs stressing. The concept of 'animality' can play a pro-pulsive role in the philosophical and ecological debate only if, para-doxically, it is emancipated from its alleged applicability to animals alone, and in particular to 'sentient' animals. Consider, to take but one example, all the efforts made by analytic philosophy to establish a criterion by which to attribute a form of 'consciousness' to nonhu-man animals, which would elect them to moral evaluation. According to Rowlands, for example, 'when a creature has a memory with the content *this is familiar*, that creature is pre-reflectively aware of itself in virtue of the fact that this content, when plugged into an appropriate context – one comprising a milieu of meta-cognitive capacities – would guarantee that the creature also has a memory with the content *I have seen this dog before*' (2016: 11). At least two observations can be made here: 1) Rowlands attributes thoughts to a sentient animal that would be

formulated through English-language statements. The point is that this is not expedient, for it would be more complex, if not impossible, to formulate them *in any way* without such a linguistic 'translation'. Indeed, those concepts only exist for a linguistic mind, and to attribute them to animals is wholly unjustified. It's not that animals think *somewhat* like us: the point is that they do not think linguistically at all. 2) The notion of the 'I' cannot be separated from language, and therefore there can be no thoughts without language. From this point of view the idea of a 'pre-reflective awareness of the self' only serves the purpose of including *some* animals into the 'moral circle' (Singer 2011). This is a righteous move, on the political level (at least for those few lucky animals we decide to treat better than others that lack this particular form of awareness), but a complete failure on the philosophical level, for it simply applies to some living beings the very same notions that are applied to humans. The point is not that 'many animals are persons' (Rowlands 2016: 16); on the contrary, the ethico-juridical concept of 'person' should be dismantled. The problem is not that of transforming a dog into a 'quasi-person'; the goal is to get out of the world of persons. Only in such a world will humans, dogs and stones finally be able to coexist.

Coda

Although nature resolves everything into its constituent particles, she never annihilates anything.

(Lucretius 2001: 9, I, 216–17)

The book you are about to conclude, if you have made it this far, deals with animality – yet not, properly speaking, with animals. It mostly focuses on a single living being belonging to the species *Homo sapiens*, one who has always defined itself as different from all (other) animals. And yet it too is, clearly, an animal (it eats animals, and it can be eaten by other animals). The meaning of this book lies within this paradox of an animal that claims not to be an animal. And its not being an animal is so true that, even when admitting to being an animal (for today this sort of admission is very fashionable), it doesn't however stop being a very special animal. A cat doesn't need to affirm its being a cat: it simply is a cat. A human being that *has* to state its animality is implicitly undermining what it is trying to claim. Between being and saying there is, precisely, language. The argument of this book is that 'speaking', more than just a means of communication, is a metaphysical machinery (what Agamben called an anthropological machine). The performance of language, as such a metaphysical machinery, severs the speaker from the world and from other speakers. For this reason, the problem of language is the real topic of this book: if speaking produces distance and separation (and the most metaphysically powerful linguistic sign is 'no'), then the members of the species *Homo sapiens* are not animals, because language splits the voice that says 'I' from the body that produces that very voice. Language is a dualism-engendering machinery. If we are looking for human animality we should look for it in a human being who has 'come to terms' with language, i.e., with the radical dualism that language ever again reproduces. Human animality comes *after* language. In this sense, human animality is intrinsically posthuman. In an extraordinary passage in *A Thousand Plateaus*, Deleuze and Guattari show how 'becoming-animal' encompasses all other possible forms of becoming. Indeed, 'becoming-animal' does not so much designate a movement towards a particular and determinate condition as represent the prototype for all other modes of *becoming*. 'Becoming' is neither a stable condition, nor yet another manifestation of the human person/subject. It does not indicate a subject 'becoming' something else; the point is rather that of accepting becoming as one's own condition: the subject is to be dissolved into becoming. In this sense, becoming is always impersonal, and non-subjective. So animality is not an ethical problem, because becoming – the dissolution of the subject – is beyond the traditional field of ethics. Deleuze and Guattari thus challenge us to take becoming seriously, as *pure becoming*. It should not be thought as something happening to a substance, as for example a human zygote turning into a foetus. The process of becoming should rather be seen as primary; in this sense zygote, embryo and foetus are simply linguistic distinctions, arbitrarily isolating (although there can be good medical or legal reasons for doing so) a single *flux* of becoming. Indeed, in biology, it is increasingly clear how distinctions drawn within the vital cycle of the 'same' organism, between one phase (for example a pupa in the case of an insect) and another (the 'adult' specimen), are largely arbitrary:

> There are many reasons, empirical and theoretical alike, to regard development as a segment of life whose two ends can be fixed by stipulation only. Arguably, we may also have good practical reasons to conventionally fix the origin of a new individual at a specified biological transition, be it fertilization, or the beginning of translation of the zygotic genome, or some other. However, from a theoretical point of view, we must acknowledge that our choice is not irrevocably dictated by the internal logics of the phenomena to which we need to apply a periodization. Still more, opening our views to the whole range of developmental sequences of the most diverse animal species (not to speak of the other living beings) invites such a relaxation of our customary anthropocentric (or at least vertebratocentric) views, to suggest the need for a currently wanting comprehensive theory of development. (Minelli 2011: 13)

Taking becoming seriously means that *the becoming that becomes* is not to be thought of as a *substance* that becomes something else. Deleuze and Guattari are indeed proposing a wholly different ontology, not one grounded on substances with properties (the subject-predicate scheme), but rather based on interlinked fluxes of becoming, perpetually in the process of becoming. This is why 'becoming-animal' encompasses all other possible forms of becoming:

Becoming-animal is only one becoming among others. A kind of order or apparent progression can be established for the segments of becoming in which we find ourselves; becoming-woman, becoming-child; becoming-animal, -vegetable, or -mineral; becomings-molecular of all kinds, becomings-particles. Fibers lead us from one to the other, transform one into the other as they pass through doors and across thresholds. Singing or composing, painting, writing have no other aim: to unleash these becomings. Especially music; music is traversed by a becoming-woman, becoming-child, and not only at the level of themes and motifs: the little refrain, children's games and dances, childhood scenes. (Deleuze and Guattari 1987: 272)

But what does it mean for every becoming to be a becoming-*animal*? The animal is neither a substance nor a subject, and even less so a personal individuation. Nor is the animal an instinct as opposed to reason, or nature as opposed to culture, or life against death. All these dualisms are dissolved in the animality of the animal, for otherwise we could not comprehend what there is in common between becoming-woman and becoming-music, or between becoming-mineral and becoming-child (Gardner and MacCormack 2017). The object of interest is becoming itself, not *what* becoming becomes. For example, becoming-woman pertains to both women and men – many women indeed still have not become-women. In truth, each of these becomings embodies a 'line of flight'. Deleuze and Guattari specify that lines of flight do not pertain to 'freedom' – a religious and juridical notion – but they are more simply and more radically 'lines of deterritorialization' (Deleuze and Guattari 1986: 34), perennially tracing new escape routes where none were present. Becoming-animal, just like the mole burrowing underground, always finds an escape route. At the same time, becoming-animal is a '[d]esire [that] is not form, but a procedure, a process' (1986: 8). Desire, then, is neither lack (of a now absent form), nor transcendence (towards a form to come) – it is a procedure or a process. This is a desire that lacks nothing, a desire of fullness and fluxes: 'starting from . . . the subject one is, the organs one has, or the functions one fulfills, becoming is to extract particles between which one establishes the relations of movement and rest, speed and slowness that are *closest* to what one is becoming, and through which one becomes' (Deleuze and Guattari 1987: 272). Already evident in this formulation is the link between becoming-animal, as an exemplary form of becoming, and the complex field of the posthuman. The becoming-woman of a man, for example, means exploring ways of being of a male body that exceed masculine identity; the same goes for the becoming-woman of a woman, i.e., the exploration of bodily ways of being that exceed those of a woman (indeed, if the 'animal' is an *animot*, the 'woman' is a *femmot*). The theme of the posthuman, then, pertains to all those ways in which a body can offer itself to becoming-animal, i.e., to a post-subjective and post-personal hybridisation. In this sense, human animality will either be posthuman or it will not be animal at all:

> Thomas Nagel advocates that humans should imaginatively attempt to become the bat they cannot be; the Renaissance poet Henry Vaughan asks his readers to acknowledge the vital vegetal life that we all possess; Geoffrey Chaucer . . . imagined himself as iron between two magnets. Are such imaginative acts of becoming-nonhuman antihumanist, posthuman-ist, neohumanist? (Harris 2012: 293–4)

Human animality is posthuman. But what is 'post-' about this kind of posthumanism? Rosi Braidotti writes that 'my anti-humanism leads me to object to the unitary subject of Humanism, including its socialist variables, and to replace it with a more complex and rela-tional subject framed by embodiment, sexuality, affectivity, empathy and desire as core qualities' (2013: 26). Braidotti's proposal touches all the critical points of the classical humanist project, yet does not intend to completely get rid of them. Indeed, even a 'complex and relational subject framed by embodiment, sexuality, affectivity, empathy and desire' would not cease to be a *subject*, i.e., a substance which, as self-aware and self-critical as it might be, would still remain a terminus for the process of becoming. What Braidotti is seeking is a posthuman subject: getting rid of the 'flaws' of traditional human-ism but still preserving some of its fundamental traits. This kind of posthumanism seeks a different, nonhumanist subject – but a subject nonetheless: 'subjectivity is rather a process of auto-poiesis or self-styling, which involves complex and continuous negotiations with dominant norms and values and hence also multiple forms of accountability' (Braidotti 2013: 35). The desired outcome is indeed explicitly defined as a 'posthuman subjectivity' (2013: 37). On the contrary, the trajectory outlined in this book tries to imagine a con-dition utterly beyond the subject: human animality is posthuman because it is post-subjective.[1] Something that has a stronger and more intrinsic resonance with the image of the posthuman presented in this book is Donna Haraway's 'cyborg feminism', which arose precisely out of 'the breakup of versions of Euro-American feminist human-ism in their devastating assumptions of master narratives deeply

Coda

indebted to racism and colonialism' (Haraway 1991: 1). Human animality is an unknown animality, since *Homo sapiens* – insofar as it is *loquens* – has never been an animal. Human animality needs to be constructed, but neither in the jungle nor in the Pleistocene, as evolutionary psychology would suggest. The point is precisely that of *constructing* an animality that never was. From this point of view Haraway's cyborg is tantamount to the attempt to 'neutralise' the artificiality that characterises the human species:

> the cyborg is a creature in a post-gender world; it has no truck with bisexuality, pre-oedipal symbiosis, unalienated labour, or other seductions to organic wholeness through a final appropriation of all the powers of the parts into a higher unity. In a sense, the cyborg has no origin story in the Western sense. . . . The cyborg skips the step of original unity, of identification with nature. (1991: 150–1)

The paradox of the cyborg consists in its being both maximally artificial – for it has no 'original' nature to recover, nor to transgress – yet, potentially, also maximally natural, for its life knows no artificiality. It is a being whose *Umwelt* coincides with the exclusively human *Umgebung*, an identity causing the ultimate collapse of this venerable metaphysical dualism: '[n]ature and culture are reworked; the one can no longer be the resource for appropriation or incorporation by the other' (1991: 152). What needs stressing is that the cyborg is a constructed, contaminated and radically anti-substantialist body (Bogue 2015); from this point of view then, when Haraway – in the years that followed the publication of her *Manifesto* – concerned herself with the transformative nexus between dogs and humans (Haraway 2008), she was actually exploring the same question: the becoming-animal of the human through non-subjective processes of hybridisation. A human-machine hybrid (or a human-animal hybrid) is still a *hybrid*. Becoming-animal is a hybrid.

But if the posthuman is a cyborg, does this mean that it lacks a body? Or, more precisely, that its body is meaningless, since – according to the original project of artificial intelligence – what matters is simply how an artificial body functions rather than how it is materially constructed (Turing 1950)? According to Cary Wolfe 'posthumanism . . . isn't posthuman at all – in the sense of being "after" our embodiment has been transcended – but is only posthu-man*ist*, in the sense that it opposes the fantasies of disembodiment and autonomy, inherited from humanism itself' (Wolfe 2010: xv). As we have seen, 'posthuman' essentially means post-subjective. The point of contention is not the body, but rather the separation – and the human being *is* this very separation – between 'person' on the one hand and 'bare life' on the other. The posthuman questions the mind/body dualism. Thus, the posthuman has nothing to do with speculations – which are indeed fully compatible with the traditional humanist project – of a future, more-than-human, humanity. '[T]ranshumanism should be seen as an intensification of humanism' (Wolfe 2010: xv). The posthuman, then, is a space for experimentation, wherein a human body – a talking body – ventures beyond the borders of subjective identity. This space is at once human – because the humanity of the human cannot be erased through a sheer act of will (for the subject exercises its will, and the renunciation of the will is still a voluntary, and subjective, act) – and beyond the human, since the encounter with the animal triggers combinations and assemblages (Deleuze and Guattari's *agencements*) that produce wholly unpredictable effects. In this sense, the posthuman

> forces us to rethink our taken-for-granted modes of human experience, including the normal perceptual modes and affective states of *Homo sapiens* itself, by recontextualizing them in terms of the entire sensorium of other living beings and their own autopoietic ways of 'bringing forth a world' – ways that are, since we ourselves are human *animals*, part of the evolutionary history and behavioral and psychological repertoire of the human itself. But it also insists that we attend to the specificity of the human – its ways of being in the world, its ways of knowing, observing, and describing – by (paradoxically, for humanism) acknowledging that it is fundamentally a prosthetic creature that has coevolved with various forms of technicity and materiality, forms that are radically 'not-human' and yet have nevertheless made the human what it is . . . this includes the most fundamental prostheticity of all: language in the broadest sense. (Wolfe 2010: xxv–xxvi)

Human animality is, properly speaking, a posthuman – i.e., post-subjective – animality. This is the most crucial point, because all the consequences of the human derive from it: the question of the Anthropocene, for example, could not even be posed without a human subject that *has* self-consciousness, a body to 'govern', and the 'right' to private property all at once. Animals *use* the world – only the human sees it as an economic resource to be *consumed*. Unlike the human, the body of becoming-animal is not subjugated by a reflective consciousness. For this reason, it is a body of absolute immanence, because only a body that has become-animal can adhere to life in all of its power, without residue. This is the body of the

194

posthuman, a body capable of forming unpredictable connections with the world, both living and non-living: a rhizomatic body, a body constrained by no law and that no biopolitical machinery can restrain. Such a body cannot even be said to be free, because it cannot be forced to obey, for it is a body without a Super-Ego. A body that no economic system can grasp, because becoming-animal does not believe in money, in desire, and not even in God: 'all becomings are ... molecular' (Deleuze and Guattari 1987: 272), they engender confusion and contaminations, they are beyond the pure and the impure. Thus, '[i]t is a question of composing a body with the animal, a body without organs defined by zones of intensity or proximity' (1987: 274). Since bodies touch each other – precisely because they do not believe in transcendence and abstraction – they are materialist by definition (with no need to formulate a materialist philosophy).

Because of its uncertain and intensive nature, the key concept of becoming-animal is that of 'assemblage' (*agencement*), the other – prehensile – face of 'desire': 'desire is always assembled; it is what the assemblage determines it to be' (Deleuze and Guattari 1987: 229). A desire does not presuppose a void to be filled but, on the contrary, is an always-full fullness, affirmative, and without hesitations: becoming-animal is therefore 'a circulation of impersonal affects ... that disrupts signifying projects as well as subjective feelings ... an irresistible deterritorialization' (1987: 233). Animality is this power that always again deterritorialises, that intuits movements no one had thought of, that establishes connections that are unnatural by definition (immanence has no Super-Ego, and no Oedipus), and that sees what everyone thought was invisible. For this reason, becoming-animal is yet another mode of presentation of the 'virtual'. There is an extraordinary example of this in *Difference and Repetition*, when Deleuze describes a child taking his first steps. His movements are either guided by external stimuli (such as those coming from the mother) or by an internal drive to stand on his legs and try to walk. But these two vectors do not exhaust what happens within the child, because there is another vector to be added – the 'virtual' one – that is neither external nor internal. This third vector is neither potential nor actual, and yet it is at work in the bodily exploration of the infant. Properly speaking, without such a space the child could never learn how to walk, since it is necessary for experimenting with a still-absent walking:

A child who begins to walk does not only bind excitations in a passive synthesis, even supposing that these were endogenous excitations born of its own movements. No one has ever walked endogenously. On the one hand, the child goes beyond the bound excitations towards the supposition or the intentionality of an object, such as the mother, as the goal of an effort, the end to be actively reached 'in reality' and in relation to which success and failure may be measured. *But on the other hand and at the same time*, the child constructs for itself another object, a quite different kind of object which is a *virtual* object or centre and which then governs and compensates for the progresses and failures of its real activity: it puts several fingers in its mouth, wraps the other arm around this virtual centre, and appraises the whole situation from the point of view of this virtual mother. The fact that the child's glance may be directed at the real mother and that the virtual object may be the goal of an apparent activity (for example, sucking) may inspire an erroneous judgement on the part of the observer. Sucking occurs only in order to provide a virtual object to contemplate in the context of extending the passive synthesis; conversely, the real mother is contemplated only in order to provide a goal for the activity, and a criterion by which to evaluate the activity, in the context of an active synthesis. (Deleuze 2001a: 99)

The 'virtual' is always a becoming-animal, a deterritorialisation, an escape route. The becoming-animal of the human is this never-ending opening of unthought and unthinkable spaces for movement: unthinkable because they cannot be thought, since all thought is categorial and cannot dwell *between* the categories; unthought because the virtual always 'lacks something in itself, since it is always half of itself, the other half being different as well as absent' (2001a: 102). Animality is always this lack that lacks nothing, lack-in-itself, without anything to match nor identities to reach; in this sense it immediately transforms itself into a pure presence. The animality of becoming-animal, as was the case with Lacan's *objet petit a*, always eludes us, like a bumblebee flying erratically around the kitchen, at once fearful and fearless. In this sense, Deleuze continues, the 'virtual' is ungraspable by thought, precisely because to think means to assign a determinate place to what is thought, to place it within a category, i.e., a *word*. The 'virtual', then, is the 'becoming-animal' of thought:

The virtual object is a *partial* object – not simply because it lacks a part which remains in the real, but in itself and for itself because it is cleaved or doubled into two virtual parts, one of which is always missing from the other. In short, the virtual is never subject to the global character which affects real objects. It is – not only by its origin but by its own nature – a fragment, a shred or a remainder. It lacks its own identity. (2001a: 100–1)

The animality of 'becoming-animal' is a shred, never whole, never a complete form identical to itself. Lacan, in his Seminar XX, presents the woman in precisely the same terms. For Lacan 'woman is defined by a position that I have indicated as "not whole" (*pas-tout*) with respect to phallic jouissance' (1998: 7). 'Phallic jouissance' is the 'jouissance of the Other', i.e., that mandated by the Law, the Super-Ego, the financial market. This is 'allowed' jouissance, and indeed encouraged: '[t]he superego is the imperative of jouissance – Enjoy!' (1998: 3). With respect to this imperative, the status of the woman position is one of 'not whole'. That is to say, the woman cannot be defined by means of a unitary category – *the* woman (the *femmot*, as I have proposed to call it). There is always something left of the woman, of her singularity ('the remainder [*reste*] I call object *a*' [1998: 6]), because she is 'not whole'. The masculine position, on the other hand, is entirely under the dominion of the Super-Ego – in Lacanian terms, of castration. The male position can have access to jouissance – the only jouissance available to him – by passing through the Oedipus, i.e., the interdiction of the mother's jouissance. Not so for the feminine position: for Lacan the woman is always 'not whole' (*pas toute*). There is always something ungraspable in the woman. Properly speaking, the woman *is* this ungraspability. It should be noted that Lacan is not simply repeating, in his own words, that the woman is an instinctive or natural creature; on the contrary the woman is 'not whole' precisely due to the existence of the Super-Ego, the Law of culture that makes the members of the species *Homo sapiens* fully human, that is, under the mark of castration. A female cat is 'not whole' because its felinity does not depend on the acceptance of a cultural interdiction. But the woman *can become* 'not whole' only because she can completely subtract herself from castration. Consequently, '[t]hat is what defines what? Woman precisely, except that Woman can only be written with a bar through it. There's no such thing as Woman, Woman with a capital *W* indicating the universal. There's no such thing as Woman because, in her essence . . . she is not-whole' (1998: 72–3).

Thus, Lacan takes a stand against any substantialist representation of the woman as a living being with a particular *nature*. Conversely, he argues, the distinctive character of the feminine position is precisely that of being radically 'not whole' (there is no essence which can 'capture' her). But, for this very reason, the feminine is a position and not a bodily essence: it follows that there can be women who do not assume this position and men who do. The problem is not that of opposing a feminine to a masculine, but rather that of breaking the dualistic machinery of genders, as well as the monism of those who would rather merge them: '[b]isexuality is no better a concept than the separateness of the sexes. It is as deplorable to miniaturize, internalize the binary machine as it is to exacerbate it; it does not extricate us from it' (Deleuze and Guattari 1987: 276). 'Becoming-animal', when applied to gender, amounts to the adoption of a feminine position, one that cannot be caged into a universal category. Consider the example of Antigone, who repeatedly casts into turmoil the thought of the Law, of the universal and of the whole. Antigone debates with her sister, Ismene, who reminds her of the place that society assigned her:

> And now we two, the last ones left – consider
> How much worse death will be for us if we
> Defy the law and flout the rulers' vote . . . I'm forced
> To act as I do, and I'll obey the rulers. (Sophocles 2001: 55–6)

When Antigone insists that she does not want to renounce giving a proper burial to their brother Polyneikes, Ismene replies that – and the Law is here speaking through her – 'it's wrong to go hunting for what's impossible' (2001: 57). This is animality: the becoming of the impossible. Antigone's desire – that, like the chorus sings, 'does not know to bend amidst her troubles' (2001: 74) – is her 'becoming-woman' i.e., her 'becoming-animal'.

Indeed, in his interpretation of Sophocles' work in Seminar VII on 'The Ethics of Psychoanalysis', Lacan presents Antigone's stance as something utterly unique and beyond argumentation: when words, language and the signifier enter into play, something may be said, and it is said in the following way: '[m]y brother may be whatever you say he is, a criminal . . . As far as I am concerned, the order that you dare refer me to doesn't mean anything, for from my point of view, my brother is my brother' (Lacan 1997: 278). That is it, and nothing else can be added. Indeed, Antigone's stand 'is not developed in any signifying chain or in anything else' (1997: 278). Antigone does not offer reasons for her opposition to Kreon, and even if she had some (for example by appealing to blood ties over duties towards the *polis*), these would still fail to motivate her gesture, which indeed is beyond any motivation. Antigone simply does not respect the Law, and that is all. She is 'not whole' with respect to the universality of the Law of the *polis*. It should be stressed that Antigone is able to subtract herself from the Law only because the Law is *already* in existence: 'Antigone invokes no other right than that one, a right that emerges in the language of the ineffaceable character of what is – ineffaceable, that is, from the moment when the emergent signifier freezes it like a fixed object in spite of the flood of possible transformations' (Lacan 1997: 279). Antigone thus inverts the Law's position, using language *against* it. Her gesture, born of language yet arresting it, is absolutely real – it is there, like Deleuze's 'shreds'. It is a *virtual* 'shred' that Antigone digs down, like a mole cricket burrowing deep in the soil, allowing her to find an escape route from a situation that seemed to have no resolution but unsatisfactory ones. Animality is this ability to position oneself – in the face of the Law – as an animal would, merely looking for a way to escape. In this case, Antigone's escape takes the form of an obstinate and obtuse (because without reasons) opposition to the Law: '[w]hat is, is, and it is to this, to this surface, that the unshakeable, unyielding position of Antigone is fixed' (Lacan 1997: 325). Becoming-woman is on the 'surface' (it could not be otherwise), in the immanence of the world, draping itself over its surface like an infinite Möbius strip. The world has no hierarchies, no above or below – it is all *surface*.

For Deleuze and Guattari becoming-animal is also a 'becoming-child'. More precisely, 'Spinozism is the becoming-child of the philosopher' (1987: 256). Indeed, the philosophical principle of Spinozism is simple, so simple that even a child could understand it: the world is all *there is*, and *only* what there is. Everything else – hierarchies, values, abstractions and universals – does not exist. This is such an elementary stance that even a spider, were it to dabble in philosophy, would agree with it. In the final analysis, a spider is Spinozian, precisely because it has no interest in philosophy. And there is a reason for the spider's lack of interest: philosophy is a thought of the world, i.e., philosophy can only exist because of the dualism between thought and world. As we know, the spider is not a dualist, for it cannot be separated from its '*Umwelt*'; the spider *is* the world, the world *is* the spider. Indeed, Spinoza writes, '[b]y reality and perfection I understand the same thing' (Curley 1994: 116). On the other hand, imperfection is nothing but the separation between '*Umwelt*' and '*Welt*', which lies at the very origin of philosophy. The child, then, is a human who can (still) experience the world as a spider would. The child is a talking spider. This is a crucial point, because it entails that language can also be used in a non-dualist manner. After all, we have always known that even the most sophisticated poetry has something infantile about it. Indeed, poetry is the 'becoming-animal' of language: '[w]hat is poetry if not an operation in language that deactivates and renders inoperative its communicative and informative functions in order to open them to a new possible use?' (Agamben 2017a: 55).

But what is the 'child' of 'becoming-child'? Once again, psychoanalysis can shed some light on this question, through what is arguably its most momentous (and always again suppressed) discovery: human psychosexual development. This pertains to that sexuality that – this is Freud's discovery – manifests itself many years prior to 'adult' and reproductive sexuality – the 'normal' form of sexuality at the service of the reproduction of the species. Indeed, Freud's *Three Essays on the Theory of Sexuality* are a large and detailed catalogue of a wholly 'virtual' sexuality, because they explore the limitless possibilities for jouissance that the body affords – first to the *infans*' experimentation and, later, to the adult 'pervert'. A body that enjoys pleasure without any Super-Ego or Law dictating how and why it should enjoy it. This condition, with no equivalents in the animal world (where sexuality seems almost always subordinated to reproduction),[2] is defined by Freud, with a famous formula: the *infans*' 'polymorphously perverse disposition' (2000: 57). The body of the *infans* enjoys itself. Freud – with a sexist and misogynist note that cannot but remind us of Lacan's 'not whole' woman – claims that 'children behave in the same kind of way as an average uncultivated woman in whom the same polymorphously perverse disposition persists' (2000: 57). However, sublimation and Super-Ego notwithstanding, 'this same disposition to perversions of every kind is a general and fundamental human characteristic' (2000: 57). But what does 'polymorphously perverse disposition' mean, exactly? Here again Spinoza can help us clarify the issue. In the fourth section of the *Ethics*, he writes about the affects of the human body, arguing that:

> *Whatever so disposes the human body that it can be affected in a great many ways, or renders it capable of affecting external bodies in a great many ways, is useful to man; the more it renders the body capable of being affected in a great many ways, or of affecting other bodies, the more useful it is; on the other hand, what renders the body less capable of these things is harmful.* (Curley 1994: 221)

The body is not an autonomous substance: it coincides with its power of touching and merging with other bodies. The newborn that suckles, kicks, touches and puts everything in its reach into its mouth is an extraordinary example of a Spinozian body. For this reason, the newborn – having not yet become-human – is an unstoppable 'deterritorialising' force, precisely because it has no personal identity to safeguard or to impose upon others: the newborn is 'the assemblage [that] extends over or penetrates an *unlimited field of immanence* that makes the segments melt and that liberates desire from all its concretizations and abstractions or, at the very least, fights actively against them in order to dissolve them' (Deleuze and Guattari 1986: 86). Becoming-child, then, is not a condition to be reached, but rather the process of becoming the act of becoming itself. That is because in the child, like in the animal, 'everything . . . is a metamorphosis' (1986: 35), a metamorphosis that never reaches a 'final' stage, but is rather an endless corridor, an infinite summer afternoon, a sunrise that blurs into a sunset:

> The only way to get outside the dualisms is to be-between, to pass between, the intermezzo – that is what Virginia Woolf lived with all her energies, in all of her work, never ceasing to become. The girl is like the block of becoming that remains contemporaneous to each opposable term, man, woman, child, adult. It is not the girl who becomes a woman; it is becoming-woman that produces the universal girl. . . . It is certain that molecular politics proceeds via the girl and the child. But it is also certain that girls and children draw their strength neither from the molar status that subdues them nor from the organism and subjectivity they receive; they draw their strength from the becoming-molecular they cause to pass between sexes and ages, the becoming-child of the adult as well as of the child, the becoming-woman of the man as well as of the woman. The girl and the child do not become; it is becoming itself that is a child or a girl. (Deleuze and Guattari 1987: 277)

All these various forms of becoming – becoming-woman, becoming-child, becoming-molecular, becoming-animal – finally converge in the most 'perfect' of becomings: becoming-music. Music, indeed, is the becoming-animal of language, i.e., of the 'anthropologic machine': the machinery that institutes all the dualisms we have encountered throughout this book. Becoming-animal is only possible when language is 'captured and neutralized' (Agamben 2016: 267). Language, along with all the innumerable biopolitical apparatuses that derive from it, is a 'machine' that produces the primordial dualism between a subject/person on the one hand and a body reduced to 'bare life' on the other. This dualism cannot be resolved, because the human being *is* this very dualism. Therefore, the becoming-music of language is also the becoming-animal of the human. Language becomes music in literature, in nursery rhymes and in poetry. The latter, in particular, represents the defusing of the subjectivising power of language. Poetry does not communicate anything, it is neither informative nor personal, even when composed by a well-known author. In this respect poetry is really like music, a tautology: poetry says itself, just like music affirms its own being musical, and nothing more. After all, this is how we can explain the perennial human fascination for animal calls. Not because we recognise, in those calls, a kind of 'communication'. But on the contrary because they have always reminded us of 'natural' sounds – like the wind, the roar of the sea, the sudden crack of a tree branch. A voice both unmistakable and meaningless. Zoosemiotics has always sought to reveal the signs hidden in animal voices, but perhaps the time has come for us to look for an animal voice in language. Music then, as pure manifestation of becoming. This is why '[m]usic is never tragic, music is joy' (Deleuze and Guattari 1987: 299). Not because music would indeed lack a 'content' capable of lifting the spirit, but because music – as a pure becoming – brings about movement: it puts bodies into contact, produces molecular connections, and therefore increases their 'rhizomatic' power. In the section dedicated to 'becoming-music' in *A Thousand Plateaus* – which could be considered as a kind of summary of the generative mechanism of the book as a whole – Deleuze and Guattari discuss the process that both links and opposes the 'refrain' to the becoming-music of music. Just as not every woman becomes-woman, so not all music accepts the challenge of becoming-music. The most exemplary case of a 'refrain' is that famously discussed by Freud in *Beyond the Pleasure Principle*: the '*Fort/Da*' that, according to the Viennese psychiatrist, is used by the child to manage the anxiety caused by the mother's departure. The refrain here delimits a 'space', territorialises an experience, assigning it a place: '[c]hildren's, women's, ethnic, and territorial refrains, refrains of love and destruction: the birth of rhythm' (Deleuze and Guattari 1987: 300). The 'refrain' is the systole of becoming, it delimits and it circumscribes: '[t]he refrain is rather a means of preventing music, warding it off, or forgoing it' (1987: 300). In the end, the refrain is the becoming-language of music, the omnipresent danger of subordinating music to meaning and to signifiers: 'music exists because the refrain exists also, because music takes up the refrain . . . because it forms a block with it in order to take it somewhere else. *The child's refrain, which is not music, forms a block with the becoming-child of music'* (1987: 300).

Finally, the becoming-music of music always again breaks the closed circle of the refrain, making it fluid and mobile: '[m]usic is a creative, active operation that consists in deterritorializing the refrain. Whereas the refrain is essentially territorial, territorializing, or reterritorializing, music makes it a deterritorialized content for a deterritorializing form of expression' (Deleuze and Guattari 1987: 300). The play between 'refrain' and 'music' allows us to introduce, at last, a question that has so far been avoided throughout this book. Is there actually a place for 'becoming-animal'? Or more precisely, is there a place for a politics of becoming-animal? The answer to this, as is all too often the case with important questions, is both *yes* and *no*. Yes, because animality is everywhere by now, and it has already produced an indubitable effect: 'the veritable explosion of animal studies over the past twenty years has led to an altogether salutary deconstruction not just of the human/animal divide, but also of the category of "the animal" itself and perforce, therefore, of "the human" too' (Wolfe 2018: 534). Today, it is impossible to speak of the human in a neutral way. This awareness has been translated into an absolutely extraordinary effort to safeguard animal life, although too little attention (both practical and theoretical) is still paid to forms of animal life that are different from mammals (which are both morphologically and psychologically very close to humans). This lack of attention to all those forms of life that are truly different from us (and that represent the majority of living beings – there are less than 7,000 species of mammals against millions of other animal and plant species (Burgin et al. 2018)), should alert animal rights advocates that perhaps this 'love' for animals is not so disinterested after all. However, I do not believe that this increased attention paid to animality will ultimately change anything at all in the relationship between *Homo sapiens* and the natural world. *Homo anthropocentricus* will keep consuming the world, because the anthropologic machinery fully coincides with the humanity of the human. So, I believe that a negative answer to the question is also appropriate: no, there is *no* space for a politics of animality, because animality and politics cannot be in agreement – where there is politics there are subjects and private property, and therefore no animality (and vice versa). What remains – and I believe this to be the 'ethical' lesson taught by Deleuze (and Guattari, who represented Deleuze's becoming-animal) – is the singular move (that for this reason cannot but swing between ethics and aesthetics) of those who find an 'escape route' in the present situation:

> the 'old' demarcation between ethics and aesthetics rested on the 'old' philosophy which traded on the distinction between Being and Act. In his last philosophical statement Deleuze therefore pointed to a way of moving beyond both these distinctions – life, with its associated philosophic *a prioris*, for him supplants the distinction between ethics (the correlative of Being) and aesthetics (the correlative of Act). Only in this way can life be lived as a work of art, that is, something at once powerful and blissful. (Surin 2011: 152)

There is no ethics – and, of course, no politics – of a singular gesture that can be a rule in itself, because a private rule is not a rule. To behave according to a rule means to acknowledge it as both a political and an ethical entity. However, animality is precisely something for which no rule can exist. Yet this does not exclude the possibility that such a gesture might also have ethical and political consequences. Human animality is the vector that always again, even in the depths of despair, finds a 'virtual' that was not there, and yet was always already there. The eyes of a mole were necessary to reveal it. Of course, the animality discussed in this book has nothing to do with ethics, and neither does it concern science or, even less so, consciousness. But since '[t]here is nothing that is major or revolutionary except the minor' (Deleuze and Guattari 1986: 26), animality is untimely, it is the perennial untimeliness of becoming. Fleeing into becoming: this is animality. Ultimately, such a possibility is always there, lurking – like a cat stalking a lizard, or the spider patiently waiting for the fly to be caught by its web. It is up to each and every one of us to rise to this challenge, which poses itself at any time, since the 'virtual' is stronger than the power/act couple. Let us conclude, then, with Agamben's words. To *exploitation* (always proprietary, territorialised and personal) he always prefers *use*, which is discreet, impersonal and light. Consider how a seagull 'uses' the air that lifts its wings during flight, or how an ant 'uses' the soil onto which its tiny legs frantically run, or again how a jellyfish 'soars' through the water. Animality is this use that does not wear out, without an 'I', and with no calculations nor savings:

> What is decisive here is the separation between contemplation and consciousness and between affectability and personality. Contrary to the prestige of consciousness in our culture, it is always necessary to recall anew that sensation and habitual praxis, as use-of-oneself, articulate a

zone of non-consciousness, which is not something like a mystical fog in which the subject loses itself but the habitual dwelling in which the living being, before every subjectivation, is perfectly at ease. If the gestures and acts of the animal are agile and graceful ('no animal is at a loss in use-of-itself'), this is because for it no act, no gesture constitutes a 'work' of which it is posited as responsible author and conscious creator. (Agamben 2016: 63–4)

The animal is what it is because it does not 'work': it uses the world without appropriating it. It will not be surprising, then, that in his *Creation and Anarchy: The Work of Art in the Religion of Capitalism*, Agamben describes the artist in the same way, as someone who does not produce artworks – since only a subject can produce something, and without a subject there is no object to be produced. Here we finally encounter the only possible 'ethics' of animality: to make an art out of one's 'imperceptible, . . . indiscernible, . . . impersonal' (Deleuze and Guattari 1987: 279) worldly presence – that is to say to become a poet, someone who is 'at the mercy of one's own impotential' (Agamben 2019: 19).

Notes

1. Braidotti believes that this emphasis on the 'subjective' dimension of the posthuman is justified by ethical and political considerations:

    The posthuman subjectivity I advocate is rather materialist and vitalist, embodied and embedded, firmly located somewhere, according to the feminist 'politics of location'. . . . Why do I stress so much the issue of the subject? Because a theory of subjectivity as both materialist and relational, 'nature-cultural' and self-organizing is crucial in order to elaborate critical tools suited to the complexity and contradictions of our times. A merely analytical form of posthuman thought does not go far enough. More especially, a serious concern for the subject allows us to take into account the elements of creativity and imagination, desire, hopes and aspirations without which we simply cannot make sense of contemporary global culture and its posthuman overtones. We need a vision of the subject that is 'worthy of the present'. (2013: 51–2)

    But a 'materialist' subjectivity is no less subjective and personal than an 'idealist' one, since both have been constituted through the 'anthropological machine'. The posthuman challenge is far more radical: it is not a matter of weakening the subject, nor of inventing a new – more fragile and 'embodied' – one. It rather means taking animality seriously. From this point of view, when feminist thought approaches animality, for example, by taking animals as new and upcoming 'social actors' (Birke and Holmberg 2017: 118), this represents an important but still theoretically unsatisfactory move. It is not enough to 'take seriously multiple subjectivities' (2017: 120) – including those of animals – rather it is necessary to consider the hypothesis of a human being living like an ant. That this hypothesis sounds ludicrous to us – if not downright offensive – demonstrates just how much unacknowledged anthropocentrism still lingers in our self-image: 'feminist theory about embodiment . . . can offer insights into human/animal relationships as intercorporeal. So, too, can animals contribute to feminist thinking . . . for example [by means of the] exquisite sensitivity of many nonhumans to our actions, even before we do them, [which] underscores the importance of nonverbal, bodily ways of knowing, which produce co-actions' (2017: 122). The animal is sensitive because it can understand us, but the opposite never seems to occur: a human being sensitive to the animal. Most of all, the fact remains that a 'nonverbal' way of knowing is still dependent on the 'anthropological machine'. Once we become humans – linguistic animals – all of our abilities, both affective and cognitive, are influenced by language and subjectivation. If the encounter of feminist thought and animality goes no further than this 'alliance' between new 'subjectivities', no real step forward from the classical humanist thought is taken. After all, for von Uexküll animals are 'subjects', but this did not stop Heidegger – who grounded his thought on the Estonian biologist's research – from formulating a radically anti-animalist philosophy. The 'subject' is always humanist, no matter which form it takes.

2. However, there seem to be examples of animal sexual behaviour – for example that of the bonobos described by de Waal (1995) – which undermine this assumption.

Bibliography

Acampora, Christa Davis and Acampora, Ralph (eds) (2004) *A Nietzschean Bestiary: Becoming Animal Beyond Docile and Brutal*. New York: Rowman & Littlefield.

Agamben, Giorgio (1998) *Homo Sacer: Sovereign Power and Bare Life*. Stanford: Stanford University Press.

Agamben, Giorgio (1999) *Potentialities: Collected Essays in Philosophy*. Stanford: Stanford University Press.

Agamben, Giorgio (2004) *The Open: Man and Animal*. Stanford: Stanford University Press.

Agamben, Giorgio (2006) *Language and Death: The Place of Negativity*. Minneapolis: University of Minnesota Press.

Agamben, Giorgio (2007) *The Coming Community*. Minneapolis: University of Minnesota Press.

Agamben, Giorgio (2013) *The Highest Poverty: Monastic Rules and Form-of-Life*. Stanford: Stanford University Press.

Agamben, Giorgio (2016) *The Use of Bodies*. Stanford: Stanford University Press.

Agamben, Giorgio (2017a) *The Fire and the Tale*. Stanford: Stanford University Press.

Agamben, Giorgio (2017b) *Autoritratto nello Studio*. Milano: Edizioni Nottetempo.

Agamben, Giorgio (2018a) *Pulcinella or Entertainment for Children*. Chicago: Seagull Books.

Agamben, Giorgio (2018b) *What is Philosophy?* Stanford: Stanford University Press.

Agamben, Giorgio (2019) *Creation and Anarchy: The Work of Art and the Religion of Capitalism*. Stanford: Stanford University Press.

Alderson-Day, Ben and Fernyhough, Charles (2015) 'Inner Speech: Development, Cognitive Functions, Phenomenology, and Neurobiology'. *Psychological Bulletin* 141(5): 931–65.

Aloi, Giovanni (2011) 'Different Becomings'. *Art & Research: A Journal of Ideas, Contexts and Methods* 4(1): 1–10.

Aloi, Giovanni (2012a) 'Deconstructing the Animal in Search of the Real'. *Anthrozoos* 25: 329–46.

Aloi, Giovanni (2012b) 'Beyond Zoocentrism. An Interview with Giovanni

Aloi', by Ariane De Blois. Available at <http://esse.ca/en/beyond-zoocen trism-interview-giovanni-aloi>

Aloi, Giovanni (2012c) *Art and Animals*. New York: Palgrave.

Alpi, Amedeo et al. (2007) 'Plant Neurobiology: No brain, No gain?' *Trends in Plant Science* 12(4): 135–6.

Amberson, Deborah and Past, Elena (eds) (2014) *Thinking Italian Animals: Human and Posthuman in Modern Italian Literature and Film*. New York: Palgrave.

Anderson, Michael and Leigh Anderson, Susan (eds) (2011) *Machine Ethics*. Cambridge: Cambridge University Press.

Aristotle (1993) *De Anima. Books II and III*, trans. D. W. Hamlyn. Oxford: Clarendon Press.

Baker, Steve (2000) *The Postmodern Animal*. London: Reaktion Books.

Baker, Steve (2013) *Artist|Animal*. Minneapolis: University of Minneapolis Press.

Baluska, Frantisek, Gagliano, Monica and Witzany Guenther (eds) (2018) *Memory and Learning in Plants*. Berlin: Springer.

Barbaj, Vanessa (2015) 'The Matter of Death: Posthumous Wildlife Art in the Anthropocene'. In Human Animal Research Network Editorial Collective (eds) *Animals in the Anthropocene: Critical Perspectives on Non-human Futures*. Sydney: Sydney University Press, 89–105.

Behuniak, Susun (2011) 'The Living Dead? The Construction of People with Alzheimer's Disease as Zombies'. *Ageing and Society* 31(2): 70–92.

Bene, Carmelo and Deleuze, Gilles (2012) *Sovrapposizioni*. Macerata: Quodlibet.

Bennett, Jane (2010) *Vibrant Matter: A Political Ecology of Things*. Durham: Duke University Press.

Bennett, Jane (2015) 'Systems and Things: On Vital Materialism and Object-Oriented Philosophy'. In R. Grusin (ed.) *The Nonhuman Turn*. Minneapolis: University of Minnesota Press, 223–39.

Bentham, Jeremy (1823) *An Introduction to the Principles of Morals and Legislation*. Oxford: Clarendon Press.

Benveniste, Émile (1971) *Problems in General Linguistics*. Miami: University of Miami Press.

Berger, John (2009) *Why Look at Animals?* London: Penguin.

Bergson, Henry (1991) *Matter and Memory*. New York: Zone Books.

Bermond, Bob (1997) 'The Myth of Animal Suffering'. In M. Dol et al. (eds) *Animal Consciousness and Animal Ethics*. Assen: Van Gorkum, 125–43.

Bimbenet, Étienne (2011) *L'animal que je ne suis plus*. Paris: Gallimard.

Birke, Linda and Holmberg, Tora (2017) 'Intersections: The Animal Question Meets Feminist Theory'. In C. Åsberg and R. Braidotti (eds) *A Feminist Companion to Posthumanities*. Berlin: Springer, 117–28.

Bjørkdahl, Kristian and Parrish, Alex (eds) (2018) *Rhetorical Animals:*

Boundaries of the Human in the Study of Persuasion. Lanham: Lexington Books.

Blazina, Chris and Kogan, Lori (eds) (2016) *Men and Their Dogs*. Dordrecht: Springer.

Bogue, Ronald (2015) 'The Companion Cyborg: Technics and Domestication'. In J. Roffe and H. Stark (eds) (2015) *Deleuze and the Non/Human*. New York: Palgrave, 163–79.

Bonaparte, Marie (1994) *Topsy: The Story of a Golden-haired Chow*. London: Transaction Publishers.

Boysen, Sarah, Berntson, Gary and Prentice, James (1987) 'Simian Scribbles: A Reappraisal of Drawing in the Chimpanzee (*Pan troglodytes*)'. *Journal of Comparative Psychology* 101(1): 82–9.

Braidotti, Rosi (2013) *The Posthuman*. Cambridge: Polity.

Braidotti, Rosi (2017) 'Four Theses on Posthuman Feminism'. In R. Grusin (ed.) *Anthropocene Feminism*. Minneapolis: University of Minneapolis Press, 21–48.

Brandl, Johannes (2016) 'The Puzzle of Mirror Self-recognition'. *Phenomenology and the Cognitive Sciences* 17(2): 279–304.

Breazeal, Cynthia and Brooks, Rodney (2005) 'Robot Emotion: A Functional Perspective'. In J.-M. Fellous and M. Arbib (eds) *Who Needs Emotions?: The Brain Meets the Robot*. Oxford: Oxford University Press, 271–309.

Brentari, Carlo (2015) *Jakob von Uexküll: The Discovery of the Umwelt Between Biosemiotics and Theoretical Biology*. Berlin: Springer.

Broglio, Ron (2011) *Surface Encounters: Thinking with Animals and Art*. Minneapolis: Minneapolis University Press.

Brooks, Rodney (1999), *Cambrian Intelligence: The Early History of the New AI*. Cambridge, MA: MIT Press.

Buchanan, Brett (2008) *Onto-Ethologies: The Animal Environments of Uexküll, Heidegger, Merleau-Ponty, and Deleuze*. New York: SUNY Press.

Burgin, Connor, Colella, Jocelyn, Kahn, Philip and Upham, Nathan (2018) 'How Many Species of Mammals are There?' *Journal of Mammalogy* 99(1): 1–14.

Caffo, Leonardo and Sonzogni, Valentina (2015) *An Art for the Other: The Animal in Philosophy and Art*. New York: Lantern Books.

Calarco, Matthew (2008) *Zoographies: The Question of the Animal from Heidegger to Derrida*. New York: Columbia University Press.

Calvo, Paco (2016) 'The Philosophy of Plant Neurobiology: A Manifesto'. *Synthese* 193: 1323–43.

Carboni, Massimo (2017) *Il genio è senza opera. Filosofie antiche e arti contemporanee*. Milano: Jaca Book.

Castellucci, Claudia, Kelleher, Joe, Ridout, Nicholas, Castellucci, Romeo and Guidi, Chiara (2008) *The Theatre of Societas Raffaello Sanzio*. London: Routledge.

Castellucci, Romeo (2000) 'The Animal Being on Stage'. *Performance Research* 5(2): 23–8.

de Castro, Eduardo Viveiros (2019), *Cosmological Perspectivism in Amazonia and Elsewhere*. London: Hau Books.

Cavalieri, Paola (2015) 'The Meaning of the Great Ape Project'. *Politics and Animals* 1(1): 16–34.

Cavalieri, Paola and Singer, Peter (eds) (1994) *The Great Ape Project: Equality Beyond Humanity*. New York: St. Martin's Press.

Chaudhuri, Una (2017) *The Stage Lives of Animals: Zooësis and Performance*. London: Routledge.

Ciccarelli, Roberto (2008) *Immanenza. Filosofia, diritto e politica della vita dal XIX al XX secolo*. Bologna: Il Mulino.

Cimatti, Felice (2000) *La scimmia che si parla. Linguaggio, autocoscienza e libertà nell'animale umano*. Torino: Bollati Boringhieri.

Cimatti, Felice (2002a) *La mente silenziosa*. Roma: Editori Riuniti.

Cimatti, Felice (2002b) *Mente e linguaggio negli animali. Introduzione alla Zoosemiotica* Cognitiva. Roma: Carocci.

Cimatti, Felice (2015) 'Ten Theses on Animality'. *Lo sguardo* 18(2): 41–59.

Cimatti, Felice (ed.) (2016) *Psicoanimot. L'animale psicoanalitico*. Perugia: Graphe.it.

Cimatti, Felice (2017) 'Arte e linguaggio. Il problema dell'esperienza estetica visiva'. *Rivista Italiana di Filosofia del Linguaggio* 11(2): 30–50.

Cimatti, Felice (2018) *Cose. Per una filosofia del reale*. Torino: Bollati Boringhieri.

Cimatti, Felice and Vallortigara, Giorgio (2015) 'So Little Mind, So Much Brain: Intelligence and Behavior in Non-human Animals'. *Italian Journal of Cognitive Sciences* 1: 9–24.

Coccia, Emanuele (2018) *La vita delle piante. Metafisica della mescolanza*. Bologna: Il Mulino.

Coetzee, John Maxwell (1999) *The Lives of Animals*. Princeton: Princeton University Press.

Collias, Nicholas and Collias, Elsie (1984) *Nest Building and Bird Behavior*. Princeton: Princeton University Press.

Crutzen, Paul and Brauch, Günter (eds) (2016) *Paul J. Crutzen: A Pioneer on Atmospheric Chemistry and Climate Change in the Anthropocene*. Berlin: Springer.

Curley, Edwin (ed.) (1994) *A Spinoza Reader: The Ethics and Other Works*. Princeton: Princeton University Press.

D'Addosio, Carlo (1992) *Bestie delinquenti*. Napoli: Flavio Pellegrino Editore.

Danesi, Marcel (2016) *Language and Mathematics*. Berlin: De Gruyter Mouton.

Danto, Arthur (1992) *Beyond the Brillo Box: The Visual Arts in Post-historical Perspective*. Berkeley: University of California Press.

Davis, Whitney (1992) 'Sigmund's Freud Drawing of the Dream of the Wolves'. *Oxford Art Journal* 15(2): 70–87.

de Fontenay, Elisabeth (1998) *Le silence des bêtes. La philosophie à l'épreuve de l'animalité*. Paris: Fayard.

De Mauro, Tullio (1999 (1965)) *Introduzione alla Semantica*. Bari: Laterza.

De Mauro, Tullio (2018 (1982)) *Minisemantica dei Linguaggi non Verbali e delle Lingue*. Bari: Laterza.

de Saussure, Ferdinand (2002) *Écrits de linguistique générale*. Paris: Gallimard.

De Waal, Frans B. M. (1995) 'The Bonobo Sex and Society'. *Scientific American* 272(3): 82–8.

Deacon, Terrence (2006) 'The Aesthetic Faculty'. In M. Turner ed. *The Artful Mind: Cognitive Science and the Riddle of Human Creativity*. Oxford: Oxford University Press, 21–53.

Deleuze, Gilles (1990) *Spinoza: Expressionism in Philosophy*. New York: Zone Books

Deleuze, Gilles (2001a) *Difference and Repetition*. London: Continuum.

Deleuze, Gilles (2001b) *Pure Immanence: Essays on a Life*. New York: Zone Books.

Deleuze, Gilles (2007) 'On Spinoza'. Available at <https://deleuzelectures. blogspot.com/2007/02/on-spinoza.html>

Deleuze, Gilles and Guattari, Félix (1986) *Kafka: Towards a Minor Literature*. Minneapolis: University of Minnesota Press.

Deleuze, Gilles and Guattari, Félix (1987) *A Thousand Plateaus: Capitalism and Schizophrenia 2*. Minneapolis: University of Minnesota Press.

DeLoache, Judy (2004) 'Becoming Symbol-Minded'. *Trends in Cognitive Sciences* 8(2): 66–70.

Derrida, Jacques (2008) *The Animal That Therefore I Am*. New York: Fordham University Press.

Despret, Vinciane (2002) *Quand le loup habitera avec l'agneau*. Paris: les Empêcheurs de penser en rond.

Despret, Vinciane (2009) *Penser comme un rat*. Versailles: Quæ éditions.

Despret, Vinciane and Porcher, Jocelyne (2007) *Etre bête. L'Esprit des étables*. Arles: Actes Sud Nature.

Di Matteo, Piersandra (ed.) (2015) *Toccare il reale. L'arte di Romeo Castellucci*. Napoli: Cronopio.

Diamond, Cora (2008) 'The Difficulty of Reality and the Difficulty of Philosophy'. In S. Cavell et al., *Philosophy and Animal Life*. New York: Columbia University Press.

Dissanayake, Ellen (2015) '*Aesthetic Primitives*: Fundamental Biological Elements of a Naturalistic Aesthetics'. *Aisthesis. Pratiche, linguaggi e saperi dell'estetico* 8(1): 6–24.

Dretske, Fred (1969) *Seeing and Knowing*. London: Routledge and Kegan Paul.

Esposito, Roberto (2008) *Bios: Biopolitics and Philosophy*. Minneapolis: University of Minnesota Press.

Esposito, Roberto (2011) *Immunitas: The Protection and Negation of Life*. Cambridge: Polity.

Esposito, Roberto (2012a) *Living Thought: The Origins and Actuality of Italian Philosophy*. Stanford: Stanford University Press.

Esposito, Roberto (2012b) *Third Person: Politics of Life and Philosophy of the Impersonal*. Malden: Polity.

Esposito, Roberto (2015) *Persons and Things*. Cambridge: Polity.

Esposito, Roberto (2018) *Politica e negazione*. Milano: Einaudi.

Fagot, Joël (ed.) (2000) *Picture Perception in Animals*. Hove: Psychology Press.

Fagot, Joël, Thompson, Roger and Parron, Carole (2010) 'How to Read a Picture: Lessons from Nonhuman Primates'. *PNAS* 107(2): 519–20.

Faria, Catia (2014) 'Equality, Priority and Nonhuman Animals'. *Ilemata* 14: 225–36.

Ferrari, Armando (2005) *Il pulviscolo di Giotto. Saggi psicoanalitici sullo scorrere del tempo*. Milano: Angeli.

Flaubert, Gustave (1999) *Three Tales*. Oxford: Oxford University Press.

Foucault, Michel (1978) *The History of Sexuality, Volume I: An Introduction*. New York: Pantheon Books.

Foucault, Michel (2008) *The Birth of Biopolitics. Lectures at the Collège De France*, 1978–79. Basingstoke: Macmillan.

Foucault, Michel (2014) *Wrong-doing, Truth-telling: The Function of Avowal in Justice*. Chicago: University of Chicago Press.

Freud, Sigmund (1961) *Beyond the Pleasure Principle*. New York: W. W. Norton.

Freud, Sigmund (1979) *Introduzione alla psicoanalisi (nuova serie di lezioni)* Torino: Boringhieri.

Freud, Sigmund (2000) *Three Essays on the Theory of Sexuality*. New York: Basic Books.

Freud, Sigmund (2002) *The 'Wolfman' and Other Cases*. London: Penguin.

Freud, Sigmund (unpublished) 'Letter to Maria Bonaparte'.

Freud, Sigmund and Lou Salomè (1972) *Letters*. New York: W. W. Norton.

Fusco, Giuseppe and Minelli, Alessandro (2010) 'Phenotypic Plasticity in Development and Evolution: Facts and Concepts'. *Phil. Trans. R. Soc. B.* 365: 547–56.

Gallese, Vittorio (2003) 'The Roots of Empathy: The Shared Manifold Hypothesis and the Neural Basis of Intersubjectivity'. *Psychopathology* 36(4): 171–80.

Gallup, Gordon (1970) 'Chimpanzees: Self-recognition'. *Science* 167(3914): 86–7.

Gardner, Allen and Gardner, Beatrice (1969) 'Teaching Sign Language to a Chimpanzee'. *Science* 165(3894): 664–72.

Gardner, Colin and MacCormack, Patricia (eds) (2017) *Deleuze and the Animal*. Edinburgh: Edinburgh University Press.

Garroni, Emilio (1995 (1986)) *Senso e Paradosso. L'Estetica, Filosofia non Speciale*. Bari: Laterza.

Garroni, Emilio (2003 (1976)) *Estetica ed Epistemologia: Riflessioni sulla Critica del Giudizio*. Milano: Unicopli.

Garroni, Emilio (2005) *Immagine, linguaggio, figura*. Roma-Bari: Laterza.

Garzón, Paco and Keijzer, Fred (2011) 'Plants: Adaptive Behavior, Root-brains, and Minimal Cognition'. *Adaptive Behavior* 19(3): 155–71.

Gehlen, Arnold (1988) *Man: His Nature and Place in the World*. New York: Columbia University Press.

Genosko, Gary (1993) 'Freud's Bestiary: How Does Psychoanalysis Treat Animals?' *Psychoanalytic Review* 80(4): 603–32.

Gibson, James (1966) *The Senses Considered as Perceptual Systems*. Boston: Houghton Mifflin.

Gilbert, Scott, Sapp, Jan and Tauber, Alfred (2012) 'A Symbiotic View of Life: We Have Never Been Individuals'. *The Quarterly Review of Biology* 87(4): 325–41.

Ginzburg, Carlo (1982) 'Freud, l'uomo dei lupi e i lupi mannari'. In *Miti emblemi spie. Morfologia e storia*, Torino: Einaudi.

Gluck John (1997) 'Harry F. Harlow and Animal Research: Reflection on the Ethical Paradox'. *Ethics & Behavior* 7(2): 149–61.

Grandin, Temple and Johnson, Catherine (2005) *Animals in Translation*. New York: Harvest Book.

Grusin, Richard (ed.) (2015) *The Nonhuman Turn*. Minneapolis: University of Minnesota Press.

Gualtieri, Mariangela (2018) 'Subumano e covraumano'. Available at: <webzine.sciami.com/subumano-e-sovraumano>

Guenther, Katja (2017) 'Monkeys, Mirrors, and Me: Gordon Gallup and the Study of Self-recognition'. *Journal of the History of the Behavioral Sciences* 53(1): 5–27.

Guidi, Chiara, Castellucci, Romeo, Castellucci, Claudia (2001) *Epopea della polvere. Il teatro della Socìetas Raffaello Sanzio 1992–1999*. Milano: Ubulibri.

Guthrie, Dale (2005) *The Nature of Paleolithic Art*. Chicago: Chicago University Press.

Hall, Matthew (2011) *Plants as Persons: A Philosophical Botany*. New York: SUNY Press.

Haraway, Donna (1991) *Simians, Cyborgs, and Women: The Reinvention of Nature*. New York: Routledge.

Haraway, Donna (2008) *When Species Meet*. Minneapolis: Minnesota University Press.

Harlow, Harry, Robert, Dodsworth and Harlow, Margaret (1965) 'Total Social Isolation in Monkeys'. *Proc. Natl. Acad. Sci. USA* 54(1): 90–7.

Harris, Jonathan Gil (2012) 'Animal, Vegetable, Mineral: Twenty Questions'. In J. Cohen (ed.) *Animal, Vegetable, Mineral: Ethics and Objects*. Washington, DC: Oliphaunt Books, 289–95.

Harvey, David (2005) *A Brief History of Neoliberalism*. Oxford: Oxford University Press.

Hauser, Marc and Konishi, Mark (eds) (1999) *The Design of Animal Communication*. Cambridge, MA: The MIT Press.

Hauser, Marc, Chomsky, Noam and Fitch, Tecumseh (2002) 'The Faculty of Language: What Is It, Who Has It, and How Did It Evolve?' *Science* 22(298): 1569–79.

Hegel, G. W. F. (1975) *Aesthetics: Lectures on Fine Art, Volume I*. Oxford: Clarendon Press.

Hegel, G. W. F. (2004) *Philosophy of Nature*. Oxford: Clarendon Press.

Heidegger, Martin (1962) *Being and Time*. Oxford: Blackwell.

Heidegger, Martin (1993) *Basic Writings*. San Francisco: HarperCollins.

Heidegger, Martin (1995) *The Fundamental Concepts of Metaphysics: World, Finitude, Solitude*. Bloomington: Indiana University Press.

Hess, Elizabeth (2008) *The Chimp Who Would Be Human*. New York: Bantam Books.

Holtug, Nils and Lippert-Rasmussen, Kasper (eds) (2007) *Egalitarianism: New Essays on the Nature and Value of Equality*. Oxford: Clarendon University Press.

Horta, Oscar (2016) 'Egalitarianism and Animals', *Between the Species* 19(1): 109–45.

Huber, Ludwig and Gajdon, Gyula (2006) 'Technical Intelligence in Animals: The Kea Model'. *Animal Cognition* 9(4): 295–395.

Huber, Ludwig, Range, Friederike, Voelkl, Bernhard, Szucsich, Andrea, Virányi, Zsófia and Miklosi, Adam (2009) 'The Evolution of Imitation: What Do the Capacities of Non-human Animals Tell Us About the Mechanisms of Imitation?' *Philosophical Transactions of the Royal Society B: Biological Sciences* 364 (1528): 2299–309.

Hyde, Daniel (2011) 'Two Systems of Non-symbolic Numerical Cognition'. *Frontiers in Human Neuroscience* 5: 1–8.

Ingold, Tim (ed.) (2016) *What is an Animal?* New York: Routledge.

Jun, Nathan and Smith, Daniel (eds) (2011) *Deleuze and Ethics*. Edinburgh: Edinburgh University Press.

Kafka, Franz (1952) *Selected Short Stories of Franz Kafka*: New York: Random House.

Kafka, Franz (1979) *The Basic Kafka*. New York: Pocket Books.

Kant, Immanuel (1991) *The Metaphysics of Morals*. Cambridge: Cambridge University Press.

Kant, Immanuel (2006) *Anthropology from a Pragmatic Point of View*. Oxford: Oxford University Press.

Khandker, Wahida (2014) *Philosophy, Animality and the Life Sciences.* Edinburgh: Edinburgh University Press.

Köhler, Wolfgang (1927) *The Mentality of Apes.* London: Kegan Paul.

Kubiak, Anthony (2012) 'Animism: Becoming-Performance, or Does This Text Speak to You?' *Performance Research* 17(4): 52–60.

Lacan, Jacques (1952a) 'Séminaire sur l'homme aux loups'. Available at <http://espace.freud.pagespro-orange.fr/topos/psycha/psysem/homoloup.htm>

Lacan, Jacques (1952b) *The Wolfman.* Available at <https://www.freud2lacan.com/docs/WOLFMAN-NOTES-bilingual.pdf>

Lacan, Jacques (1997) *The Ethics of Psychoanalysis 1959–1960. Seminar of Jacques Lacan, Book VII.* New York: W. W. Norton.

Lacan, Jacques (1998) *On Feminine Sexuality: The Limits of Love and Knowledge, Book XX, Encore 1972–1973.* New York: W. W. Norton.

Lacan, Jacques (2001) *Autres écrits.* Paris: Seuil.

Lacan, Jacques (2007) *The Seminar of Jacques Lacan: The Other Side of Psychoanalysis, Book XVII.* New York: W. W. Norton.

Lacan, Jacques (2011) 'Seminar XXVII, Dissolution!, Overture to the First International Encounter of the Freudian Field, Caracas, 12th July 1980', trans. A. R. Price. *Hurly-Burly* 6, 17–20.

Lacan, Jacques (2014) *Anxiety: The Seminar of Jacques Lacan, Book X.* Cambridge: Polity.

Lacan, Jacques (2016) *The Sinthome: The Seminar of Jacques Lacan, Book XXIII.* Cambridge: Polity.

Lacan, Jacques (2018) *Seminar IV: The Object Relation and Freudian Structures 1956–1957.* Available at <http://www.lacanianworks.net/?p=11980>

Lawrence, D. H. (1994) *The Man Who Died.* New York: Ecco Press.

Lawrence, D. H. (2006) *The Woman Who Rode Away/St. Mawr/The Princess.* London: Penguin.

Lemm, Vanessa (2009) *Nietzsche's Animal Philosophy: Culture, Politics, and the Animality of the Human Being.* New York: Fordham University Press.

Leopardi, Giacomo (1976) 'Elogio degli uccelli'. *Operette morali.* Milano: Feltrinelli.

Lestel, Dominique (1995) *Paroles de singes: L'Impossible dialogue homme-primate.* Paris: Éditions la Découverte.

Lévi-Strauss, Claude (1964) *Totemism.* London: Merlin Press.

Linden, Eugene (1974) *Apes, Men and Language.* New York: Penguin Books.

Lucretius (2001) *On the Nature of Things.* Indianapolis: Hackett.

Lyn, Heidi (2012) 'Apes and the Evolution of Language: Taking Stock of 40 Years of Research'. In J. Vonk and T. Shackelford (eds) *The Oxford*

Handbook of Comparative Evolutionary Psychology. Oxford: Oxford University Press, 356–78.

McCracken, Peggy (2012) *The Floral and the Human*. In J. Cohen (ed.) *Animal, Vegetable, Mineral: Ethics and Objects*. Washington, DC: Oliphaunt Books, 65–91.

Macphail, Euan (1987) 'The Comparative Psychology of Intelligence'. *Behavioral and Brain Sciences* 10(4): 645–56.

Macphail, Euan (1998) *The Evolution of Consciousness*. Oxford: Oxford University Press.

McWhorter, Ladelle and Stenstad, Gail (eds) (2009) *Heidegger and the Earth: Essays in Environmental Philosophy*. Toronto: University of Toronto Press.

Mäekivi, Nelly and Maran, Timo (2016) 'Semiotic Dimensions of Human Attitudes Towards Other Animals: A Case of Zoological Gardens'. *Sign Systems Studies* 44(1/2): 209–30.

Malaparte, Curzio (1948) *Kaputt*. London: Alvin Redman.

Manzotti, Riccardo (2017) *The Spread Mind: Why Consciousness and the World Are One*. New York: Or Books.

Marchesini, Roberto (2016) 'Philosophical Ethology and Animal Subjectivity'. *Angelaki: Journal of the Theoretical Humanities* 21(1): 237–52.

Marchesini, Roberto (2017) *Over the Human: Post-humanism and the Concept of Animal Epiphany*. Berlin: Springer.

Marcoaldi, Franco (2006) *Animali in versi*. Torino: Einaudi.

Marder, Michael (2013) *Plant-Thinking: A Philosophy of Vegetal Life*. New York: Columbia University Press.

Marr, David (1982) *Vision: A Computational Investigation into the Human Representation and Processing of Visual Information*. New York: Freeman.

Martin, Raymond and Barresi, John (2008) *The Rise and Fall of Soul and Self: An Intellectual History of Personal Identity*. New York: Columbia University Press.

Mazzeo, Marco (2009) *Contraddizione e melanconia. Saggio sull'ambivalenza*. Macerata: Quodlibet.

Michaels, Claire and Carello, Claudia (eds) (1981) *Direct Perception*. Englewood Cliffs: Prentice-Hall.

Miller, Jacques-Alain (2001) 'Lacanian Biology and the Event of the Body'. *Lacanian Ink* 18: 6–29.

Miller, Jacques-Alain (2004) 'Pièces détachées'. *Orientation lacanienne III*, 6: 1–210.

Miller, Jacques-Alain (2017) 'The Real Unconscious'. *Lacanian Ink*, 50: 22–41.

Minelli, Alessandro (2011) 'Animal Development, An Open-Ended Segment of Life'. *Biological Theory* 6(1): 4–15.

Minelli, Alessandro (2016) 'Scaffolded Biology'. *Theory Biosci.* 135: 163–73.

Morgan, C. Lloyd (1903) *An Introduction to Comparative Psychology.* London: W. Scott.

Morris, Desmond (1962) *The Biology of Art: A Study of the Picture-Making Behaviour of the Great Apes and Its Relationship to Human Art.* London: Methuen.

Moyle, Tristan (2017) 'Heidegger's Philosophical Botany'. *Continental Philosophy Review* 50(3): 377–94.

Næss, Arne (1973) 'The Shallow and the Deep Long-range Ecology Movement. A Summary'. *Inquiry* 16(1): 95–100.

Nagel, Thomas (1974) 'What Is It Like to Be a Bat?' *The Philosophical Review* 83(4): 435–50.

Nagel, Thomas (1986) *The View From Nowhere.* Oxford: Oxford University Press.

Nancy, Jean-Luc (2008) *Corpus.* New York: Fordham University Press.

Nietzsche, Friedrich (2001) *The Gay Science.* Cambridge: Cambridge University Press.

Nietzsche, Friedrich (2007) *Ecce Homo: How One Becomes What One is.* Oxford: Oxford University Press.

Obholzer, Karin (1982) *The Wolf-man Sixty Years Later.* New York: Routledge & Kegan Paul.

Odling-Smee, John, Laland, Kevin and Feldman, Marcus (2003) *Niche Construction: The Neglected Process in Evolution.* Princeton: Princeton University Press.

Oriel, Elizabeth (2014) 'Whom Would Animals Designate as "Persons"? On Avoiding Anthropocentrism and Including Others'. *Journal of Evolution and Technology* 24(3): 44–59.

Ovid (1958) *The Metamorphoses.* New York: Viking Press.

Parikka, Jussi (2010) *Insect Media: An Archeology of Animals and Technology.* Minneapolis: University of Minneapolis Press.

Parker, Heidi and Ostrander, Elaine (2005) 'Canine Genomics and Genetics: Running with the Pack'. *PLoS Genetics* 1(5): 507–13.

Parron, Carole, Call, Josep and Fagot, Joël (2008) 'Behavioural Responses to Photographs by Pictorially Naïve Baboons (*Papio anubis*), Gorillas (*Gorilla gorilla*) and Chimpanzees (*Pan troglodytes*)'. *Behavioural Processes* 78: 351–7.

Pasolini, Pier Paolo (2001) *Teatro.* Milano: Mondadori.

Patterson, Charles (2002) *Eternal Treblinka: Our Treatment of Animals and the Holocaust.* New York: Lantern Books.

Payson Evans, Edward (1896) *Criminal Prosecution and Capital Punishment of Animals.* London: Heinemann.

Pepperberg, Irene (1999) *The Alex Studies: Cognitive and Communicative Abilities of Grey Parrots.* Cambridge, MA: Harvard University Press.

Perrone-Bertolotti, Marcela, Rapin, Lucile, Lachaux, Jean-Pierre, Baciu, Monica and Lœvenbruck, Hélène (2014) 'What Is That Little Voice Inside My Head? Inner Speech Phenomenology, Its Role in Cognitive Performance, and Its Relation to Self-monitoring'. *Behav. Brain Res.* 261: 220–39.

Pierantoni, Ruggero (1977) *Riconoscere e comunicare. I messaggi biologici.* Torino: Boringhieri.

Plotnik, Joshua, de Waal, Frans and Reiss, Diana (2006) 'Self-Recognition in the Asian Elephant and Future Directions for Cognitive Research With Elephants in Zoological Settings'. *Zoo Biology* 28: 1–13.

Ponge, Francis (1974) *The Voice of Things.* New York: McGraw-Hill

Rancière, Jacques (1999) *Dis-agreement: Politics and Philosophy.* Minneapolis: University of Minnesota Press.

Regan, Tom (1983) *The Case of Animal Rights.* Berkeley: California University Press.

Regan, Tom (2003) *Animal Rights, Human Wrongs: An Introduction to Moral Philosophy.* Lanham: Roman & Littlefield.

Renoult, Julien (2016) 'The Evolution of Aesthetics: A Review of Models'. In Z. Kapoula and M. Vernet (eds) *Aesthetics and Neuroscience.* Berlin: Springer, 271–99.

Rieber, Robert W. and Carton, Aaron S., eds (1997) *The Collected Works of Lev Vygotsky, Volume 4: The History of the Development of Higher Mental Functions.* Dordrecht: Kluwer.

Rieber, Robert W. and Carton, Aaron S., eds. (1999) *The Collected Works of Lev Vygotsky, Volume 6: Scientific Legacy.* Dordrecht: Kluwer.

Rilke, Rainer Maria (1975) *The Duino Elegies* and *The Sonnets to Orpheus.* Boston: Houghton Mifflin.

Ritvo, Harriet (2007) 'On the Animal Turn'. *Dedalus* 136(4): 118–22.

Rizzolatti, Giacomo, Fadiga, Luciano, Fogassi, Leonardo and Gallese, Vittorio (1999) 'Resonance Behaviors and Mirror Neurons'. *Archives italiennes de biologie* 137(2): 85–100.

Rizzolatti, Giacomo and Sinigaglia, Corrado (2006) *So quel che fai. Il cervello che agisce e i neuroni specchio.* Milano: Raffaello Cortina Editore.

Rock, Irvin (1997) *Indirect Perception.* Cambridge, MA: The MIT Press.

Rowlands, Mark (2016) 'Are Animals Persons?' *Animal Sentience* 10(1): 1–18.

Russell, Nerissa (2012) *Social Zooarcheology: Humans and Animals in Prehistory.* Cambridge, MA: Cambridge University Press.

Safran Foer, Jonathan (2009) *Eating Animals.* New York: Little, Brown & Company.

Saito, Aya, Hayashi, Misato, Takeshita, Hideko and Matsuzawa, Tetsuro (2014) 'The Origin of Representational Drawing: A Comparison of Human Children and Chimpanzees'. *Child Development* 85(6): 2232–46.

Samuelsson, Lars (2013) 'At the Centre of What? A Critical Note on the

Centrism-terminology in Environmental Ethics'. *Environmental Values* 22(5): 627–45.

Sartre, Jean-Paul (2007) *Existentialism is a Humanism*. New Haven: Yale University Press.

Sauret, Marie-Jean (2005) 'Les Hommes aux loups'. *Psychanalyse* 1(2): 53–82.

Savage-Rumbaugh, Sue and Lewin, Roger (1994) *Kanzi: The Ape at the Brink of the Human Mind*. New York: John Wiley & Sons.

Schooler, Jonathan and Engstler-Schooler, Tonya (1990) 'Verbal Overshadowing of Visual Memories: Some Things are Better Left Unsaid'. *Cognitive Psychology* 22(1): 36–71.

Sebeok, Thomas A. and Ramsay, Alexandra (2011) *Approaches to Animal Communication*. Berlin: De Gruyter.

Semenowicz, Dorota (2016) *The Theatre of Romeo Castellucci and Sòcietas Raffaello Sanzio: From Icon to Iconoclasm, From Word to Image, From Symbol to Allegory*. New York: Palgrave Macmillan.

Shaviro, Steven (2015) 'Consequences of Panpsychism'. In R. Grusin (ed.) *The Nonhuman Turn*. Minneapolis: University of Minnesota Press, 19–44.

Silvertown, Jonathan and Gordon, Deborah (1989) 'A Framework for Plant Behavior'. *Annual Review of Ecology and Systematics* 20: 349–66.

Simondon, Gilbert (2013) *L'individuation à la lumière des notions de forme et d'information*. Grenoble: Millon.

Singer, Peter (1975) *Animal Liberation*. New York: HarperCollins.

Singer, Peter (2011) *The Expanding Circle: Ethics, Evolution, and Moral Progress*. Princeton: Princeton University Press.

Skinner, Burrhus (1951) *How to Teach Animals*. San Francisco: Freeman.

Skrbina, David (2017) *Panpsychism in the West*. Cambridge, MA: The MIT Press.

Smith, Daniel (1973) 'Systematic Study of Chimpanzee Drawing'. *Journal of Comparative and Physiological Psychology* 82(3): 406–14.

Sneddon, Lynne, Elwood, Robert, Adamo, Shelley and Leach, Matthew (2014) 'Defining and Assessing Animal Pain'. *Animal Behaviour* 97: 201–12.

Soler, Colette (2014) *Lacan: The Unconscious Reinvented*. London: Karnc.

Sophocles (2001) *Antigone*. Oxford: Oxford University Press.

Stone, Jennifer (1992) 'A Psychoanalytic Bestiary: The Wolf Woman, the Leopard, and the Siren'. *American Imago* 49(1): 117–52.

Strand, Mark (2016) *Collected Poems*. New York: Knopf.

Strawson, Galen (2006) 'Realistic Materialism: Why Physicalism Entails Panpsychism'. *Journal of Consciousness Studies* 13(10–11): 3–31.

Surin, Kenneth (2011) '"Existing Not as a Subject But as a Work of Art": The Task of Ethics or Aesthetics?' In N. Jun and D. Smith (eds) *Deleuze and Ethics*. Edinburgh: Edinburgh University Press, 142–53.

Tanaka, Masayuki (2007) 'Recognition of Pictorial Representations by Chimpanzees (*Pan troglodytes*)'. *Animal Cognition* 10: 169–79.

Tattersall, Ian (1998) *Becoming Human: Evolution and Human Uniqueness.* New York: Harcourt Brace.

Taylor Parker, Sue, Mitchell, Robert and Boccia, Maria (eds) (1994) *Self-Awareness in Animals and Humans: Developmental Perspectives.* Cambridge: Cambridge University Press.

Terrace, Herbert et al. (1979) 'Can An Ape Create a Sentence?' *Science* 23(206): 891–902.

Terrace, Herbert (1987) *Nim: A Chimpanzee Who Learned Sign Language.* New York: Columbia University Press.

Theofanopoulou, Constantina et al. (2017) 'Self-domestication in Homo Sapiens: Insights From Comparative Genomics'. *PLoS One* 12(10): e0185306.

Thompson, Jennifer, Krovitz, Gail and Nelson, Andrew (eds) (2003) *Patterns of Growth and Development in the Genus Homo.* Cambridge: Cambridge University Press.

Timofeeva, Oxana (2018) *The History of Animals: A Philosophy.* London: Bloomsbury Academic.

Tomasello, Michael (2017) 'What Did We Learn From the Ape Language Studies?' In H. Brian and Y. Shinya (eds) *Bonobos: Unique in Mind, Brain and Behavior.* Oxford: Oxford University Press, 96–104.

Trewavas, Anthony (2014) *Plant Behaviour and Intelligence.* Oxford: Oxford University Press.

Triebenbacher Lookabaugh, Sandra (1998) 'Pets as Transitional Objects: Their Role in Children's Emotional Development'. *Psychological Reports* 82(1): 191–200.

Tugendhat, Ernst (2016) *Egocentricity and Mysticism.* New York: Columbia University Press.

Turing, Alan (1950) 'Computing Machinery and Intelligence'. *Mind* LIX(236): 433–60.

Valéry, Paul (1989) *Dialogues.* Princeton: Princeton University Press.

Valéry, Paul (2010) *Cahiers/Notebooks 4: 1973–74.* Frankfurt: Peter Lang.

van Duijn, Marc, Keijzer, Fred and Franken, Daan (2006) 'Principles of Minimal Cognition: Casting Cognition as Sensorimotor Coordination'. *Adaptive Behavior* 14: 157–70.

Vicedo, Marga (2009) 'Mothers, Machines, and Morals: Harry Harlow's Work on Primate Love From Lab to Legend'. *Journal of the History of the Behavioral Sciences* 45(3): 193–218.

Virno, Paolo (2013) *Saggio sulla negazione. Per un'antropologia linguistica.* Torino: Bollati Boringhieri.

von Frisch, Karl (1953) *The Dancing Bees: An Account of the Life and Senses of the Honey Bee.* New York: Harvest Books.

von Uexküll, Jakob (2010) *A Foray into the World of Animals and Humans, with a Theory of Meaning*. Minneapolis: University of Minnesota Press.

Vygotsky, Lev and Luria, Alexander (1993) *Studies on the History of Behavior: Ape, Primitive, and Child*. Hillsdale: Lawrence Erlbaum Associates.

Vygotsky, Lev and Luria, Alexander (1994) 'Tool and Symbol in Child Development'. In René van der Veer and Jaas Valsiner (eds) *The Vygotsky Reader*. Oxford: Blackwell.

Waller, Sara (2012) 'Science of the Monkey Mind: Primate Penchants and Human Pursuits'. In J. Smit and R. Mitchell (eds) *Experiencing Animal Minds: An Anthology of Animal-Human Encounters*. New York: Columbia University Press, 79–94.

Wallman, Joel (1992) *Aping Language*. New York: Cambridge University Press.

Wang, Guo-Dong et al. (2016) 'Out of Southern East Asia: The Natural History of Domestic Dogs Across the World'. *Cell Research* 26: 21–33.

Watanabe, Shigeru (2012) 'Animal Aesthetics from the Perspective of Comparative Cognition'. In S. Watanabe and S. Kuczaj (eds) *Emotions of Animals and Humans*. Dordrecht: Springer, 129–62.

Watanabe, Shigeru (2015) 'Aesthetics and Reinforcement: A Behavioural Approach to Aesthetics'. In T. Hoquet (ed.) *Current Perspectives on Sexual Selection: What's Left After Darwin?* Dordrecht: Springer, 289–307.

Watanabe, Shigeru, Sakamoto, Junko and Wakita, Masumi (1995) 'Pigeons' Discrimination of Paintings by Monet and Picasso'. *Journal of Experimental Analysis of Behavior* 63(2): 165–74.

Weil, Kari (2010) 'A Report on the Animal Turn'. *Differences. A Journal of Feminist Cultural Studies* 21(2): 1–23.

Weisman, Ronald and Spetch, Marcia (2010) 'Picture Perception in Birds: Determining When Birds Perceive Correspondence Between Pictures and Objects: A Critique'. *Comparative Cognition & Behavior Reviews* 5: 117–31.

Wheeler, Wendy (2018) 'Meaning'. In L. Turner, U. Sellbach and R. Broglio (eds) *The Edinburgh Companion to Animal Studies*. Edinburgh: Edinburgh University Press, 337–53.

White, T. H. (ed.) (1960) *The Book of Beasts*. New York: Putnam.

Wiese, Heike (2003) *Numbers, Language, and the Human Mind*. Cambridge: Cambridge University Press.

Wittgenstein, Ludwig (2009) *Philosophical Investigations*. Oxford: Wiley-Blackwell.

Wolfe, Cary (2003) *Zoontologies: The Question of the Animal*. Minneapolis: University of Minnesota Press.

Wolfe, Cary (2009) 'Human, All Too Human: *Animal Studies* and the Humanities'. *PMLA* 124(2): 564–75.

Wolfe, Cary (2010) *What is Posthumanism?* Minneapolis: University of Minneapolis Press.

Wolfe, Cary (2018) 'Afterword: Who Are These Animals I Am Following?'. In L. Turner, U. Sellbach and R. Broglio (eds) *The Edinburgh Companion to Animal Studies*. Edinburgh: Edinburgh University Press, 533–45.

Wynne, Clive (2007) 'What are Animals? Why Anthropomorphism is Still Not a Scientific Approach to Behavior'. *Comparative Cognition and Behavior Reviews* 2: 125–35.

Yasnitsky, Anton and van der Veer, René (eds) (2016) *Revisionist Revolution in Vygotsky Studies: The State of the Art*. London: Taylor & Francis.

Zavershneva, Ekaterina and van der Veer, René (eds) (2018) *Vygotsky's Notebooks: A Selection*. Berlin: Springer.

Index

223

Index